Reminiscences

of

Vice Admiral Charles S. Minter, Jr., USN (Ret.)

Volume I

U. S. Naval Institute
Annapolis, Maryland

June 1981

Preface

Volume I of the taped interviews with Vice Admiral Charles S. Minter, Jr. contains copies of the first seven in a series of thirteen. They were all conducted in the Admiral's home in Providence, Annapolis, Maryland, during 1979. He read the original transcript and made the necessary corrections. The manuscript was re-typed and a subject index has been added for convenience.

The Admiral has had an extraordinary career in the navy; one which made demands upon all his abilities, his total dedication and his commanding personality. Volume I includes much of the career that was dedicated to naval aviation. Minter got his wings in early 1941 in time to participate in the neutrality patrol of the North Atlantic. After the outbreak of hostilities he served in several "hot spots" such as Iceland and the Caribbean. Subsequent duty on the newly commissioned carrier RANDOLPH took him to the Pacific, to raids over Tokyo and the battles for Iwo Jima and Okinawa. A burning ambition was realized in 1950 when he was sent to the Patuxent Naval Air Station. After that he was stationed in Japan and saw service over Korea. In June 1953 he returned to the U. S. Naval Academy as Executive Officer of the Physical Education Department. This duty made heavy demands upon his skill in dealing with the complexities of the athletic program of that day. Minter's natural presence and his strong personality proved to be powerful assets. From June 1956 to 1958 he served as Project Manager for the ill-fated P6M Seaplane Weapons System, an assignment that called for unusual dedication, tact and perseverance. There followed a year at sea as skipper of the carrier INTREPID and a stay with the Sixth Fleet in the Mediterranean.

Subsequent events in this significant career are covered in Volume II of the Reminiscences.

John T. Mason, Jr.
Director of Oral History

June 1981

VICE ADMIRAL CHARLES S. MINTER, JR., UNITED STATES NAVY

Charles Stamps Minter, Jr., was born in Pocohontas, Virginia, on January 23, 1915, son of C. S. and Nan (DuPuy) Minter. He attended Bluefield (West Virginia) Junior College, prior to entering the U. S. Naval Academy, Annapolis, Maryland, on appointment from his native state in 1933. Graduated and commissioned Ensign on June 3, 1937, he subsequently advanced in rank, attaining that of Vice Admiral, to date from March 1, 1971.

Following graduation from the Naval Academy in 1937, he joined the USS HOUSTON. In June 1939 he was detached for duty as Communications Watch Officer on the Staff of Commander Cruisers, Scouting Force, USS CHICAGO flagship. In August 1940 he reported for flight training at the Naval Air Station, Pensacola, Florida, receiving his designation as Naval Aviator on March 7, 1941. During the period May 1941 to June 1942 he served as Communications and Watch Officer with Patrol Squadron SEVENTY-THREE, which was based consecutively in Argentia; Iceland (for convoy coverage); and at the Naval Air Station, Quonset Point, Rhode Island. "For meritorious achievement...as Pilot of a Bomber Plane engaged in anti-submarine patrols and convoy coverage flight in the North Atlantic Area during the winter of 1941-1942..." he was awarded the Air Medal.

In June 1942 he transferred to Patrol Squadron FIFTY-THREE, serving first as Flight Officer and from September 1942 to June 1943 as Executive Officer. That squadron, based in Trinidad, participated in anti-submarine patrol and convoy coverage. In December 1942, he piloted an aircraft in a night attack on a German submarine trailing a convoy, with resultant damage to the submarine. He next reported as Executive Officer of Headquarters Squadron NINE, based at Quonset Point, Rhode Island, and from July 1943 to August 1944 commanded that squadron.

He assisted in the fitting out of the USS RANDOLPH, an aircraft carrier which was commissioned on October 9, 1944. He served on board as Assistant Air Officer and later Air Officer. While attached to the RANDOLPH he saw action in the first and second carrier raids on Tokyo; the Iwo Jima and Okinawa Campaigns and participated in the Victory Cruise against the Japanese Homeland (July-August 1945). He was awarded the Bronze Star Medal with Combat "V."

Detached from the RANDOLPH in August 1946, he next served as Administrative Officer at the Naval Air Station, Patuxent

River, Maryland. In June 1948 he became Assistant Director of Tactical Test at the Naval Air Test Center, Patuxent River, and in June 1950 assumed command of Patrol Squadron TWENTY-EIGHT, which deployed to Itami Air Base, Japan, to engage in reconnaissance missions, antisubmarine patrols, photographic and flare dropping illumination missions against enemy Korean forces. He was awarded a Gold Star in lieu of the Second Air Medal.

Detached from command of Patrol Squadron TWENTY-EIGHT in February 1952, he then joined the Staff of Command Fleet Air Wing TWO as Operations Officer. In June 1953 he returned to the Naval Academy for duty as Executive Officer of the Physical Education Department and remained there until August 1955. After instruction at the National War College, Washington, D.C., he served from June 1956 to July 1958 first as P6M Seaplane Weapons System Project Manager and later Head of the Aviation Ships and Shore Based Aero Equipment Branch, Office of the Deputy Chief of Naval Operations (Air), Navy Department, Washington, D. C.

He commanded the USS ALBEMARLE from August 1958 until April 1959, then reported as Assistant Chief of Staff for Readiness to the Commander Naval Air Force, U. S. Atlantic Fleet. He assumed command of the USS INTREPID in September 1960 and in June 1961 reported as Commandant of Midshipmam at the U. S. Naval Academy, Annapolis, Maryland. On January 11, 1964 be became Superintendent of the Naval Academy, with additional duty as Commandant, Severn River Naval Command. He was relieved as Commandant, Severn River Naval Command on January 1, 1965 when that regional command was abolished and encompassed in the newly established Naval District Washington, D.C. "For exceptionally meritorious conduct...from June 2, 1961 to January 11, 1964 as Commandant of Midshipmen, and from January 11, 1964 to June 12, 1965 as Superintendent, United States Naval Academy..." he was awarded the Legion of Merit.

In July 1965 he reported as Deputy Assistant Chief of Staff for Plans and Policy to the Supreme Allied Commander, Europe and for "exceptionally meritorious service in that assignment was awarded a Gold Star in lieu of the Second Legion of Merit. In October 1967 he assumed command of Carrier Division SIXTEEN and for his direct contribution to the improved antisubmarine warfare capabilities of the U. S. Atlantic Fleet was awarded a Gold Star in lieu of the Third Legion of Merit. He became Commander Fleet Air Wings, Pacific/Commander Fleet Air Moffett, with headquarters at the Naval Air Station, Moffett Field, California, in July 1969 and during November and December of that year was assigned additional duty as Commander Antisubmarine Warfare Force, U. S.

Pacific Fleet. He was awarded the Distinguished Service Medal and cited in part as follows: "...Charged with both operational and type command functions, (he) initiated and implemented major plans and programs that resulted in Pacific Fleet Patrol Aviation Forces reaching and maintaining an outstanding high level of anti-submarine proficiency and readiness..."

In February 1971 he reported as Deputy Chief of Naval Operations (Logistics), Navy Department and in April 1973 became Deputy Chairman of the North Atlantic Treaty Organization Military Committee, Navy Department. His retirement from the Navy came in September 1, 1974.

In addition to the Distinguished Service Medal, the Legion of Merit with two Gold Stars, the Bronze Star Medal with Gold Star and Combat "V," and the Air Medal with Gold Star, Vice Admiral Minter has the American Defense Service Medal with Bronze "A"; American Campaign Medal; European-African-Middle Eastern Campaign Medal; Asiatic-Pacific Campaign Medal; World War II Victory Medal; Navy Occupation Service Medal; China Service Medal; National Defense Service Medal with bronze star; Korean Service Medal; United Nations Service Medal; and the Philippine Liberation Ribbon. He also has the Korean Presidential Unit Citation Badge.

His home town address is 216 Prospect Street, Covington, Virginia. He is married to the former Mary Margaret Skeehan of Beverly Hills, California, and they have three children, Lieutenant Commander Charles S. Minter, III, USN, David M. Minter and Meredith Ann Minter.

NAVY - Office of Information
Biographies Branch (OI-0111)
6 June 1973

DECLARATION OF TRUST

The undersigned does hereby appoint and designate as his (her) Trustee herein, the Secretary-Treasurer and Publisher of the United States Naval Institute to perform and discharge the following duties, powers, and privileges in connection with the possession and use of a certain taped interview between the undersigned and the Oral History Department of the United States Naval Institute.

1. Classification of Transcript.

( )a. If classified OPEN, the transcript(s) may be read or the recording(s) audited by the qualified personnel upon presentation of proper credentials, as determined by the Secretary-Treasurer of the U.S. Naval Institute.

(✓)b. If classified PERMISSION REQUIRED TO CITE OR QUOTE, the user will be required to obtain permission in writing from the interviewee prior to quoting or citing from either the transcript(s) or the recording(s).

( )c. If classified PERMISSION REQUIRED, permission must be obtained in writing from the interviewee before the transcribed interview(s) can be examined or the tape recording(s) audited.

( )d. If classified CLOSED, the transcribed interview(s) and the tape recording(s) will be sealed until a time specified by the interviewee. This may be until the death of the interviewee or for any specified number of years.

2. It is expressly understood that in giving this authorization, I am in no way precluded from placing such restrictions as I may desire upon use of the interview at any time during my lifetime, nor does this authorization in any way affect my rights to the copyright of my literary expressions that may be contained in the interview.

Witness my hand and seal this 9th day of January 19 81.

I hereby accept and consent to the foregoing Declaration of Trust and the powers therein conferred upon me as Trustee:

Interview #1 with Vice Admiral Charles S. Minter, Jr.
U.S. Navy

Place: Adm. Minter's residence, Annapolis, Maryland

Date: Thursday morning, 17 May 1979

Subject: Biography

By: John T. Mason, Jr.

Q: Well, Sir, I've been looking forward to this series of interviews with you. This is, as you know, a talking biography, so would you begin in the proper way with a biography and tell me something about yourself - first, where you were born, the date and place of your birth, something about your family background, your early life.

Adm. M.: All right. I was born in Pocahontas, Virginia, a very small town - about 500 people - on the 23rd of January, 1915. My father was a lawyer. He practiced law with his father, who was a lawyer/minister. My Grandfather Minter died in Pocahontas, Virginia, when I was about three years old and shortly thereafter we moved to Logan, West Virginia, where my father opened a law practice; and it was a very successful one, initially.

Q: Was he involved in local politics as well?

Adm. M.: No, he was not. Dad wasn't a politician - he was strictly a lawyer. He did not really do too well in the partnership he had there and when the depression came along, he had a rather hard time of it.

I graduated from Logan High School at the age of 15 in 1930, and -

Q: Would you like to say something about your mother, also?

Adm. M.: Oh, yes. Yes, I will. Mother was a native Virginian, as was my father, and Mother was a graduate of Farmville, which has since become - I'm trying to think - Longwood, I believe, is the name of the school now, but Mother was a teacher when she met my father.

My father was not a college graduate, but he went to Washington and Lee University for one year and I have recently contacted Washington and Lee and gotten a transcript of his academic record there. He crammed the better part of two years in one years' work. As I say, he didn't graduate so he didn't have a degree in law, but he passed the Virginia bar exams to qualify as a lawyer.

Q: That's quite a remarkable achievement, though,

isn't it?

Adm. M.: Well, yes, it was. His father, as I mentioned, was a lawyer and a minister.

Q: What kind of a clergyman was he?

Adm. M.: He was Presbyterian. As I say, my dad pretty much put himself through the year of law school at Washington and Lee - I think 1909 was the year he was there.

I mentioned I graduated from Logan High School at 15 - and that's not said to indicate any terrific academic prowess - I've looked back on it many times and I think it was a mistake to have allowed me to graduate that early. At the time I was coming up through grade school and junior high school, there was a procedure in effect that I think is an incorrect one, but they allowed one to skip a grade - I wasn't really that smart at all, but -

Q: You mean, so that you not get bored, I suppose.

Adm. B.: Well, that was the theory, but I really believe it's a mistake; I think a youngster matures intellectually, as well as physically, better if he stays with his peer group unless he's an exceptionally gifted youngster and I certainly wasn't that.

But, in any event, my parents permitted me to skip a couple of grades and I graduated at age 15.

Q: Did you have any brothers and sisters?

Adm. M.: I have two brothers. I'm the oldest of three. One brother is four years younger than I am, one is thirteen years younger.

After graduating from high school in 1930, my father was simply financially unable to do more than let me go to a junior college, where I lived with relatives in Bluefield, West Virginia - Bluefield Junior College. And this is when -

Q: Now, that was the time of the Depression, wasn't it?

Adm. M.: Oh, it was, it was indeed, and dollars were pretty hard to come by. This is where I first got my real interest in the Naval Academy. The people I lived with were an aunt of mine, my mother's sister, and her husband, who was a doctor, Dr. Stuart, in Bluefield, West Virginia. He had two brothers who were naval officers, both graduates of the Naval Academy. One had been a rear admiral at the time of his retirement and the other was a navy captain at the time of his retirement.

Q: Did you meet them?

Adm. M.: Yes. No, I didn't meet the admiral - I met the captain. When he was a lieutenant, I met the captain, on a visit to the Naval Academy. But seeing pictures of this navy background and getting some sort of a feel for the navy through them, I developed an interest in the Naval Academy. This coupled with the fact that I was quite certain I was not going to be able to go to college - at least the prospects looked rather dim - the possibilities of going into the Naval Academy began to appeal more and more to me.

Q: How did your father react to this?

Adm. M.: Oh, Dad was quite pleased. As a matter of fact, right after getting out of high school, I had tried to go to sea as a cabin boy on an ocean liner. The liners in those days, going back and forth across the Atlantic, used to have youngsters that they would take on for summertime jobs but, because of the Depression, I suppose, there were really practically no vancancies in this area and so I never was able to make that part of my dream come true.

But Dad was able to send me here to Annapolis to a "cram school" - Cochran-Bryan, which no longer exists. It used to be located out on Franklin Street, and it existed as a cram school - purely to cram for the Naval Academy; no other purpose in life.

Q: Like the Werntz School.

Adm. M.: Bobby Werntz was another one that was here. I was here for a six-week period, trying to cram for the Naval Academy, and I was unsuccessful the first go-around. I did not pass the exams given here in Annapolis in the post office.

Q: Your high school preparation hadn't been adequate, then?

Adm. M.: Well, no, it had not, and neither had my junior college experience of one year really done that much for me. So, the following year I lived in Fincastle, Virginia, with an uncle of mine who was a lawyer. Fincastle is about 40 miles from Covington, Virginia, and this uncle of mine was a partner-in-law of my father's. And I studied on my own there, and had a former superintendent of schools give me extra instruction in mathematics. And that year I was successful - that was 1933 and I qualified for

Minter, Jr. #1 - 7

entrance into the Naval Academy.

Q: Did you have a Congressional appointment, or how - ?

Adm. M.: I had a Congressional appointment.

Q: What, from West Virginia?

Adm. M.: No, from Virginia. We were living in Virginia by this time. I'm sorry, I didn't mention this. My father moved from Logan, West Virginia, where he'd been practicing law, to Covington, Virginia, where he lived until he died. He moved there in 1932 and I went to the Naval Academy from Virginia, by Congressional appointment.

Q: Tommy Hart was just giving up the superintendency at that point, wasn't he?

Adm. M.: Well, he was on for that year, and then Admiral Sellers came in as the superintendent.

Q: Well, how did you take to life at the academy? The regiment, that sort of thing?

Adm. M.: I enjoyed it very much. I think I was really a pretty immature 18-year-old when I arrived - I know I was, and I feel I was immature through most of my time here - but I really took to the life at the Naval Academy. I can recall to this day the thrill and the excitement I felt the first night in Bancroft Hall. I found it hard to believe I was there, because I had been working for two years to get there and all of a sudden I was realizing a dream, and -

Q: That in itself was a lesson about life, wasn't it?

Adm. M.: Yes, it was and, as I say, I took to the regimen. I was not a model midshipman by any manner of means, but I truly enjoyed the experience. I didn't find the plebe indoctrination system all that demanding - I enjoyed it - it was in many respects like a college fraternity initiation, I suppose, except that it lasted for an entire year. I found the camaraderie of the regiment really quite stimulating. I was around a bunch of interesting people, some of course who became truly life-long friends. I enjoyed it all.

But the Naval Academy was stereotyped in those days. The academic program was such that it was sometimes a little depressing to be able to look in your regulation book and project yourself four years ahead - you could almost tell where you'd be on any single day of the year that you were going to graduate. And so that was a little stifling in a way, but all in all, I found my Naval Academy experience truly a satisfying one and exciting in many ways.

Q: How did you do with the scholastic end of things?

Adm. M.: I was quite bad. I've thought many times with embarrassment that I should have done much better. I know I could have done much better, but I didn't exert myself to the fullest, so I stood fairly low in the class.

Q: That again, I suppose, could be attributed to your immaturity –

Adm. M.: Well, I'd like to excuse myself on those grounds, but the truth of the matter was I don't think I worked nearly hard enough. I'm not one of Admiral Rickover's most ardent admirers but I must say his professed desire to have his people exert their best effort is something I wish I'd had instilled in me sooner in the game.

I had never had a foreign language, for example, when I came to the Naval Academy. I had studied Latin in high school, and I found French an extremely difficult experience. My first year here I was afraid I was going to bilge out in French. I did reasonably well in math and English and history and that sort of thing, but the foreign language was really a pretty difficult bill for me. I roomed with a fellow who has been my life-long friend; he retired as Rear Admiral - this is Pinky Baer. We roomed together four years, and we kept each other alive plebe year. I helped him in math and he pulled me through in French because he'd had three years or four years of French in high school, and therefore we sort of teamed academically to try to keep our heads above water.

Q: What about athletics? Did you go in for a thorough-going program in athletics?

Adm. M.: Yes, I did. I've always been tremendously interested in athletics. I rowed on the crew here, and I was on the football squad for one year. We didn't have in those days the intramural sports program that one has at the Naval Academy now, which is a tremendously important part of the curriculum as I see it. So, it was sort of pick up sports - if you wanted to go out and play softball or touch football or things like that. But yes, I had a keen interest in athletics and I was a tremendous admirer, as I think most of us were, of Tom Hamilton, who was the head football coach at the time I was at the Naval Academy. Of course, he was one of the all-time great sports figures of Naval Academy history, and we all were aware of his background. He was also a flier, and I flew with him once or twice

Minter, Jr. #1 - 11

here in some of the training planes. That helped initiate my interest in aviation.

Q: Do you want to comment on the sports program as a lesson in teamwork and that sort of thing, in leadership?

Adm. M.: I feel very strongly that it has a tremendous part to play, and I know it did for those of us who participated. I think it taught us values that were of major importance in later life. I'm sure there are those who would take exception to this, but organized sports, in my judgment, clearly has a large part to play in individual efforts later on.

I think I learned important lessons in rowing and on the football team - disappointments that you experience when you lose, and elation when you win - but the knowledge of how you got there, and why, is tremendously important. Learning to think and act under pressure and the appreciation for the teamwork that is so vital, of course, to success in the navy and in the military anywhere - all come from participation in sports. There's a feel for it - for the teamwork that's required - and I think it colors your whole view of how things should be done.

Q: Certainly when Admiral Hill became superintendent,

Minter, Jr. #1 - 12

he emphasized this as almost paramount - the teamwork, the sports program.

Adm. M.: Well, that's an interesting thing - most superintendents that I've known have been very high on the sports program here but for reasons best known to himself, Admiral Rickover has been totally opposed to it. He's constantly railing against organized athletics; the varsity football program and others, he feels just are a total waste of time. But, fortunately, most of the superintendents have shared my view, that varsity sports play a very important part in the life of a midshipman.

Q: Tell me about the summer cruise program when you were there - of course, this was a difficult time, I suppose, economically speaking, and so the navy was lacking in funds.

Adm. M.: Well, yes, we were lacking in funds, but even so, I'd have to say that in some respects we had better cruises in those days than midshipmen experience these days. There was such a thing as a training squadron. Three of the old battleships, the Wyoming, the Oklahoma, and the Arkansas were generally used for our summer cruises, and here again I remember that as one of the exciting parts of the Naval Academy

Minter, Jr. #1 - 13

experience: a cruise to European ports. There was a lot of work on some of those cruises but there was a lot of fun too. The ships were overcrowded to the extent that you couldn't usually be given individual jobs that meant that much from a training standpoint. I never had a major assignment in the engineering spaces, for example, and certainly you couldn't put all of us in the important positions in other departments either. But we got good group instruction. Over all, the experience was a very good one and we made some marvelous trips - we got to see ports of call or places that I'd only heard about before. My youngster cruise, for example, we went to the Mediterranean - England first, then to the Mediterranean. And so, I felt that the cruises were tremendously motivating factors for one that had never been to sea.

Q: Really educational in some capacity?

Adm. M.: Yes, I thought so. We were pretty well crowded into those ships and there was little opportunity for individual instruction. But over all, I felt that they served a very useful purpose. They did give us some opportunity to see what life was like at sea. We had of course the usual weather conditions that one experiences. But I think maybe the most exciting part about it was actually getting aboard - seeing people of different cultures, getting the first opportunity to use your foreign language. I can remember working on a stores-loading party in a French port and trying to talk to the Frenchmen around me, trying to use my limited French. It was an exciting experience.

Q: So many men seem to have found the cruise a way of verifying the fact that they wanted to be sailors.

Adm. M.: That's very true. I'd never been to sea until these cruises and this did satisfy me that the navy was going to be an exciting career. On those ships, I can recall young ensigns who had been in the regiment - and I'd known them as midshipmen - and suddenly they're junior officers of the deck and functioning in other j.o. capacities. I was able to talk to some of them, and found that they were pretty excited about it, although they tried to act nonchalant in the presence of midshipmen. As an ensign they weren't supposed to be all that excited. But it satisfied me that this was something I was truly interested in doing, and I hoped that I could make a career of it. I'm not sure that any of us really thought about whether we were going to be in it for thirty years.

Minter, Jr. #1 - 15

It's really much different now. Many young fellows that come to the Naval Academy now come primarily for the education. That's unfair to say about a lot of them - but I'm sure that many of them come just for that reason. And also resignation is so much more prevalent these days. Nobody resigned from the Naval Academy when I was there. You could get kicked out for academics or you could get kicked out for demerits, but I don't recall anybody really resigning. Here again, this was maybe a -

Q: It was not easy to get a job, was it?

Adm. M.: - result of the Depression. There was no place for you to go, and so maybe many of us stayed because of that reason. But, in any event, I became satisfied that this was something I really wanted to do, and I never thought about it any other way.

Q: Of course, there was an advantage in the cruises being made, as they were in those days, on battleships where a lot of the men were there together. Now they're scattered all over the world.

Adm. M.: Well, they are, and as I say, it was a source of real concern to me when I was here as a superintendent and I'm sure the same applies now. The lack of ship billets for these young fellows - many times they don't have a very happy experience in the summer simply because the fleet commanders can't accommodate all of them they'd like to accommodate. And they are spread all around and I'm afraid their experience is not altogether a happy or, in some instances, a motivating one.

Q: Well, why isn't the navy high command concerned about this problem? Why didn't they do something about retaining some of the battleships for this kind of thing?

Adm. M.: Well, economically it was just totally infeasible, I suppose, to keep battleships in service just for the purpose of having a training squadron, with the primary purpose of taking midshipmen to sea on summer cruises. That would be a pretty inefficient method of training and I know that such a training squadron would not even be considered these days. I was in the Navy Department in the Pentagon when Zumwalt made the decision to decommission a large number of our old ships because they were just getting to be a tremendous drain on navy resources. The hope was we would build up to a much larger fleet with newer ships, so the numbers of ships we actually have now is about half of what we had a few years ago.

Minter, Jr. #1 - 17

Q: What about aviation summer? Was there one?

Adm. M.: Well, we didn't have the same sort of experience that midshipmen do now. By that I mean the aviation summer aspects now are taken care of at Pensacola. We had a second-class summer here at Annapolis in which we did get some aviation experience in the seaplanes that were based here at the Naval Academy.

Q: It was just flying in them, though -

Adm. M.: Oh yes, that's all. You got a chance to get in the cockpit or see the pilot at work a little bit, but just the experience of getting up in the air was a pretty interesting one for me and for most of us. At the same time, you know, we made a couple of dives out here in the bay in the old R-boats, and I must say that experience satisfied me that submarine duty was not going to be my cup of tea. No, I think from second-class year on aviation was certainly a goal of mine. But as you know, I'm sure, none of us were allowed to go to specialties of that type until two years after graduation so it was a fairly long-range view, you knew you were going to have two years in the fleet before you went to submarines or aviation.

Q: But at least it was an ambition —

Adm. M.: It was something that had its start right here, yes.

Q: Did you develop any ideas while you were there as a student of what you'd like to see changed and something that you did eventually have an opportunity to do?

Adm. M.: Are you talking about the curriculum at the Naval Academy?

Q: Yes, or any of the customs or that sort of thing.

Adm. M.: I don't think I was really wise enough to have thought that through. I must say, it always seemed strange to me that young men who had been fortunate enough to have had two, and sometimes three or four years of college before coming to the Naval Academy would have to plow right back through the same material here at the Naval Academy. It seems strange in retrospect that we didn't modify the system sooner. Many of the old timers today still question whether we have been all that wise in some of the changes that have been made here in recent years because they feel that there were advantages to the old system where everyone was exposed to the identical academic experience. The U.S. Naval combat leaders of World War II were Naval Academy graduates so how much more do you need to prove that this place does the job? I've had occasion to talk, when I was the superintendent particularly, with some of our very senior naval officers, and they were pretty disturbed about many major changes to the curriculum. I had difficulty making them understand why these changes were really terribly important and in the best interest of the navy. But their concerns were that we were departing from an established tradition and from something that had proven its worth and therefore we were stepping out into the unknown and probably it wasn't a very wise move. But I can't say that when I was here as a midshipman I looked at it that way. I did envy people who had had that much background and therefore didn't have to work nearly as hard academically as some of the others did, and I suppose occasionally you might sort of get the view that it's a little bit unfair for a fellow to be able to stand so high because he had had the background that the rest of us hadn't had, but by and large I can't recall as a midshipman thinking of major changes. And certainly it never crossed my mind that I'd ever come back to the Naval Academy - in any capacity. It simply never occurred to me.

Q: What did you think, or what do you think in retrospect of the course of study, the curriculum, as you experienced it there then? Was it adequate?

Adm. M.: No, I don't think it was. Particularly in the electrical engineering area. We got a bachelor of science degree in electrical engineering upon graduation. And I must say I'd be embarrassed to take my electrical engineering knowledge at the time I graduated and put it against anyone who had been through a similar course elsewhere. I think that the mathematics course here at the Naval Academy was very sound and I think most of the other courses were also, but I believe in the electronics, electric engineering area, we were deficient. I think we were sort of stereotyped and maybe I'm not being fair about this, but I don't really believe we had people that were terribly well qualified to teach in those subjects. In those days we had a number of officers back from the fleet - the same sort of mix we have now - and the idea was good. You would expose the midshipmen to people who had had recent fleet experience, and therefore who would be able to talk about the navy in addition to the subject they were teaching. But so many of those fellows were totally unqualified, really, to serve as instructors in depth - they were maybe one jump ahead of the midshipmen themselves, if that far. And so, it was the blind leading the blind in some of those areas and the midshipman came out the loser in this.

Q: Teaching is a very special vocation.

Adm. M.: There's no question about it.

Q: Not everybody has the aptitude.

Adm. M.: No, nor the attitude - and certainly many of these people just didn't have the background qualifications. As you know, the people that come to teach now all have degrees, all have expertise in this area, and the qualifications have gotten higher and higher. Now, you pay a little penalty for that because - I think I'm correct in saying that many of the officers that come to teach would not have had as much actual fleet experience maybe as the old timers that I used to see - and these were dyed-in-the-wool navy types who'd been in a long time, maybe pretty short on the teaching background knowledge, but at least they knew the navy, better than some of the young fellows now; and this is a direct result of the amount of time that's required to get ready. You have only so many years that you're available, so if you're going to be going to postgraduate school and getting other qualifications, you're not spending that time in the fleet, therefore you relinquish that sort of background.

But I think over all the educational experience here was a good one. We used to pride ourselves on the fact that, certainly our mathematics at the Naval Academy was fully the equivalent of that received by any graduate engineer in any of the schools in the country. Incidentally, one of the people that I admired most around here during my time was the head of the mathematics department, later Admiral H.K. Hewitt; he was Captain Hewitt at that time. I got to know him quite well.

Q: Kent Hewitt?

Adm. M.: I was in his home many, many times and he was a marvelous person and, of course, a great innovative leader in World War II. He not only headed the mathematics department, he knew math as well as any instructor over there. He could do anything in mathematics. That used to really impress me that a navy captain could go right into a midshipman recitation room and, if you were puzzling over a problem at the board, he could come up there and whip it off for you in nothing flat. And few of the heads of departments were as well qualified as he in their particular subjects.

Q: Well, he was an exceptionally sharp individual.

Adm. M.: He was indeed. Oh, there's no question about that.

Q: I knew him very well, too.

Adm. M.: Well, as I say, I was in his quarters many times when I was a midshipman. I saw him infrequently during the war and afterwards. I lectured at the War College on one occasion with him in attendance. I'd gone to have dinner with him and Mrs. Hewitt the night before, and when he heard I was going to lecture, he wanted to come and hear me. I felt almost like a plebe again, standing up there with Admiral Hewitt sitting in my audience - a great man.

Q: In your time there, with some of these younger officers coming back to teach for a year or two at the academy - coming from the fleet - was there anything reflected by them on the contest that was looming up in the Pacific?

Adm. M.: No. I really don't recall any of them having ever expressed the view that war with the Japanese was imminent. There was increasing concern during my time at the Naval Academy about what was happening in Germany. It was quite obvious that Hitler was moving fast, and there were ominous signs in Europe, and I think our attention was more focused on the likelihood of war breaking out in Europe than in the Pacific.

I remember my first class summer cruise. I rowed on the crew at Poughkeepsie, and the crew races at Poughkeepsie took place after the midshipmen training squadron ships had left, and so they were forced to send us to Europe - because we didn't have transatlantic flights in those days - on a North American line cruise ship. And the captain of the ship had been a cruiser captain in the German Navy in World War I. There were fifteen of us midshipmen aboard, and he invited us up to the bridge one day and was showing us around the bridge a little bit, and he took that occasion to try to enlist either our sympathy or our support. But anyway, I recall him telling us how important it was that the United States and Germany work together - that we had common interests, and that the Reich of Hitler was going to be the ruling force in Europe. It was an interesting little discussion from a former captain of a World War I German cruiser -

Q: And a little bit of propaganda too!

Adm. M.: Yes, exactly! But that was the sort of thing that more people were concerned about in those days than the Pacific.

I guess I didn't personally get to thinking that much about the possibilities of war with Japan until I served as an ensign, as custodian of confidential and secret publications on an admiral's staff. I was able to look at the Orange Plan and some of the other plans we had. Of course, some of our war games in the Pacific when I became a young officer were postulated to reflect the possibilities of war in the Pacific. But as far as people coming back from the fleet - I just don't recall any of them that gave any indications that war with the Japanese was a very likely possibility in the near future.

Q: Well, you approached graduation - did you have any choice in your first tour?

Adm. M.: Yes, I did, and I got my first choice. Our choice was predicated on our class standing, as I recall. And, as I mentioned before, my class standing wasn't the type one really would brag about. But I did get my first choice - I wanted to go to a heavy cruiser. I talked to some younger officers who had said that cruiser duty, they felt, had certain advantages to it. The advantages they enumerated to me were that in a battleship there were so many officers that you were just one among very many and your chances for moving up, possibly, and getting a little more individual attention and possibly moving into areas of responsibility came faster in a cruiser.

The cruisers were fast, exciting-type ships - at least, I thought they were - and so I requested and got a heavy cruiser, the USS Houston.

Q: Eight-inch guns?

Adm. M.: Eight-inch guns. I went with three classmates to Houston. I never had any particular reason to feel later on that I had made a bad choice, there -

Q: Did you have a good skipper?

Adm. M.: Well, I would not say that I would classify him as a highly competent professional naval officer. He was a nervous little man, and his nervousness wasn't helped at all by having President Roosevelt aboard for two different cruises. He was terribly, terribly uneasy with the President aboard - I suppose any captain would have been, but he wasn't very impressive as a captain under even normal circumstances. I saw other cruiser captains that I admired more.

He didn't help us very much either, frankly, in his marking of the fitness reports that he gave to us. We used to be allowed to go down to the captain's office to see our fitness reports about a week before they were to be mailed off the ship. I don't recall there was ever anything written saying this was permissible, but it -

Q: It was a preview.

Adm. M.: You could see what the captain had said about you.

Q: But you couldn't do anything about it.

Adm. M.: Oh no, nothing you could do about it. And, frankly, I thought my reports were great - I was getting 3.7s and 3.8s - only to find that every place else in the fleet this was considered a rather modest sort of a mark. It was brought to my attention how poorly our skipper marked when several of our lieutenants who were under the gun for lieutenant-commander got permission from the executive officer to go talk to the captain to tell him that, while they really believed that he was marking them in accordance with what he honestly thought they deserved, that perhaps he wasn't aware of the fact that his marking standards were so much lower than his contemporaries in the cruiser scouting force - that they were going to be killed before selection boards. He apparently took this to heart, because I'm told that he checked with his cruiser captain contemporaries and he did do something about raising the marks. When I left the Houston, when I was detached, the captain called me up and really told me what a wonderful job I'd done as one of his young ensigns. I appreciated what he had to say but those kind words didn't help very much professionally. When I graduated, the procedure was that your final class standing would be determined at the end of two years. That two-year probationary period was used to factor in your fleet fitness report marks in such a way that superior performance could greatly improve your class standing on graduation and vice versa. I know classmates who jumped 30 and 40 numbers in the class as a result of two years of work under captains who were very generous. Chicago's skipper, for example, was noted for high marks - he was practically a 4.0 marker - everybody got 4.0. Our captain wasn't anywhere near as generous as that in his marks, and I had a number of people that jumped over me in class standing as a consequence of that two years.

Q: You had the same skipper for two years?

Adm. M.: Yes, I did. And, in all fairness, I really do think he thought I had done a pretty good job. He was kind enough to call me up personally to tell me all this when I left the ship. One of those officers that was up fighting for his professional life, one of the lieutenants I mentioned, was Arthur A. Agerton - you may or may not have heard of him.

Q: Oh, yes.

Adm. M.: Well, he was quite a fellow. Here he was - he had written a book on navigation, he had done a lot of things - and he was a lieutenant struggling for promotion to lieutenant-commander, and the prospects were rather bleak.

Q: Doesn't that say something about the need for greater uniformity in writing fitness reports, and also a better ability on the part of officers to write fitness reports?

Adm. M.: There's no question about that. I don't know what the ultimate would be, but I've seen the fitness report system change time after time in my career, and BUPERS always hopes to refine it to the point that it will approach uniformity -

Q: That loses significance -

Adm. M.: Of course it does. But the last revision that I had to deal with was not one that I found terribly attractive. When it came out I was on active duty in Brussels, and when my aide came in and told me there were twenty-six single spaced type-written pages of instructions to explain how to make out a one-page form, I began to realize the depths to which we had arrived in the fitness report system.

There certainly were major differences in the way people wrote fitness reports, but that's been true throughout my career. I sat on several selections boards as a flag officer and when you review thousands of records you see how differently people mark. You eventually - particularly when you're looking at people coming up for flag selection - begin to identify certain individuals as very tough markers, and you just have to make certain allowances for those individuals.

Q: I was impressed with something Robin Quigley told me when she went up to submarine school in New London. She had not too heavy duties, I guess, and she had a feeling about these fitness reports, and so she inaugurated a course to teach the officers up there how to write proper fitness reports. She felt that they didn't all know, and I thought that was a good approach to things. I suppose at the academy it would be too soon to do that.

Adm. M.: Oh, I think so. Of course, they have a

system for midshipmen peer-ranking at the Naval Academy. That's designed to give midshipmen some sort of an insight into how to mark an individual for various traits. But I think it's too early in his career for a midshipman to really understand the niceties of the fitness report system, and feel that he can learn it better in the fleet.

Q: Yes.

Adm. M.: There are some people who operate on the theory that if you truly feel that an officer is fully deserving of a promotion, why, you're going to go all out in your fitness report of him. Those that you have some doubts about, you'll mark a little less generously. But there's a tremendous tendency - just tremendous tendency - to overmark in our navy. For some reason the British are much more realistic in their marking. If you work for a British officer on an international staff, for example, and he says you're doing an excellent job, that's considered pretty high praise. We're inclined to say so-and-so is going an outstanding job and we probably mean the same thing that the British do. They're more discriminating somehow. They're tougher in their evaluations, but I don't know how they inculcate that in their marking seniors.

Q: Isn't that true, reflected in the kind of awards which they hand out? They have different gradations for the same award –

Adm. M.: Exactly.

Q: – and to make these different categories is –

Adm. M.: Exactly. Yes. That award business got to be a very sore point between the American services during the war, as you know. I think the navy was probably right in its awards standards, but the award system got to be so terribly inflated. I think the Army Air Corps, later the Air Force, got to be the worst offender – they just handed out medals for anything and everything. I saw many instances of that. When I was in Trinidad, we did all the night flying for an air corps squadron which really didn't have the airplanes to do the job. But later on I found out that they were just decorated beyond belief and our people got nothing. We did all the work but they got all the awards.

Q: Well, let's go back to the Houston and tell me about some of the adventures you had on board the Houston. Where did she serve, largely?

Minter, Jr. #1 - 33

Adm. M.: In the Pacific. I joined Houston in Mare Island Shipyard, and at the time I went aboard, she was being outfitted for a cruise with the president - President Roosevelt.

Q: Was this a fishing expedition?

Adm. M.: Yes. It just seems incredible somehow, today, to think about the president going off practically incommunicado for a couple of weeks of relaxed fishing and so on, compared to what the president today has to carry around with him when he leaves Washington.

Q: The difference is in the atom bomb, isn't it?

Adm. M.: No question. Well, that and communications in general are so much better, and world events seem to move at a much faster pace, and the president just has to stay so much closer to the real world than seemed to be the case in Franklin Roosevelt's time.

Q: This was in the Caribbean, was it?

Adm. M.: No, we sailed from the west coast and eventually took him around, through the canal, the first of our cruises and into the Caribbean where he watched part of a fleet problem, and then he disembarked at Pensacola.

He came across country - this was at a time when politics was at a fever pitch. The president was attempting to pack the Supreme Court, and he had arrived in California with a political entourage that was just almost unbelievable. On this particular occasion the Houston was in Oakland and the president was going to board there. Governor MacAdoo was with him and a lot of political hangers-on.

Q: What year was this?

Adm. M.: This was '38. Houston served as flagship for the president as he reviewed the fleet in San Francisco Bay.

I can remember an interesting little sidelight on this trip. Commander Callaghan was the naval aide for Roosevelt.

The quarterdeck, before we got underway for this trip around San Francisco Bay, was an absolute madhouse of people milling around and trying to get near the president. The officer of the deck was given a frantic communication to get to Commander Callaghan - something that Commander Callaghan had to be told. He turned to the junior officer of the deck, who was a brand new ensign out of the Naval Academy, and said: "Find Commander Callaghan and give him this message";

and this young fellow went scurrying around the quarterdeck, and the first person he saw with three stripes he saluted smartly and said, "Sir, are you Commander Callaghan?" And old Admiral Bloch unfolded his arms - he'd seen the three stripes but he hadn't seen the broad one underneath - and Bloch said, "No, I'm not Commander Callaghan. There's Commander Callaghan over there." Callaghan was surrounded by newspaper people, and he was parrying questions, and all of a sudden this young ensign felt a shove in the back, and it was Admiral Bloch - pushed him right into Callaghan, said, "Now, give him your message, whatever it is!"

Well, a few days later we were underway, things had quieted down, and this young fellow was junior officer of the deck underway. Callaghan came up on the bridge, saw him, walked over, saluted smartly, said, "Good morning, Sir! - Oh, pardon me, I thought you were the captain."

Oh, we had some great times there, with the president. My Shellback certificate was signed by President Roosevelt.

Q: Oh, really?

Adm. M.; Yes, that's one of my proud momentos of those days.

That was an interesting group with him. The secret service men we got to know pretty well. I was the junior mess treasurer, so I had to deal with those fellows as far as their wardroom mess bills were concerned. Mike Riley, who later became one of the senior secret service men with the president's detail was one of the group.

General Pa Watson was of course along with the president; and one of the memorable occasions was the Shellback-Pollywog dinner we had in the wardroom the night before crossing the line. The president came down and had dinner in the wardroom with the ship's officers, and of course all the Pollywogs were seated at the cruise mess benches in between the arms of a huge "u" shaped table at which all the Shellbacks were seated. Steven Early was spokesman for the Pollywogs. He was the press secretary for the President. General Watson had been across the line several times, and he served as spokesman for the Shellbacks. The president spoke just very briefly that night. He later signed our Shellback certificates.

Q: You also engaged in some war games, didn't you, in the Pacific?

Adm. M.: Yes, we did. We had two - I guess it was

two - battle problems that I participated in. I'm a little hazy on my timing, now. I don't remember the specific games but one included an air attack on Honolulu, and it showed what could be done with carrier aircraft.

That was something that really interested me - the attitude of the so-called "black shoe" senior officers in those days. There was a very sincere distrust of aviation in the navy on the part of some or, rather, an unwillingness to accept or acknowledge aviation capabilities. That may not be the right way to describe it, but I remember Rear Admiral Rowcliff, whom I worked for, who was ComCruScoFor at the time - he was chief umpire in one of these battle games and Houston was his flagship. Houston was hit by aircraft from Ranger - simulated strikes - and it infuriated him because nobody aboard had seen the planes in time to get us to full general quarters condition, and therefore the gun mounts were really hardly manned before the attack was over. I can remember him saying, "They didn't do a damn bit of damage, it was just a lot of noise!" And here they'd come out of the sun, they'd dive-bombed us - we were dead ducks - there was just no question in my mind about it.

But for me, as a young ensign, to hear a senior admiral disclaiming any possibility of damage from aircraft from a carrier just struck me as being absurd. I didn't know how he could possibly have arrived at that conclusion. But it was sort of indicative, I think, of —

Q: It wasn't untypical at all!

Adm. M.: No, it was not. No, it was a battleship navy in those days.

Q: Even as we approached World War II.

Adm. M.: Exactly. Oddly enough, Admiral Rowcliff was a great friend of Bill Halsey's. I used to see Halsey come aboard to visit. They were great buddies otherwise. But Admiral Rowcliff just refused to acknowledge that aviation was going to have any part to play in the war, any significant part. I remember when I was detached to go to Pensacola, he was really upset. I remember him telling me, and he wasn't joking, "Just another good man gone wrong" — and he tried to talk me out of it.

Q: Of course, at that point it was much easier to go to Pensacola than it had been a few years before.

Minter, Jr. #1 - 39

Adm. M.: Oh, it was. It was.

Q: You were really going off onto a dead-end street.

Adm. M.: Well, that's right. Of course, by this time, the possibilities of us getting into the war were getting increasingly apparent. I had requested Pensacola before, but the gunnery officer of Houston, which I was then serving in, had convinced me that it would be better for my career to stay on board. He was going to give me a division and a turret, and this was heady stuff for a young ensign. But before that promise ever came to fruition, I was whisked off to Admiral Rowcliff's staff as a communications watch officer, and once I got there they would not allow me then to resubmit my papers for Pensacola. So I spent a year as a communications watch officer on Admiral Rowcliff's staff, and then went to Pensacola.

Q: What did the two years on the Houston contribute actually to your knowledge and to your career?

Adm. M.: They were quite important to me, really, in subsequent years - as an aviator particularly.

I qualified as an officer of the deck underway, I qualified as an engineering watch officer, and this stood me in good stead because, as you will recall,

Minter, Jr. #1 - 40

many officers who were just aviators and had not had this shipboard experience. When they got along to that stage in their careers where they were commanders or captains, and were slated for surface commands, they lacked the background that those of us who had two years in the fleet before going into aviation had had.

Q: Unless they were fortunate to serve under an officer who required them to be so qualified.

Adm. M.: That's right. But, human nature being what it is, if you're an aviator, you're inclined to stick with the aviation business and not fight your way up to the bridge to try to become qualified as OOD in a carrier, for example.

So it did a lot for me. It prepared me; I feel, qualified me far better than I would have been otherwise.

Q: Did the Houston carry a plane?

Adm. M.: Yes. We had SOCs, and I used to fly in them with the aviation cadets. I roomed with an aviation cadet aboard Houston, and so I got some flight experience with the aviation unit. I used to do some of the spotting when they'd go up for spotting practice for short-range battle practice.

But I do feel that that time was really well spent. In many respects, I wish today we still could afford the luxury of having young fellows from the Naval Academy go to sea for a year or two years before going to Pensacola or before going to New London. I do believe that this is a pretty valuable experience, but I realize the constraints of time these days are such that we don't have that luxury any longer.

Actually, although I resented it at the time, the year on the staff that I was required to serve as a communications watch officer -

Q: How did you happen to get that assignment?

Adm. M.: Well, as I mentioned, the gunnery officer of Houston had told me if I would withdraw my papers for Pensacola he would make me a division officer. I had hardly gotten my papers withdrawn, and suddenly I got a set of orders, and he couldn't rescind them, for me to go to this communications watch officer -

Q: What was back of those orders?

Adm. M.: I really don't know. I think just the fact that I was available. They just needed a CWO in the commander cruiser scouting force staff, and that's where I ended up.

As I say, I resented it at the time - it made me a year later going to Pensacola than I would like to have been - but that experience, too, was an interesting one. I felt that I learned perhaps a little bit more about fleet operations than I knew. I saw it from a broader perspective working for an admiral - at least I saw how the cruiser formations worked, and also got some insight into the battle problems in a way I wouldn't have gotten otherwise. I don't mean to say I got an in-depth education, but I had a better feel for it maybe than I would have had otherwise.

Q: Well, what was he like, Rowcliff?

Adm. M.: One of the old school type - very stern, gruff-type individual. He had been the director of naval communications, so he knew quite a bit about the communications side of things. He was like a lot of those fellows, though, that I thought about later on - they didn't last very long when the war started. They were peace-time admirals.

Our operations were fairly routine. We'd go to sea on Monday, come back on Friday, everybody except those with the watch had the weekend off. You'd go to sea next Monday, you'd come back on Friday - occasionally you'd go on a lengthier cruise. But the navy, it seems to me, had sort of stagnated in the sense that it was a pretty comfortable life, I'm sure, for admirals and for captains in those days. They all lived pretty well and life didn't seem too threatening. Our enlisted men weren't leaving in droves the way they do now; they stayed, and they made it a career. And so it was a pretty stable kind of existence. But of course, the very stability breeds in some very undesirable traits, I think, in your senior officers. The fact that they weren't threatened seems to me —

Q: They're not challenged.

Adm. M.: I'm talking now as a very junior officer. My views of things may be wrong, but I really felt that so many of those fellows just didn't have very much to offer, and certainly when the war started they were weeded out pretty quickly. When Ernie King took over, things began to move, and you didn't have people that were just sort of drifting with the tide the way I'm sure a lot of them were.

There were some very able people, certainly. Bill Halsey was in that group at that time, and of course Admiral Kimmel was a cruiser division commander at the time that I was working on this particular staff, and he went right up, of course, to Pacific Fleet command. But an awful lot of them that were cruiser captains - I never saw much more of them. They were phased out pretty quickly, and some of the older admirals were, too.

Q: Were you married at that time?

Adm. M.: No, I was married en route to Pensacola in 1940.

Q: Would you then comment on the wardroom life and its importance to unmarried officers?

Adm. M.: Well, the bachelors always felt that the deck was stacked against them because the liberty routine seemed to favor the married officers pretty much.

Q: Yes, the wardroom was home actually -

Adm. M.: The wardroom was home, and that was another thing that differed in the cruisers from the battleships. The battleships, because of the large number of officers, had a JO mess; in the cruiser you had a single mess. The executive officer was the president of the mess, of course, but all cruiser ships' officers, except the Captain, ate in the same mess.

Now, I've talked to friends of mine who served in the battleships, and some of their fondest

Minter, Jr. #1 - 45

recollections as JOs was in the JO mess, where they had a relatively uninhibited sort of life, I gather. We were much more formal in our mess routine, and it was a real breach of etiquette if you came in late to dinner, or any meal, as a matter of fact. You had to have a pretty good excuse to arrive at the table after the executive officer had been seated.

So we were fairly formal, but I feel that for a junior officer it was pretty interesting experience because we could at least sit and hear the department heads and the exec in some of the discussions they had. While we were seldom asked for our advice, at least we were privy to some of the things going on that we might not have known about otherwise.

I think the wardroom experience was a healthy one for me and for my classmates who were aboard - there were four of us in the same class that went to the Houston.

Q: What about the sports program in the fleet?

Adm. M.: Well, it was fairly active, and of course if you had participated in sports at the Naval Academy, you were automatically going to be the coach of whatever team corresponded to that -

Q: So you became what?

Adm. M.: So I became the crew coach. We used to have the old whale boat races. They were called the Lysistrata Cup Races. I became the crew coach, and this got to be a real chore because the executive officer wanted me to have a good crew and he wanted us to win - but he didn't want it enough to give me any time to work with the crew during working hours. In other words, I had to try to race my people and prepare them for races at 6 o'clock in the morning or at 5 o'clock in the afternoon.

Q: Not very propitious.

Adm. M.: This didn't sit too well with the people who were married, my enlisted men who had wives ashore. It took a pretty dedicated fellow to stick it out. We did pretty well, though - we had a pretty fair crew -

Q: The competition was intense, wasn't it?

Adm. M.: Oh, indeed it was. I think we came in third or second - I've forgotten now. But anyway, we had, at least, a crew that was reasonably competitive.

We didn't have a heavy sports program in the cruisers. The battleships had more. The battleships had football teams. We didn't have football, but we had crew, and of course we had boxing, and that was about it. The ships' officers really didn't have much of anything in the way of organized sports. The JOs used to go ashore frequently in Long Beach and play touch football or play a little softball.

Q: Golf?

Adm. M.: Golf, we had - I wasn't a golfer at that time, but many of our ship's officers were. Tennis was a pretty active sport. I played a little tennis. But as far as organized sports among the officers, we had very little of that.

Q: Well, you served only a year with Admiral Rowcliff on the Chicago, and then you finally achieved your ambition to go to Pensacola. This was in 1940, was it not?

Adm. M.: It was, yes.

Q: So, would you give me a picture of Pensacola and the method of training at that point. This was on the threshold of World War II.

Adm. M.: It was, and for that very reason, I believe, the training program at Pensacola was altered rather significantly just about the time I went there. I arrived at Pensacola for a flight class convening the 26th of August.

Q: You took your wife down there?

Adm. M.: My wife, yes, we went down and we found accommodations in a little house for which I paid $50 a month to a chief petty officer. And that house still exists in a rather nice little community now.

But, in any event, I arrived there the 26th of August and just about this time the training program changed. I don't know that our class was the first one, but we were certainly one of the first that was affected by the new training procedure. What this amounted to was that the classes from my class on did not - each individual didn't - go through every phase of flight training that had previously been the case. Previously students going through Pensacola were normally there for a year or more for total flight training, in which they were exposed to every aspect of training - fighter-types, seaplanes, and so on.

Q: Yes. Much more leisurely.

Adm. M.: That's right, and more extensive. But at the time I arrived it became apparent that they weren't going to have the luxury of putting everybody through every phase of flight training, and therefore they began to specialize. If you were going to be a fighter pilot, you went one route; if you were going to be a seaplane pilot, OS-2-Us for example, or SOCs, you went different route, slightly different; and if you were going to do as I did, go into patrol planes, you had another route. The result was that you went through a primary training, which was common to all of us, but from that point on you began to move off into the various specialties. So I was never exposed to fighter training. For example, I didn't have any scouting plane experience.

Q: What did you choose as your specialty?

Adm. M.: Well, I chose patrol planes - actually, I was assigned to patrol planes. I didn't have that much choice.

Q: Were there any aptitude tests given when you arrived?

Adm. M.: You mean to determine which way you were going to go?

Q: Yes, or determine your ability to be a flier.

Minter, Jr. #1 - 50

Adm. M.: No. No, not when you first arrived. I will mention something pretty interesting that happened, though. We had some doctors there who were -

Q: Oh, yes. I hope you will tell us about that.

Adm. M.: - interested in starting a sort of an effort to determine if there was some way it could be determined whether one could get through the flight-training program or not; and they developed a series of tests to make such a determination.

Q: One of those doctors was very famous, I think.

Adm. M.: Yes. I was one of a group known as "the thousand aviators" who went through Pensacola at this time. They had 1,056 of us, all of whom were subjected to a series of tests, and all of whom have been given special physical examinations in all the years since - I still go down to Pensacola and get the "thousand aviator" physical exam, as a matter of fact. This developed into a study of the aging process using a select group of healthy young Americans - but initially it was designed to see if it could be predicted in advance whether you'd make a flier or not. They maintained, at the time I went through, that they were quite certain they could tell in about 90% of the cases whether you could get through Pensacola, by these series of tests. And some even would go so far as to say that they could predict at what phase you would wash out if you didn't get through - whether acrobatics would get you or whatever. Of course, if you really could be 95% certain of something like this and put it into effect, it would save an awful lot of money in training people that were obviously not really well qualified to go through.

There's a curious sort of a mentality about this thing. Very few people, that I know, will have the just plain guts to admit that this was not their cup of tea, once they've put their shoulder to the wheel and gone to Pensacola to be a flier. They wouldn't want to admit that they were either afraid of flying or that they really didn't think they were going to make it.

Q: This is especially true of aviation, isn't it?

Adm. M.: Well, I think it is. I can't speak for the other specialties, but it certainly is true of aviation to some degree. It was a rare fellow who would say, as one of my classmates did after his second flight - he came down and simply said - "This just isn't for me."

At this time they were doing everything they could to encourage people to stay, and so his flight instructor said, "Oh, you're giving up too quickly." And he said, "No, I'm not. I'm sure this isn't my cup of tea." He said, "Well, stay around for one more flight." So he did. The next day they went for a flight, and he came back and the instructor said, "Do you feel any different?" He said, "Listen. You're wasting your time, and I'm wasting my time, and we're both wasting the government's time. I don't want to be a flier."

Well, I admired that fellow because I know there were others that probably felt that way, some at least who just didn't have the guts to say it.

Q: Did they employ gliders at your time, then?

Adm. M.: No.

Q: That was earlier.

Adm. M.: No, we didn't have gliders -

Q: That was a technique I believe that they used in the '30s, some time or other, in order to determine aptitudes.

Adm. M.: Yes. Well, I think they thought, at least from an operational standpoint, that they could pretty well tell.

Most of the instructors felt that they could get a pretty good handle on whether fellows were going to make it or not. To be honest with you, I can't recall now when my class went through at what time we were told the type flying we were going to do. But I don't remember being in a position to say, "I would prefer fighters, or I would prefer this." It differs in respect to the way it's done now at Pensacola, as I understand it - there is an aptitude determination, and they decide which ones are going to be jet pilots and which ones are going to go into patrol planes, or helicopters.

In any event, our course was specialized, and our course was shortened. Our total flight time was not nearly as extensive as it had been before. I think I graduated from Pensacola with maybe 230 or 40 total flying hours, including the basic training course and the more extensive time in the seaplanes that we went right into.

Q: This meant that a certain amount of it had to be on the job training, then, later on - ?

Adm. M.: Yes. Well, I'm not at all sure that we went to the seaplane squadrons, which I went to - PBY outfits. I'm not sure we were any less trained than perhaps our predecessors, who had had other types of flying. I think we were as well qualified in the seaplanes as fellows who had gone through fighter training, then had patrol-plane training, and went to the fleet. But we hadn't had as well rounded an aviation background as those others did. So we were specialized in that sense.

Q: The forepart of your training was on ground, wasn't it?

Adm. M.: Oh, yes. The first two weeks we were there was a ground training course in which you learned Morse Code, and you got some instruction in maintenance of aircraft, and you got just general aeronautical background experience. It was fairly primitive by today's standards, certainly, but at least it gave you a feel -

Q: So were the planes, though.

Adm. M.: Yes, they were indeed. The old Yellow Perils, the N2Ss, and the N3Ns, were the types that we flew.

I remember well my first flight in an N3N. My instructor, who later became a great friend of mine, was a JG - I was an ensign - no, I'd just become a JG. In any event, we took off from Chevalier Field. Chevalier didn't have extensive runways. You didn't need a lot of space to land those little airplanes - they were light, they weren't very fast - and so they didn't have runways as such, just a huge asphalt mat that you landed on. And you landed, of course, in accordance with what the wind sock indicated the wind direction was. But because the wind could be kind of tricky down there, there was some danger of groundlooping these little airplanes, and I remember this instructor telling me over the gosport as we were coming in to land the first time - he said, "Now, you've got to be very careful when you get ready to land because the wind may shift a little bit, and so you've got to really pay attention or you can groundloop one of these things pretty easily." Whereupon we went in and groundlooped with the instructor at the controls and it spun around once and stopped, and he looked back and said, "See how easy it is?"

Q: Was he talking to you and so he didn't pay attention?

Adm. M.: Yes.

I think, as I mentioned a moment ago, our total flight time at Pensacola - our total instruction time - was reduced by this specialization that I mentioned. I went to Pensacola in late August of '40 and I got my wings in March of '41.

Minter, Jr. #1 - 56

Q: Well, that was speedy.

Adm. M.: So it wasn't really a very extensive course. The man who gave us our wings was Captain A.C. Read, who had been the NC4 pilot.

Q: How did Mrs. Minter take to this twist in your career?

Adm. M.: Well, she was remarkably, I think, relaxed about it. She worried, I suppose, as most of the young wives did, about the dangers associated with it. I had some trouble with one phase of the flight program. It was the 20-hour check - that was a fairly extensive check that they gave you after you had completed a certain amount of the curriculum - and I had a little difficulty with that thing, and I suppose I was a little hard to live with during the time of preparing for the check. But by and large Mary was being exposed to navy life for her first time. She was with a group of gals, many of whom are great friends of ours to this day, and they all were experiencing the same sort of thing. It was an exciting kind of a time too. We were all young aviators, most of us newlyweds, and we were all sort of in the same boat. We all lived about the same way, none of us lived very well, but we were at least comfortable and we had our little group of friends, so she could handle it pretty well.

My mother was not quite as excited about this idea as my wife was. She was more concerned I think than perhaps my wife was at the time.

Q: Was there attrition in the class?

Adm. M.: Yes. Of course we lost some through crashes - not a large number, but we did have some. The attrition was relatively low. The wash-out rate was not terribly high, and I think again this might have been sort of the temper of the times. We were obviously getting close to the time when we were going to need every pilot we could get, and so I suspect that, maybe, the rules for retention were relaxed to a degree. I think they were more lenient possibly in our time than had been the case in the past, when the competition was a little keener. In fairness, I have to say I think that many of us going through at that particular time benefitted, if that's the proper word, from perhaps a little less rigidity in the retention.

Q: Were these all navy recruits or were there others?

Adm. M.: Oh, yes, there were coast guard officers there also.

Minter, Jr. #1 - 58

Q: Were they training any foreign pilots at Pensacola at the same time?

Adm. M.: I don't recall that we were, not. There could have been some Canadians, but I just don't recall any foreign pilots. Not in any numbers like we have these days, certainly.

Q: How closely was Washington watching the training schedule down there? You were at the beginning of the new regime in training.

Adm. M.: Well, I'm sure they were watching very closely. I was so far down the totem pole that I couldn't have been really aware of major concerns on the part of the Bureau of Aeronautics, but I've been told since of course that the decision to go to that shortened and more specialized course was one that was taken at the instigation of the Bureau of Aeronautics, and I'm sure they were watching the training command very, very closely.

We had some pretty impressive people there at Pensacola - or at least people that had been associated with the early days of aviation. Captain Read was one of those. Aviation had come a long way since their active flying time. They all stayed very current, I think, and I feel that the program there was pretty well thought out, considering the fact that our airplanes were somewhat primitive and they weren't first-line. I didn't get in a PBY, for example, until right towards the end of my course, and that was the type of squadron I was going to when I got my wings.

Q: After getting your wings down at Pensacola you were assigned to Norfolk first?

Adm. M.: I was. I went to a VP-73, a PBY-5 squadron based at Norfolk. We were there less than a month, as I recall, and we were moved to Quonset Point. This was the first operational squadron to arrive at Quonset Point Naval Air Station in Rhode Island. Quonset Point was just being completed at this time.

Q: We weren't actually in the war, yet, so –

Adm. M.: No, this was May of 1941. Quonset Point hadn't even been commissioned yet as an air station. It was commissioned the first of July, 1941, but they wanted us there to start operating from there, and from there our squadron went to Argentia in Newfoundland.

Q: So you were part of what they called the neutrality patrol, were you not?

Minter, Jr. #1 - 60

Adm. M.: Oh yes, indeed we were. We did our first real operational flying out of Quonset Point. We were there most of that summer, and then we flew to Argentia. We flew active patrols out of Argentia.

I was at Argentia, as a matter of fact - we were there - at the time the Atlantic Charter was signed. This was a pretty interesting experience in the sense that of course it was being very, very closely held, the information that the president and Churchill were coming in there.

Our squadron was living - the personnel were living - aboard a little seaplane tender named Belknap. It was a converted old four-piper that had just been made into a seaplane tender, and a rather poor one at that.

Q: Named after Reggie Belknap?

Adm. M.: Admiral Belknap, yes.

I recall so well - Augusta was Admiral King's fleet flagship and she came in first. We heard the president was aboard. Speculation was rife that something big was going to happen, and sure enough, HMS Prince of Wales came in with Churchill aboard.

Argentia Air Station hadn't been completed to take land planes at that time so some participants in the coming conference flew up in seaplanes. I remember standing on the deck one time and watching a whale boat go alongside a seaplane that had flown up from Washington. They brought the personnel over to Belknap just long enough to have a ship's boat from Augusta come to pick them up properly, and among the group that came aboard was General Marshall. I had seen his pictures, I knew who he was, but I'd never seen him in the flesh before. I happened to be standing nearby, which I suppose is the reason he collared me and started asking me questions about the Argentia Naval Air Station, which was under construction in sight of the deck of the Belknap. I was a JG - I'd hardly gotten started talking to him until I felt a hand on my shoulder and turned around and Commodore Mullinnix, realizing a JG was nobody to be discussing things like this with General Marshall, pulled me to one side and took over the conversation.

I was visiting a friend aboard Augusta when Churchill was piped aboard and rendered honors prior to being received by the President for the start of their talks. One of the president's aides was his son, young Franklin. I'd rowed against young Franklin on the Harvard crew, so I knew him very, very slightly. But in any event, I was trapped in the passageway when I heard the indications that Churchill was coming aboard, and I couldn't get out of the way, and here came Admiral Ernie King steaming down the passageway.

We had no dry-cleaning facilities whatsoever - I was wearing the baggiest, crummiest-looking set of greens you can imagine, and I can still feel the stare of Admiral King as he went by JG Minter, and if he had ever been able to get hold of me, he would've strangled me, I'm sure. I couldn't wait to get off of Augusta, but I was there in time to see Churchill come up to the quarterdeck and receive his honors, and then be taken on up to meet with the president and sign the Atlantic Charter.

We were flying patrols out of Argentia and were not there very long until the decision was made to send our squadron to Iceland. We flew to Iceland in September, '41, and the squadron operated from our Icelandic base until January 1942. We'd been told by the British, who were flying Sunderlands out of there, that flying seaplanes out of Iceland after October was asking for trouble, but the submarine situation was so desperate that the decision was made in Washington that we just had to stay on, and we flew the whole time.

Q: Let's go back to Quonset. You say they were building the base - tell me something about that. What was the concept? How large was it to be? What were the facilities?

Adm. M.: It was quite a large base, because it was

to accommodate both seaplanes and carrier aircraft for training. We had a carrier aircraft service unit based there. The Ranger operated her aircraft in and out of there occasionally. Of course, I was with seaplanes, and we had major seaplane ramp facilities there and major hangars to accommodate PBYs and PBMs that we had in those days. It was quite a large base, and at the time we arrived, as I mentioned, it was just being completed. It was so new, as a matter of fact, that when the wind would blow - and it always did up there - the sand and material from the sides of the field that didn't have any sod on it filled the air. Every morning you'd go to the hangar and find your desk covered with a fine silt of this blowing sand.

We lived in very modest accommodations. When we first got there our mess hall was in a temporary little wooden structure. We finally moved into the completed BOQ, those of us that didn't have our wives there, in a very nice BOQ building that was built to accommodate personnel based or operating out of there.

It got to be quite a sizable base, and I served there two other times. The next time I came back to serve I had command of a maintenance squadron, which took care of patrol planes - seaplanes as well as land planes. Quonset was a very important base, one of the biggest ones we had on the east coast at that time, when it was finally completed.

Minter, Jr. #1 - 64

Q: Yes. What was neutrality patrol? What was your real mission? Sighting submarines, reporting them, or what?

Adm. M.: Yes, it was, and we did some convoy coverage. As a matter of fact, before we actually got into the war - could you shut that off for just a second?

Interview #2 with Vice Admiral Charles S. Minter, Jr.,
U.S. Navy

Place: Admiral Minter's residence, Providence,
Annapolis, Maryland

Date: Tuesday morning, 19 June 1979

Subject: Biography

By: John T. Mason, Jr.

Q: I've been looking forward to this chapter, Sir. You're going to talk about the neutrality patrol and the role that your Squadron 73 played in this in the early days - 1941. This is an interesting period, and not too heavily documented. Perhaps you will add to the picture for me.

Adm. M.: Well, as I mentioned before, VP-73 moved into Naval Air Station Quonset in May of 1941, which was before the commissioning of the base on the first of July, 1941. We flew training missions out of Quonset Point for the remainder of the summer of 1941, and then in late July the squadron moved to Argentia.

Argentia was in the process of development as a land base - it was then operational as a seaplane base. The tender that we operated from at that time was the

USS Albamarle. We flew patrol missions out of Argentia for better than a month before the squadron moved on to Iceland. During that time, the month of August, the Atlantic Charter signing took place. We had no part to play in that, of course, but we were actively involved in patrol missions out of Argentia. Admiral Bristol was in Argentia at that time.

Q: Mark Bristol?

Adm. M.: Mark Bristol. He died there about a year later of a heart attack, but he was conducting and controlling the neutrality patrol forces in the Atlantic Fleet at that time.

We flew a number of patrol missions out of Argentia, and I might mention just in passing, we experienced weather there that I've never seen since, in that you could have the densest fog you could imagine with a strong wind blowing, which is an unusual thing. You could have 25 or 30 knots of wind and you could have pea-soup fog.

Q: And it didn't dissipate?

Adm. M.: It didn't dissipate. I can remember many times coming back in from flights and actually seeing that fog rolling up Placentia Bay like a kind of river.

You would try to get in under, of course, before it actually closed in the base.

I might mention also that at this particular time I remember seeing my first, very primitive GCA. There was a trailer that was used for giving us guidance - a very primitive type of GCA that could lead us down, a glide path to the water. Most of us were very suspicious of it at that time because we'd not had any experience in operating with it. But we worked day after day and one of our squadron officers, who had a fairly decent electronics background and knew more about this equipment and had more faith in it than any of the rest of us, was instrumental in getting us really to realize its potentialities. With the heavy fog that you would experience up there frequently, this was a pretty valuable piece of equipment to have to bring you in.

Q: Did you have somebody from the bureau there also?

Adm. M.: There were technicians there operating this equipment. It was based on the runway, but they could give us a touchdown point maybe a thousand yards off the runway after bringing us in on a glide pattern. So, it was my first look at anything approaching GCA.

Q: What were your specific orders as a patrol squadron

at that time out of Argentia? What was your mission?

Adm. M.: Our mission was to patrol and to attempt to locate submarines - German submarines - and also, of course, any shipping other than our own U.S. shipping.

Q: And once the submarine was located, then what?

Adm. M.: Our orders were a little bit hazy on that point. If we were operating with a convoy - covering a convoy - we could attack a submarine - and this brings up an interesting point - I recall one of the pilots in our squadron who was really quite disturbed about this situation under which we were operating. I recall him telling me one night that he really wondered if he had the right to attack a German submarine, because we were not at war, and he found it difficult to square with his own conscience - attacking a submarine.

Q: It became a moral issue with him.

Adm. M.: It became a moral issue with him.
I didn't have that problem, I must tell you, because I thought that we were as close to being at war as we could be, and it was inevitable. But further than that, the submarines were obviously there to sink

our ships that we were using to get supplies to England, and so it didn't trouble me. But that was the first time I came across someone who really challenged, you might say, higher authority.

The president had earlier in that summer declared an Unlimited National Emergency and had extended the Neutrality Zone. And of course, shortly after this we had a couple of attacks on U.S. destroyers. I've forgotten the exact dates now, but I know Reuben James was sunk. Kearny was hit and limped into Iceland - we were in Iceland when she came in. So, after these episodes, there was no longer any question about what we were going to do in the event of sighting submarines.

Our squadron saw few submarines during this entire time we were there. Well, in the first place, there weren't lots of German submarines in those days - they didn't have that many and those they did have were attempting to get themselves in convoy lanes and fairly well off from our base.

Q: In large measure weren't they concentrating on the tankers coming out of the gulf?

Adm. M.: Actually, at this particular time, the convoys going to England were not hit hard at all. It wasn't until '42 that things began to really heat up in that connection - and they were concentrating more on tanker-types, yes.

As I mentioned, we left for Iceland in early September. That was, I think, about a 1500-mile flight. In any event, half of our squadron - six planes - flew to Iceland, and I was in that group. We landed and based in a fjord at Reykjavik. Our planes were PBYs - not amphibious airplanes - and so we had to use mooring buoys. Our personnel lived aboard two old converted four-pipers, <u>Belknap</u> and <u>Goldsborough</u>. Living conditions were fairly austere.

We also at this time began to build a base ashore, a bunch of Nissen huts - our crew actually constructed those and lived in them, so a large part of the squadron was actually living ashore, with many of us still living aboard -

Q: Was that the place that they called Keflavik or something like that?

Adm. M.: No, Keflavik was a base that was built later on. This was right on the banks of the fjord that we were operating from.

We had half of a PBM squadron there also and, in addition, at the time we arrived, the British were operating a few Sunderland aircraft out of there. As I mentioned before, the British advised us when we arrived that they did not believe seaplane operations were feasible in the Icelandic weather after October. The powers that be in Washington apparently decided to gamble on this. Our convoy coverage at this time was so important that no effort was made to move us. We stayed on right up until January of 1942, with the PBYs.

Q: Their advice - was it borne out?

Adm. M.: On the 15th of January - I think that's the date - 1942 we had a storm. The wind blew 90 knots or better for about eight hours. We lost seven airplanes at the buoys, and in Halfjord, where the fleet anchorage was located, ships were dragging anchor with a number of near and some actual collisions. Admiral Giffin was there - Wichita and Tuscaloosa almost hit. It was a terrible storm, but the interesting thing was, I am totally convinced we wouldn't have lost a single airplane if we had had the wisdom to have somebody aboard - a pilot and a plane captain just to turn up the engines. But aviation policy in those days was any time the wind got above 35 knots you moved all the crews off the airplanes. It does seem a little silly in retrospect because I'm sure that by just turning up the engines - obviously they were turned into the wind anyway - we could've saved all those airplanes. These planes, incidentally, were all loaded. We were to fly back to the States in these airplanes the next day. They had personal gear aboard, they had everything aboard, and we lost all of them right there at the base.

Q: It's like abandoning ship –

Adm. M.: It really is. It was a pity to stand there on the deck of the old Belknap and watch those planes go down. We could see them just getting lower and lower in the water, with nobody aboard and the waves beating over the bows and filling them up, and eventually they all went down.

Until that time, we had not had weather that I thought was so bad that we could not have operated. We didn't have a storm even remotely comparable to that prior to that time, and we operated later from the field, because we flew PBY-5As – amphibious PBYs – to replace the ones we had lost. But the British were quite concerned about the weather conditions and thought that we should move in October.

I've flown a little bit out of the Aleutians, but not in wartime, and I've talked to pilots that flew out of there, and I suspect that their weather was worse than ours. But ice and wind in the wintertime is bad enough for me, particularly in the absence of really good homing equipment to get you back to base. We lost a couple of planes that plowed into mountains up there in bad weather.

Q: I think I have a description of that very same storm from Jerry Wright, who was on the Mississippi; and she was badly battered.

Adm. M.: Oh yes, that storm was a fierce one, and it was something that was a terrible frustration for our aerologist up there. They didn't have enough weather information coming in to make really very valid forecasts, and every day we'd get just the aerologist's best guess, really. Now, we had some weather stations operating on Greenland, but communications were not always that good, and the result was that our local aerologist simply wasn't getting sufficient information to make a meaningful forecast. He hadn't the faintest clue that that storm was going to hit.

Q: It takes special indoctrination to understand that kind of weather, and our people hadn't been exposed to it.

Adm. M.: That's right.

Q: Now, the British had more knowledge of it because —

Adm. M.: They operated there.

Q: - they'd operated there.

How were you received by the Icelanders?

Adm. M.: Not very hospitably. They were very stand-offish. As a matter of fact, more than standoffish. I think they really resented our presence there, and that's not too difficult to understand. We were a sizable military presence. We had the U.S. Army, Navy, and Marines and these air contingents. The army air corps was flying planes from the Reykjavik field - fighters - and here we came in with these two squadrons of seaplanes, and the British had their seaplanes in there. The fleet anchorage was far enough away from Reykjavik that fleet personnel didn't get into town that frequently, but for all of us based right there at Reykjavik, of course, it was our only liberty port - and the Icelanders were sort of overwhelmed with military, primarily American, and not very happy about it.

Q: You were a threat to their economic life, were you not? And also, more importantly, to their womenfolk?

Adm. M.: Oh, yes. They were very concerned about that.

They really were. I wasn't senior enough at that time to be privy to the relations between our senior commanders and the Icelanders, but it became pretty apparent that every effort was being made to keep us back at the base. Our liberty hours were pretty restrictive in town, and every effort was made to develop recreational activities and so on out where we were so we wouldn't be in conflict with the Icelanders.

Q: Pretty dull life, wasn't it?

Adm. M.: It was pretty dull, but you know, it hasn't changed that much over the years. The Icelanders are still not terribly happy with our people up there, as you undoubtedly know, and the base at Keflavik that you mentioned earlier - the Icelanders to this day, as far as I know, retain police jurisdiction over that base although it's a U.S. base. They've always been very jealous of their prerogatives in this area.

Q: There's a certain amount of political involvement today.

Adm. M.: Yes, of course, you realize that particularly when the Icelanders were having their real difficulties with the British over the fishing rights a few years back -

Minter, Jr. #2 - 76

Q: The cod war.

Adm. M.: That's right, the cod war. They didn't really blackmail NATO, but it came awful close to it. They threatened the United States if the U.S. didn't back them. The threat was that we were going to have to either move out completely or certainly restrict our activities, and we've had to cut back, rather substantially, in that area.

Q: Charlie Duncan as SacLant was heavily involved in that.

Adm. M.: Oh, yes. I was in NATO at the time, and I remember it quite well, too. It was a bad time.

Q: What about the dangers of flying in Icelandic waters at that time? What precautions could you take? If you had to land in the water, you wouldn't last more than a few minutes.

Adm. M.: No, you wouldn't. But actually the PBY is a pretty good bird to be in if you're going to have to be flying in weather like that. In the first place, it has tremendous range and staying power, it cruises along at a very slow speed and even in a pretty heavy sea, you can put a PBY down, and be reasonably safe.

We didn't have any planes that had to land at sea ever, but we certainly did have weather such that you'd very gingerly grope your way back to base, because as I mentioned before, we didn't have very sophisticated homing equipment then. I can remember being out in weather when your only directional information was by the tender, sending "MOs" - that's just a radio signal. If your radio operator was really good on his direction-finding equipment, you could get a reasonably good bearing coming in, but of course you have no range information, and if the weather was such that you were in the soup, you had to be very, very careful, and your navigation had to be extremely good. In high winds the old PBY could be blown pretty well off course, and the navigators were constantly taking drift-sites to try to keep themselves on position. It took some doing.

But the PBY itself was a good bird to be in in weather like that because if you had to, you could've landed and been reasonably sure of getting away with it successfully. That wouldn't have been true - and wasn't true - of the PBY-5A. When they got that heavy landing gear in there, that wasn't the greatest water airplane going. It was kind of a clumsy bird, as a matter of fact.

Q: What type of convoys were you observing and

watching over?

Adm. M.: The convoys that we covered were really quite far out, because the mid-ocean meeting point for the convoys was well south of Iceland, as was the subsequent convoy track. Of course with the PBY, with 12 hours' endurance - you could still spend a fair amount of time over a convoy. But these convoys we normally covered were going from Halifax across to Londonderry.

Q: To the U.K.?

Adm. M.: Oh, yes. All to the U.K.

Q: This was before the Murmansk - ?

Adm. M.: Yes. We didn't get in on any of the Murmansk stuff.

Actually, our convoy coverage, I think, was reasonably good, but our squadron did not get an actual submarine attack at any time during the time I was there - that was from September through January. We didn't get an attack on a German submarine while on convoy patrol, but we did sink one submarine that one of our pilots on just routine patrol located and sank.

Incidentally, that was a sort of amusing story. Dan Gallery was the base commander then.

Q: He had come out from the U.K.

Adm. M.: That's right. And he had gotten really upset over the fact that we weren't getting any kills on submarines in that area, and so he established the policy that the "O" club was closed until we got a submarine. You may remember a man with your name down in Argentia - "sighted sub, sank same" - who was credited with two submarine kills. When our pilot sank his submarine he sent, "Sank sub, open club."

Q: And Dan's sense of humor - prevailing. Probably as early as that he began to think that he was going to capture a German sub some time or other!

Adm. M.: A remarkable fellow. He really was something. He was a commander then, and a very avid baseball player. We played a lot of softball up there on the base.

I just might mention something else about this time. I was the squadron communications officer and became the squadron intelligence officer. During this time in Iceland, the early days, we had a joint intelligence committee comprised of representatives from the marines, from the British forces, from the U.S. Army, and the U.S. Navy, and I was the Navy representative.

Q: This was based on Iceland?

Adm. M.: Well, we rotated it around. The meetings would take place one time at our base, one time at the marines' or Army base, and one time the British would have us.

I think we met maybe once every couple of weeks, and the purpose of it was simply cross-pollination of what information we had. We'd exchange notes on what we were doing. I'd give them all the convoy coverage material that we had - the British would tell us anything they had. It wasn't a tremendously productive organization, but at least it gave us some rapport with the other services and some opportunity to get an idea of what each of us was attempting.

Q: Was it in any sense tied in with Washington?

Adm. M.: No. This was a local affair. I would simply report back to my squadron and give a report to my commanding officer, but I don't think it ever got higher than that - it was local type of intelligence.

Talking about the navigation in that area, we had very poor charts of Iceland itself - they were quite old and outdated.

Q: Didn't the Icelanders have their own charts? Could you borrow those? Were they generous in letting you have them?

Adm. M.: No, I might be wrong about this, but my recollection is our first charts we got from the British. They may in turn have gotten them from the Icelanders. But for aerial navigation purposes they were really pretty bad.

I remember one instance when we lost an airplane. Fortunately, we didn't lose anybody aboard. One of the flights one of our planes made was to take some army officers up a fjord on the east coast of Iceland, not too far from Reykjavik, maybe an hours' flight or something like that. The pilot had never been in that fjord before, and we had no one that had been, and he wasn't absolutely certain that he'd picked the right fjord when he turned up. The weather was not all that good, and all of a sudden the end of the fjord loomed up ahead, and he had no place to turn, no place to go. He just chopped his engines and set her down, had to force her down; knocked the bottom out of the airplane, but they hit and bounced and what was left of the airplane rolled up on the beach. The plane was a total loss. Everybody aboard was safe, fortunately, but it was sort of indicative of the fact that we just didn't have that much information about what our bases were like up there.

Q: It's just a continuous series of fjords.

Adm. M.: It was, in Iceland! The Icelandic coast, if you've ever seen it, is just one fjord after another and, as I say, you have to have pretty accurate charts to fly in this area very sensibly.

Q: You said off-tape that you came back to pick up some new-type planes to bring back to Iceland to replace the ones that were lost in the storm.

Adm. M.: Yes. The half of VP-73 that had been in Argentia and Quonset during the time the rest of us were in Iceland flew up to replace the group returning in January of 1942. We were returned to Quonset Point aboard <u>Albemarle</u>, the major seaplane tender. The half of the squadron that had lost its airplanes was returned to Quonset Point, and we then picked up the PHB-5As – the amphibious PBYs – flew in them for training missions out of Quonset Point.

One near tragedy I might mention that happened during this time: One of our PBY-5As out on a patrol near Block Island, coming back to Quonset Point, sighted a submarine at periscope depth right on the boundary of the restricted zone which was established for U.S.

submarine operations in Long Island Sound. Approaching the boundary from the north was a U.S. tanker moving into the Sound. The pilot of the PBY faced a terribly difficult decision. He thought the submarine was outside the quarantined area - just outside, but he was quite certain it was outside - and he saw the tanker moving directly towards the submarine, and therefore had to decide whether he would attack or not - he had depth charges aboard. Finally, he decided to attack, and he did, and fortunately he wasn't successful, although he shook up the submarine. It was a U.S. submarine, on a training mission, and they were using the tanker as a target. Of course, the submarine swears he was inside the quarantine zone, and I guess if I had to make a judgment I would probably say the submarine was more than likely to be correct, because I'm sure he kept his position better than our pilot did.

In any event, it created quite a stir, and things didn't settle down between New London and Quonset Point for some little time thereafter. But it alerted everyone to the possibilities of a terrible and tragic accident, and therefore I think we were all more concerned from there on about the operations in that particular area.

Q: And tightening up on communications?

Adm. M.: Exactly.

Well, after our training there at Quonset in May of 1941, I was the senior pilot for three of the PBY-5As that were to be ferried to our squadron operating then in Iceland. The PBY-5A doesn't have the range of the PBY, or the endurance, because of the additional weight of that landing gear, and so the trip had to be made in stages. We flew from Quonset Point to Argentia, where I was temporarily placed under the command of the commanding officer of VP-84, a land-based PBO squadron that was operating out of Argentia then. This was the squadron of which Lieutenant Mason of "sighted sub, sank same" fame was a member. For about ten days or two weeks I was retained there with these three planes to assist VP-84 in some special convoy coverage, particularly night flights (we did a lot of night flying during that time.) I was eventually released and the three of us flew on to Greeland because we couldn't make it direct from Argentia to Iceland in one flight, and that flight to Greenland was one that I'd just as soon never have to do again.

Once again, the weather information was really very sketchy, and you took your chances with the accuracy of a weatherman's prediction. We had gotten on the day of our departure a quite favorable report for our flight conditions between Argentia and Bluie West I, the base that we were going to land at in Greenland. But I must say it turned out about 180 degrees out of phase with what actually happened.

We took off, and had hardly gotten airborne, when we went into the soup, and we stayed in it until we finally climbed out at about six or seven thousand feet, and we were over a solid overcast the entire flight to Greenland. What made this particularly unpleasant was the fact that Bluie West I was about 30 miles up a very narrow fjord, with no homing information available other than a homing ship at the entrance to the fjord. Furthermore, the surface conditions in that vicinity of Greeland at that time of year can be considerably less than ideal. There are a lot of icebergs.

Q: That's Davis Strait?

Adm. M.: Yes, that's right. And so, two or three times during the flight one of us would drop down as low as we dared go, our altimeter being of some concern, to see what kind of a ceiling we had. We found we had a 200 or 300-foot ceiling, and icebergs made this a rather chancy operation. We were actually making plans to strip the airplanes, and throw overboard everything we didn't have to have, because we thought we were going to have to make an emergency landing at the end. We didn't see any way of getting in that fjord, and our intention was, if we had to, to make an open sea landing and either anchor or simply stay on the water until the weather conditions improved.

Fortunately, at the end of this flight, we found a fairly sizable hole, just off Cape Farwell, that we could go down through and get underneath. We had been in sketchy communication with Bluie West I, alerting them to our difficulties, and they sent an amphibious light plane - one of the Grumman Ducks - out, and this plane led the three PBYs up the fjord into Bluie West I, and I've never seen a sight more welcome than that runway.

Bluie West I was an interesting base. It had one marston strip mat. You land going up slope, towards the glacier, and you take off going down slope, and it's so protected that wind seemed to make very little difference in there, so you always landed going uphill, and you took off going downhill. The fjord was really quite narrow, and for an airplane like the PBY, which can't turn on a dime like a fighter, it took a little doing.

The base was operated by the Army Air Force, and they were most cordial to us, I must say. We were there just overnight. We took off the next morning and flew across the Greenland ice cap. We had to go up to about 15,000 feet, and that doesn't sound like very much to a fighter pilot, but to a guy struggling in a PBY it gets to be a little higher than you normally are accustomed to in that airplane. So we went across the ice cap and on into Iceland without further incident.

Q: Bluie West was primarily a base for the ferrying of planes, wasn't it?

Adm. M.: Yes, very much so. The ferry route used to take the airplanes from the United States up into Halifax, Argentia, then Bluie West, Iceland, and then on across, the ones that were Preswick bound.

Q: And there was more than one Bluie West.

Adm. M.: Oh yes, there were several. I've forgotten how many Bluies there were, but this is the only one that I had any personal experience with.

Q: I've always been amazed at the name. It's a very curious name - Bluie West.

Adm. M.: Well, it was interesting. I remember, I was invited in after I landed, the jeep picked me up and took me over to the commanding officer's office, and as I walked in the door he said, "Is everything all right?"

I said, "Fine."

He said, "Well, if it isn't, here's something for you," and I noticed a red cross sign on a large cabinet and it said "First Aid for Visiting Pilots."

I said, "What's that?" and he said, "Well, open it up." I opened it up and there was a bottle of Scotch and a bottle of bourbon. Appropriate medication after a flight like that.

Well, as I mentioned, we flew these planes on into Iceland, and I was detached shortly after that along with three other pilots from VP-73, and had orders to return and to assist in the formation of a new PBY squadron based at Norfolk for commissioning, VP-53. Our transportation back to the States was aboard Belknap, the tender I mentioned, the old four-piper that had been used as our tender. I had been a senior watch-stander aboard Houston when I was a junior officer, so I immediately became an officer of the deck underway instead of a passenger going back to Quonset Point.

Belknap had a bent shaft. She apparently had hit some kind of submerged object on her way up to Iceland, and had been unable to effect repairs, and when she turned up above 15 knots, the whole ship vibrated. But the commanding officer simply wouldn't listen to the chief engineer about the possibilities of this bent shaft giving them real troubles if we got up to 18 to 20 knots. She was capable of making, I think, 22 knots flank speed. But he was determined he was going to crank on all speed, and away we went, over the chief engineer's violent protests, that shaft thumping away.

We pulled into Argentia and refueled, and then immediately left to go to Quonset Point. As we pulled into Narragansett Bay and started up the channel to Quonset Point, the captain had to back down on one occasion, and the port propeller fell off, right in the center of the channel. And I can still see the chief engineer back on the propeller guard with a swab handle, jobbing down the water, and shouting up to the bridge, "I told you, Captain! It's gone! It's gone!

Q: Rejoicing -

Adm. M.: Yes, his prediction had finally come true.

But we got into Quonset Point and, as I mentioned, I had orders to report to VP-53 as one of the commissioning officers. I went as the operations officer. This was again a PBY squadron - PBY-5, not the 5A - and this particular squadron operated in the south Atlantic.

Q: Yes - quite welcome to have a change in scenery

and weather!

Adm. M.: I didn't mind that a bit.

Q: We're turning our attention now to the Caribbean, which turned out to be a very hot theatre as far as German submarine activity was concerned.

Adm. M.: Yes, it did. This was in 1942, when the German submarine activity off the east coast of the United States had gotten to be extremely alarming. They were sinking ships just off our coast. Many of our beaches, including Virginia Beach, used to have oil wash up from sinkings of tankers practically in sight of Cavalier Hotel. So the antisubmarine effort was an intense one, and our squadrons were used as intensively as could be for antisubmarine warfare purposes.

VP-53, the squadron that I just mentioned I had gone to as the operations officer, was formed in Norfolk, commissioned in Norfolk, and we were immediately sent to Key West, where we operated for about six weeks, doing just coastal patrol pretty much because there were no convoys of any significance in that particular area. But we did coastal patrol work off Key West and trained in the Key West area. Then in the early fall of that year, we were sent to Trinidad, where the squadron was based for the rest of that winter, 1942 and 1943.

Trinidad was a focal point for many of the convoys. Many of them formed in Trinidad and left from there, and others that we covered passed not too far from Trinidad. The antisubmarine warfare effort in that area was particularly intense. We had squadrons operating out of South American bases, PBMs pretty much, and we had PBYs there in Trinidad. When we first arrived in Trinidad, the Army Air Corps was flying an old plane, the B-18. They were using them for antisubmarine warfare patrol, but they were totally ineffective - they were very poor airplanes in the first place. The first thing we found after arriving was that the army wanted us to take over all the night patrol operations because they were just concerned about the B-18 as an instrument airplane, a night-flying airplane. The result was, I think our squadron logged more night time than day time in patrols out there.

But submarine activity was pretty intense and for the first time our squadron began to really get in on some of it, not all of which had a happy result.

I remember one of our pilots, who had the best chance to sink a submarine anyone has ever had, and who made such a complete botch of it that I wonder to this day why he wasn't court-martialed. I'm serious about that. By this time I was the executive officer of the squadron - perhaps I have some responsibility for not pursuing this.

We had just received a new antisubmarine weapon called the hedge-hog bomb. It was a contact-fuse weapon, and the idea was that you would carry depth charges to work on a submarine if it was surfaced or had just submerged and hedge hogs for use after the sub had submerged completely. One hedge-hog hit was supposed to completely put a submarine out of commission. If it hit, the explosive was such that it would just tear the submarine apart.

So we commenced the practice of loading our PBYs with Mk 54 depth charges under one wing, and hedge-hogs under another wing.

Q: Did they more or less balance?

Adm. M.: Oh, yes. They were close enough to the centerline that the weight distribution wasn't a problem. But it did require a pretty complete knowledge of the wiring circuit of the PBY. You had to throw your switch one way to drop your depth charges, you threw your switch another way to drop your hedge-hogs; and we drilled everyone very carefully in this. But one other complicating factor - more and more proof was required that you'd actually sunk a submarine. Everyone was claiming submarine sinkings, and the facts were not always that way.

Q: And there were pretty wild claims -

Adm. M.: Everybody who saw a submarine go down thought he had sunk the thing, obviously, and so there were all kinds of claims, and the Navy Department was getting very selective about giving credit for actually sinking a submarine. So photographs were pretty much an order of the day.

This particular attack took place about 300 and some miles out of Trinidad. Our pilot, flying through the clouds, spotted a fully surfaced submarine with the entire crew on deck, or a good part of them, sunbathing. Obviously they hadn't seen him. He came down out of the clouds, and instead of having his bow gunner with his 30-caliber gun operating, he had stationed a photographer in the bow to be sure he had a picture of this attack he was about to make.

He came swooping down over the submarine, had his switches thrown the wrong way, dropped his hedge-hog weapons first. By this time the submarine had gone to general quarters, and their people were scrambling down the conning tower, and by the time he had circled around and come back for another attack the submarine was going down, and this time he didn't have his switches thrown and couldn't drop his Mk-54 charges. The submarine got away scot-free.

We'd gotten the report that he was making an attack, and everybody was waiting at the base to see what the results were. He came back after dark, and I was the first one aboard the airplane. I knew by this time that the attack had been a total failure. We had been so hungry to get one submarine - this was the first real good chance we had - and he had botched it completely. I got aboard and before anybody could do anything I said to the pilot, "Show me how your switches were thrown, right now. I want to see exactly what you did." And it was obvious he didn't know how they should have been thrown. The result was we just lost a wonderful chance.

Q: But he had been trained?

Adm. M.: Oh, of course he had. He was a plane commander, and, as I say, I was a fairly young lieutenant and - well, in fairness, I think our squadron commander was not the strongest guy in the world, and he just couldn't bring himself to do anything more than censure the fellow verbally.

Q: This points up the fact that training is basic, and there are certain people who, regardless of whether they get excited or filled with fear, can still rely on their training to do an accurate job, but there are others who can't, who lose their heads.

Adm. M.: Yes, completely - and he had such a beautiful opportunity. There was no excuse at all for not creaming that submarine.

Q: His excitement just got the best of him.

Adm. M.: Well, Admiral Hoover sent really a strong message to the squadron about this, as you can well imagine. I don't want to make myself appear the hero of this thing, but fortunately, I got an attack a few nights later, which took a little of the heat off us because I had the same load he had. I had the hedgehogs and the Mk-54 depth charges. I was covering a tanker convoy headed for the Mediterranean. These tankers were desperately needed in the Med at this time, and this convoy had surface coverage. I think I'm right in saying there were 15 or 16 tankers in this convoy, and a wolf pack got amongst them after they got beyond our air coverage area, and I think only about seven or eight actually made the Med. So they were really being hit very hard.

But I was giving the air cover on the night of the 28th of December, and flying a standard patrol search around the convoy. On one leg, coming up towards the convoy, I saw a surfaced vessel - I could see the wake below me, and I knew it couldn't be one of the convoy ships. I was at about 1,000 feet - broken cloud cover, a little moonlight - but a little rain also in the area. It wasn't until I got directly on top and looked down that I realized that it was a submarine, surfaced, and heading straight for the convoy.

From 1,000 feet in a PBY you can't do an Immelmann and get right down on a submarine, you have to take your time, and by the time I got down and in attack position the submarine had already submerged. I felt he had been submerged long enough it would be pointless to drop any depth charges, so I pulled up and contacted the convoy commodore and told him there was a submarine astern, trailing the convoy, and that I would go back and attempt to reestablish contact. I assume, although I don't know, that he put some of his escort ships back in that area.

In any event, I went back parallel to the course that I had just flown to the ship, and twice made two sweeps at a much lower altitude, and the second time I spotted my friend again on the surface. He'd come back up again and he was heading in. He spotted me about the same time I spotted him, at least, I think he did because he immediately made a sharp turn and a crash dive. I was leading as best I could in the somewhat restricted visibility, and I dropped my depth charges. I think I dropped them long - I was too close to him. But then I circled around - and this was exactly why we'd loaded the airplanes the way we did - because now he was going down, at least I saw the swirl of the conning tower and I knew he was making a right turn, and I dropped a string of hedge-hogs across the submerged submarine.

One of the waist gunners reported seeing one of the hedge-hogs go off. That meant it hit the submarine. I've never been satisfied that that was actually the case. I think it was wishful thinking on all our parts, hoping we'd killed the submarine.

But I stayed in the area, and by daylight - this was late at night - there was, not debris, but a fair amount of oil in the area. The plane that relieved me on station got on and gave coverage the rest of the night. So I got back to base and we made the report that this attack had been made, and initially, we were given credit for a kill. It turns out we did not kill the submarine, but we damaged him so badly that he had to return to Germany.

Q: This was learned after the war, I suppose?

Adm. M.: Yes, it was learned after the war. As a matter of fact, I just last year found the name of the commanding officer of that submarine, which was the U-214. I got his name through the Naval Institute, and I was curious to know if the fellow was still alive. I contacted the German language exchange officer at the Naval Academy, a Commander, Krupp, and asked if he could find out whether the skipper of the U-214 was still around. To my surprise he said, "Yes, I think I know who he is."

He contacted the German Embassy. They in turn got word back to me that the fellow was an admiral, still living and named Reeder, identified myself, told him my interest in that particular attack, and asked if he recalled it. I got a nice letter back from him stating that he remembered it quite well, that we had knocked out his master gyro, and it couldn't be repaired, and that he had to go back to Germany to get repairs. He apologized for not being able to give me more information because he said he was relying totally on his memory, because after getting back to Germany he had to be hospitalized, not because of this attack but for some other reason, and U-214 sailed, after being repaired, without him, and was lost on the next patrol with all hands. Therefore, he had none of his shipmates that he could rely on, and he said his own home, personal possessions, everything was lost during the war, so he was going solely on his memory. But he recalled this, and this was the way he remembered the thing.

Q: Interesting. He had surfaced several times - you observed him twice. Was he going to use his guns on the convoy

Adm. M.: Oh, no, I don't think so. I think what he was doing was, he was closing the convoy as rapidly as possible.

This convoy was reasonably fast. It was a ten or twelve-knot convoy. These were tankers and they could move fairly fast. Although he didn't tell me in the correspondence we had, I've always assumed that he simply found himself well astern of the convoy and realized that his best chance of catching them was at night, and he was going to run on the surface until he was up close enough to submerge, possibly, and do something about it or maybe get ahead of them and have them come to him.

There were escort ships in that convoy, and it would have been interesting to me to know exactly what his tactics were going to be.

Incidentally, in the letter I got from him, he said that although he was damaged by us and rendezvoused with another U-boat, which gave him spare parts to assist in repairing his master gyro - they worked for about a week and were never able to do it - in spite of this damage, he did get one more ship before he sailed back to Germany. Not out of this convoy, but an independent ship that was in the area.

Q: Did the U-boats have a tender near?

Adm. M.: Yes, they did. In the south Atlantic during that time there were tenders. Our squadron never saw any of them, but they obviously had rendezvous areas well offshore, of course, where these tenders could actually do repairs and refueling, and all these other things for the submarines.

But he made no reference to any tender that he tried to get to in his letter to me. He simply said that he had rendezvoused with another - just a second, I've got this thing here -

Q: It was a very exciting year that you spent in the Caribbean, with many real submarines to attack. Did you have anything to do with the French at Martinique?

Adm. M.: No.

Q: Guadeloupe?

Adm. M.: No. We had no relations with them at all, actually.

During the time we were there in Trinidad, Churchill came through there on one occasion, on a seaplane flight.

Q: He had a conference in Bermuda, did he not?

Adm. M.: I can't recall now what the conference was. A British club - used as a club during normal times - was turned over to us for our use during this particular period. We did so much night flying that after every night flight the pilots were authorized to go over to this British club and spend the day. There was a nice beach over there and individual cottages and a club house. I recall that we were told during a particular week that the club would not be available for anybody for several days, and it turns out that this was the time that Churchill was coming through. I really don't recall what his destination was. It might have been the Bermuda Conference.

Q: You speak of the night flying and night patrols - what can you accomplish?

Adm. M.: At that particular time we were beginning to get fairly decent results with radar, which was still in its infancy. I remember the first radar I ever saw aboard a PBY. We used to have a group of radar antennae around the bow of those airplanes, and we had to be very careful coming alongside a buoy to keep from knocking off those little antennae that were sticking out. It was pretty primitive stuff.

Our operators, of course, were not really terribly well trained. It was kind of on-the-job training. But we were beginning to get to the point where we had some reasonable assurance of success with radar. It took an extremely skilled operator, somebody who really knew what he was doing, to distinguish between a large ship and a small ship, for example, in those days. The blip on the screen was such that only the fellows that really worked at it and understood were able to distinguish them.

Frequently you had disappearing radar contacts. Of course, you always thought it was a submarine. It might well have been just radar-operator error that gave you this, but at least we felt we were keeping them down; and of course, this was at a time when the submarine, once you got him down, was pretty helpless. Your convoy, if that was what you were covering, could get away and he might never catch up again. So, suppression was almost as important as attack in some cases. The object was to get the ships across, and using these night patrols - of course, there were attacks at night, just like I mentioned and there were others that attacked submarines at night. Sometimes the submarines would stay on the surface and fight against a plane if the sub were damaged. I know of one occasion when a PBM was held at bay by a submarine that got his machine guns manned and was able to keep the PBM from coming in to finish him off, just using a machine gun for defensive purposes.

Q: Were you using blimps in any way in that area?

Adm. M.: Not in our area. Blimps were used all along the Atlantic coast. I think they were of questionable value. But at least they served the purpose of surveillance of a fairly sizable area. They weren't capable of doing very much in the way of attacking, because they weren't fast enough - they couldn't maneuver.

Q: They were awfully vulnerable, too.

Adm. M.: Oh, yes. But they could keep a pretty sizable area under surveillance, and if a submarine were sighted by a blimp, planes could be called out to either locate him or hold him down, so, they served that purpose.

We used a tremendous number of different types of aircraft to attempt to do the ASW problem, because that '42-'43 year was a desperate one. We just lost thousands of tons of shipping to German submarines. We were so slow in learning such obvious lessons. The east coast stayed pretty well lit up during that time and I read subsequently that - it shouldn't come as a surprise to anyone - submarines were able to see ships silhouetted against the coastline. You'd have thought the whole thing would've been blacked out. The west coast did a better job of this than the east coast did after the war started because they were more afraid of Japanese attack on the west coast, and the east coast wasn't that concerned. But it sure made the ASW problem easier for the submarines than it did for us.

Q: You mentioned a wolf pack down there in the Caribbean - I thought that was more typical of the tactics in the Atlantic itself.

Adm. M.: It was, and the wolf pack operation I was talking about really was the concentration, well out in the Atlantic, against this tanker convoy that I was covering en route to the Mediterranean. They really got in them well out in the Atlantic. This wasn't close to the Trinidad area at all.

Q: There they were largely operating as single units?

Adm. M.: Pretty much so, and they had pretty good hunting because that was a very heavily traveled area for shipping. A lot of convoys formed at Trinidad, and moved up and down that area.

Q: And that oil came largely from Venezuela, did it not?

Adm. M.: Venezuela, Curacão -

Q: Aruba?

Adm. M.: Yes.

Q: You're becoming a very skillful patrol-plane operator against the German submarines, and now you're leaving the Caribbean to go to Quonset Point once again.

Adm. M.: Yes, I had orders to Quonset Point to be executive officer of what was known as headquarters squadron 9-1. That was a maintenance squadron, which had the responsibility for major maintenance care for patrol squadrons transitting the Quonset area, and there for periods of very intensive training.

The Quonset area lent itself to this sort of thing. In the first place, it was a very fine base, and secondly, there were ranges where torpedoes could be fired, and there were targets that could be used for services. Submarines out of New London could occasionally be made available for an ASW squadron to operate against. That sort of service was kind of hard to come by because our submarines were usually otherwise occupied.

In this particular time, in aviation, we were beginning to experiment, to some degree at least, with streamlining the squadrons. The plan was to have a major maintenance squadron, such as the one I was in there at Quonset, which would do major maintenance jobs, and the squadron itself would be responsible for minor maintenance. Squadrons were self-sufficient in that they could take care of the normal routine day-to-day maintenance, but changing an engine, or a major component replacement, or something like that would normally be done by a squadron such as the one that I went to.

Q: How many men had been assembled for a squadron of that sort for maintenance purposes?

Adm. M.: Well, I was quite astonished when I arrived. I'd never had any association with these squadrons before, and I found out shortly after I got there that I was going to be the commanding officer at a fairly tender age - I'd just become a lieutenant commander. I had about 1400 men.

Our counterpart for the carrier aviation was what they called a "CASU" - Carrier Aviation Service Unit. Quonset Point had one of those units at the field. My squadron was based at the seaplane hangars, where the ramps were, where we did seaplane operations, although we maintained land-based patrol seaplanes as well as seaplanes.

Q: You were an ideal assignment for that job, because you had so much operational experience at sea.

Adm. M.: Well, it certainly helped. Looking back on it, I realize how very, very inexperienced from a command standpoint many of us were, who were pushed into command positions that early in the game. But that was an interesting assignment to me because I saw and appreciated maybe for the first time, how well-trained our maintenance personnel were. Most of my officers in that squadron, in a maintenance capacity, were ex-chief petty officers who had been promoted to lieutenants or JGs or whatever. They were absolutely superb in maintenance techniques, and they knew the problems of the petty officers they were dealing with to a degree that the average regular naval officer wouldn't have known, because he wasn't raised through that hierarchy. I had some absolutely superior people, and I thought the world of them. I could, hopefully, provide the leadership, the overall direction in which we moved, but these fellows were top-notch in every way.

I took command maybe a month or two after I arrived - the man who was commanding the squadron when I arrived was sent up to the wing staff, and I took command. At this time, I had my first experience with the product of the Quonset Point AVS school. These fellows were really top-flight in every way. I don't know of a single one that I didn't think was really a pretty superior fellow.

Q: Well, with superior backgrounds -

Adm. M.: They all had. They were all obviously potentially very successful young businessmen. At that particular time, the bulk of them were graduates of Harvard and Yale and Princeton. The Ivy League schools. My squadron, along with several others, benefitted tremendously from these fellows. I had my legal officer, I had my administrative officer, I had officers in other capacities who had gone through the AVS school, and all they needed was just a word or two about which way to go, and they were off and running. They didn't understand the navy all that well at that time, but they were superior, and the melding of that kind of talent with the outstanding maintenance capability that we had down below, made this command a pleasure to be associated with.

Q: Did you run into Luis de Flores?

Adm. M.: I saw him occasionally - yes, I did. Of course, he wasn't associated with my squadron in any way -

Q: No, because he was associated with that program.

Adm. M.: Oh, yes, indeed he was. And that was really a tremendously successful program. I don't know of anybody who didn't give it just the highest marks.

Q: Did you also run into Gus Reed?

Adm. M.: No, I didn't know Gus Reed.
I remember so well how impatient many of these fellows were with the red tape that frequently is associated with an organization such as the navy, just not understanding that certain things have to be done certain ways.

The commanding officer of the naval air station at that time was a Captain Gale Morgan. One of his administrative assistants had been ordered right out of the school, was a Wall Street broker in civilian life, and apparently arrived in his office and found that he didn't have a typewriter. He asked the first lieutenant when he would get a typewriter. Well, typewriters were in short supply, he was told, and it might be a week or two.

He said, "But I've been given a job to do. How am I going to do it without a typewriter?"

"Well," he said, "You'll just have to wait."

He picked up the telephone, called his New York office, had a typewriter put in a taxicab and driven up to Quonset Point and delivered to his office. The next day he was in business. He wasn't going to put up with any of this nonsense of waiting for normal supplies.

That was almost typical of the way those fellows were prepared to go. All you really had to do was give them a little guidance.

I had one man, much older than the others, who in civilian life ran a restaurant, a very successful one, in Providence. But he was so desperately anxious to be a part in the war effort that although he was way older than me or anyone else in the squadron, he became my almost permanent squadron duty officer. Nothing delighted him more than to help visiting pilots get into Providence or do a little shopping, or take care of them some way. It was heartening to see somebody who was so dedicated that whatever he could do to make that war move in our direction, he was prepared to do. And these fellows were all like that. Everyone of them that I dealt with were just really anxious to do their part.

It's interesting to me as I think back on it, the pitfalls a very young and somewhat inexperienced commanding officer can fall into. I can understand better now than I could when it happened why the Unified Code of Military Justice was actually established the way it was. Because in peacetime before World War II, of course the articles for the government of the navy gave the commanding officer of any outfit fairly broad disciplinary control. I still feel that is badly needed, but there were serious abuses, obviously, of this sort of power during the inevitable war time expansion of the military services. It came about many times through inexperience, other times through just plain sadistic —

Q: In the hands of a martinet type.

Adm. M.: That's right. It could be very bad, so it's not difficult to understand why it was changed. I can remember commanding officers issuing 100 or 150 hours extra duty to a man. The war would practically be over before you work off that amount of extra duty and restriction and so on.

Q: Contrary to common sense.

Adm. M.: That's right.

Thinking back on that time, I really had very few serious disciplinary problems. There were a lot of reasons for it, when I think about it. In the first place, I think the leadership at the lower level was just top-notch. The men working for the ex-chiefs knew these chiefs knew what they were doing, and therefore had real respect for them. Secondly, and not too unimportantly, after all, it was shore duty. A lot of these fellows weren't all that eager to get out in the Pacific. There were some who didn't want to fight the war at sea quite as much as others did. So while our hours were pretty long, they were fairly regular, and the men were with their families, and so there wasn't any particular reason for having really serious disciplinary problems.

I had only a few that required recommendations for general court-martial. I had very few that I can recall that were deserters. I had some AWOLs, some overleave people, but my problems were not serious.

I did have occasion to recommend discharge of an officer, but he was not one of my AVS fellows. He was a photographer in civilian life, and really

quite good, but the most irresponsible individual
I've ever known. It's too long a story to tell, but
I had to recommend his discharge.

Q: Sort of an artist type.

Adm. M.: Pretty much. Time meant nothing to him.
If he went to New York, as he did, for a weekend, and
it didn't end until the next Wednesday, why, he didn't
see anything wrong with that. The fact that the office
was just struggling along in his absence didn't bother
him very much, so I recommended, and we discharged him.

Q: Don't you think another very important reason why
you didn't have many problems in discipline is illustrated by the man with the typewriter in the taxicab?
This spirit was pretty general. People wanted to do
their bit.

Adm. M.: They certainly did, and it's never been that
way since, in my experience. The Korean War was a
different kettle of fish, and certainly Vietnam was
totally different. I've just thought so many times
how I never again expect to see my fellow citizens
as totally united as they were in World War II.
Everyone. If you wore a uniform downtown in New
York City, you'd be beseiged by people that wanted

Minter, Jr. #2 - 114

to help you or buy you a drink or whatever. You could hardly pay your bill in any place, because the country was totally devoted to what we were doing.

Q: Wasn't this true only after Pearl Harbor? Before Pearl Harbor there was great division.

Adm. M.: Oh, yes. You know how close we came not to even having the draft - it won by just one vote.

After Pearl Harbor there was no question about it at all. I've thought many times my sympathy has been with some of the younger fellows that have gone through the Vietnam experience because public reaction was so totally different from what we experienced in World War II, when people were dedicated to just one goal, and that was to win.

Q: Well, that was a broadening experience for you in the development of your career, and even as a young, very junior-type commanding officer you learned fast.

Adm. M.: Yes, I did.

I remember something else during that time, though. Pilot's intuition sometimes is something that is interesting. I mentioned the fact that I had absolutely superior maintenance personnel, and of course, they went pretty much by the book. You changed an engine after X number of operating hours, or if there was a serious malfunction in the engine, but you didn't do it just because a pilot came in and said, "Gosh, there's something wrong with this engine. I'd like to have you change it."

An interesting thing happened. A fellow that later got to be a very close friend of mine, and worked for me at Patuxent River years later, was a pilot in the squadron that Tom Moorer was the skipper of and they were there for this advanced training that I mentioned earlier. After one of his flights he came back in and on the yellow sheet, which is the discrepancy sheet you turn in after a flight, he squawked one of his engines. But he wasn't very specific, he just said it didn't run right. Well, our people were always coming to me and saying, "Captain, can't you get these fellows to tell us in a little more detail what's wrong - 'doesn't run right' means anything!"

Well, he said it ran rough. My night check crew took the plane out on the ramp, turned up that engine to full power, ran up and down - nothing they could find wrong. So they didn't do anything. They reported okay.

He took the plane out a couple days later, came back - "Engine doesn't run right." The squadron was just about to leave, by the way, to go to England by way of Recife in South America and across the South

Atlantic, and he was concerned about this engine conking out on him somewhere along the way. He finally came to see me personally, and he said, "I wish you'd tell your folks to change that engine."

I said, "Oh the basis of what they find, they don't have any reason to change that engine. It turns up perfectly on the ground. You can't quarrel with it."

He said, "There's something wrong with that engine."

And I guess he was right, because they got into Recife and the engine had to be changed down there. He never let me forget that after the war. He said, "You know, I knew there was something wrong with that engine, and I could not get your fellows to understand that."

Q: Maybe they were less resistent in Recife, and he was more persuasive.

Adm. M.: No, he said he landed with a prop feathered, so he proved himself right.

But it was an interesting experience. I'd just become a lieutenant commander, and this was my first command. It was exciting, of course, to have a command, and although it wasn't an operational command, it was one that I felt, and still do feel, did a tremendous job in preparing me for subsequent assignments.

Q: In retrospect, you saw the value of it, but I bet at the time you didn't want to take this command.

Adm. M.: No, I didn't. As a matter of fact, I was quite concerned. The real war, as far as I was concerned, was out in the Pacific. I was not a carrier pilot, and therefore my chance of getting into that end of the game was pretty remote. I was a patrol-plane pilot, and while our job was an important one, it somehow lacked the excitement of other type flying. You just spent hour after frustrating hour flying out over that Atlantic Ocean, usually not seeing anything except the Atlantic Ocean, so the opportunities for doing anything very spectacular weren't very good.

So, going to that particular command was not the most exciting thing that could have happened to me. But I eventually did get carrier duty with my then wing commander, Captain Felix Baker, when he got orders to be prospective commanding officer of Randolph, which was being built in Newport News. I was asked to go with him as his assistant air officer, which I did.

Q: If you had access to the monthly statistics on the sinkings, however, in the Atlantic, this must have been some evidence to you that you had a terribly important job.

Adm. M.: Oh, there's no question about that. We did have evidence. We knew what the sinking rate was. And we were getting better - we, I mean the antisubmarine forces were improving. We were beginning to make our presence felt. There were more ASW aircraft squadrons, ships were getting better in the use of their sonar, radar was making more of a contribution, and so, the tide was beginning to turn. It was an important operation that we were engaged in.

Q: At your level, was there any evidence of an exchange with the British in terms of their experience and their equipment and so forth?

Adm. M.: Not at my level. I was aware of the fact that this exchange was taking place, but I learned it more through the wing headquarters than I did down at my particular level. I had no relationships with the British personally, other than that time in Iceland.

Q: I thought of that when you mentioned the hedge-hog because, if I remember rightly, that was a British invention.

Adm. M.: I'm not sure that's correct. The hedge-hog I think was a U.S. design, and I think the British had a weapon that was called a hedge-hog, but I think that was a different one from the one I mentioned.

Q: They had a hedge-hog, I know they did.

Adm. M.: Yes. It might be the same. I think their hedge-hog was actually fired, was it not? A distance away from a destroyer, fired from a catapult?

Q: I believe you're right.

Adm. M.: - to cover an area. It might have been a variant of that.

An interesting thing to me, thinking back on it - we had a number of our top scientists, I'm sure, working on the ASW problem, and we had a number of fairly complicated patterns you were supposed to fly once you knew there was a submarine in the area. You flew so many minutes on a leg, and so many minutes on a leg, and so on. But I thought many times that we really weren't very sophisticated, and it seems to me that we could've done much better somehow. I feel like our tactics could have been - and should have been - far better than they were. It was hit or miss, a lot of this antisubmarine effort.

Looking back on it, I don't think we had nearly the guidance that might have been made available to us for the sort of tactics that you would use once you got into an area. We were simply given a patrol area to cover, for example, unless you were covering an actual convoy, and I know that we had information that might have been - certainly wasn't accurate down to within a mile or two - but we certainly had area information. Our Hf/df stations were beginning to zero in on submarines. Somebody who was in that business might quarrel with me, but I never felt, and I don't feel now, that the operating units got as much specific information as they needed to do a better job than we did in our patrol coverage.

I'm sure there has been a survey done - I know there was - of the number of flying hours as opposed to the number of sightings of actual submarines in those days when we didn't have radar that was too effective, and your eyeball was the way you determined a submarine.

An astonishing amount of effort went into every single sighting that was ever achieved. Somehow I feel that we were lacking in the sort of intelligence information that should have been made more available at the squadron level.

Q: Would you think that perhaps one reason for this was that there was very little carry-over from World War I experience to World War II in this area, and that we were actually starting from zero, and building up in terms of experience, and equipment, and everything else?

Adm. M.: We were, but I've read articles and of course I've been associated with ASW quite a bit in my career, and I still have a feeling that our effort wasn't misdirected, but it just wasn't given as effective direction as it might have.

I'm being very vague about this, but with all the talent and the brainpower we had, I still feel that the guidance to the ASW squadrons was not anything like what it could have been, and might have made us much more effective instruments for ASW purposes than was actually the case.

Interview #3 with Vice Admiral Charles S. Minter, Jr.
U.S. Navy (Retired)

Place: His residence in Providence; Annapolis, Maryland
Date: Thursday morning, 19 July 1979
Subject: Biography
By: John T. Mason, Jr.

Q: Well, Sir, we're going to go to the carrier Randolph today. You were assigned to her before she was commissioned, I believe.

Adm. M.: Yes, that's correct.

Q: And this was in the year 1944?

Adm. M.: 1944. I'd been serving as the squadron commander of Headquarters Squadron 9-1 at Quonset Point, and my wing commander at that time was Captain Felix Baker. When I heard that Captain Baker was going to get command of a then-building aircraft carrier I asked what possibilities there were that I might join him, and he was kind enough to get orders for me to the ship as assistant air officer. I was so assigned and moved over in August of 1944 to Newport to the precommissioning detail for the Randolph.

Q: Are you going to tell me about your role in the precommissioning period? What did you do?

Adm. M.: Yes. This was fairly standard practice for carriers that were going into commission. The precommissioning detail formed at Newport, and this was simply a shore-based unit, the skeleton of what was going to be eventually the entire crew of the carrier. This was while the ship was still being built in the yard. The departments simply got themselves organized ashore and established administrative routines. Of course, you couldn't do any actual operational work with the flight-deck crews, for example, and the catapult crews, and others, but the basic organization was being formed, the department regulations were being prepared, and we were having daily discussions about how we were going to operate the ship.

Q: Training was required, too, wasn't it, for some of the new recruits?

Adm. M.: Yes, indeed, but, of course, many of the lower ratings were actually being trained at special schools, and we eventually all joined forces aboard the ship itself at commissioning time.

I'd never served aboard a carrier as a ship's officer. Therefore, it was somewhat new to me. I'd had cruiser duty and I'd had qualification as an officer of the deck underway, and so I didn't feel strange about going to a ship, but my flying background was in the patrol-plane part of the navy, not in the carriers, and therefore this was somewhat new to me. My air officer was a veteran fighter pilot named Roy Simpler, who had flown F6Fs in the Guadalcanal campaign and had a fair amount of flying experience, but he himself had had scant carrier operation experience. Therefore, we were starting out really from scratch.

We did have the benefit in those days of those who had gone through this before. We had the ship's manuals, we had the organizational manuals available to us and, of course, constantly we were attempting to learn from those who had just come back from combat aboard carriers, to get ideas about the major things to look out for with a green crew. All these things were terribly important in our precommissioning work.

Q: What about night operations, did you anticipate any of those?

Adm. M.: At this stage of the game, we didn't get into that. We were getting the skeleton organization of the ship put together and the operational background was going to come later when we actually got to sea and actually started working with the ship and with the air group.

As it turned out, Jack, it was a good thing that we did as much of this advance preparation as we did because - maybe I'm jumping the gun a little bit here - but the Randolph was the first carrier that never returned to her building yard after her shakedown. We went right straight through the canal and out to the Pacific, and we were in combat four months from the time the ship was commissioned.

Q: I noticed that from the record. What special precautions did you take, if any, for damage control?

Adm. M.: Here again there's just so much that you can do ashore before you actually get to the ship. Study of the ship's plans, and study of the fire-fighting systems aboard, many of which were new to most of us. The foam system, for example, was something I previously had not been exposed to. The actual fueling system for the aircraft had to be studied in great detail by our fueling crews and by everybody in the air department. All these things had to be studied and considered and plans made for how we were going to operate them, but until you actually get your hand on a piece of the equipment and you actually see how it really functions aboard an operating carrier, there's not much more you can do.

Damage-control schools were held, again for our special people, for people in the repair parties, and they got specialized instruction in training schools. But those of us in the precommissioning detail in Newport had nothing very much that you could really use for that actual training experience. That had to come when you got aboard the ship.

Q: Well, it sounds like a busy time.

Adm. M.: It was terribly busy. It was sort of frantic.

Q: How many weeks was this?

Adm. M.: I guess we were there about six weeks.

Q: Commissioning was on the 7th of October.

Adm. M.: 9 October 1944. I can't tell you when the first personnel arrived at Newport. I personally arrived there about the middle of August, and then we moved the entire crew down two or three days before we went aboard for the commissioning, which was on the 9th of October, in Newport News. So we

Minter, Jr. #3 - 127

had roughly six weeks in Newport.

Q: What sort of a complement was in her?

Adm. M.: Well, let's see. We must have had about, in total, 3,300 people in the carrier.

Q: That's tremendous.

Adm. M.: It was a huge ship and, of course, the Air Department was a big part of it, but you've got the engineering and the navigation, communications, and all the other departments that I didn't have responsibilities for, but we all had to function together as a team, certainly.

Q: Well, you commissioned her on the 9th. Was there a ceremony in connection with that?

Adm. M.: Oh, yes, quite a ceremony. Our commanding officer, Captain Baker, I feel in all honesty, has never gotten the credit that he really deserves, and maybe he was hoist by his own petard. He was desperately anxious to get the ship to the Pacific and, I think, "desperately anxious" is not overstressing the feeling that he had about it. It was obvious that things were going our way by this time in late 1944. The war in the Pacific was moving very favorably and, while there were many big battles yet to be fought, I think the handwriting was beginning to be on the wall that we were going to be victorious there. And he was terribly anxious, after all this work, to get our ship out to get her part of the big show, so he pushed. He pushed awfully hard, and he insisted on long hours for us and hard training, but the interesting thing is I don't recall people being the least bit concerned about that sort of thing. He infected the crew with a desire to get the job done and to get ourselves as ready as we possibly could be.

When I mentioned a moment ago that he was hoist by his own petard, we actually got to the war zone probably before we were really ready to go, and when we moved in with those old-timers there, the Essex and the Ticonderoga, the Bon Homme and all the rest of them -

Q: Were you in Mitscher's task force?

Adm. M.: Yes, we were operating under Mitscher and under Halsey and Spruance. We alternated.

But what I was saying is that Captain Baker pushed so hard. I mentioned earlier that we did not go back to our building yard, we went straight through the canal and got our 40-millimeter sponsons installed in the shipyard at San Francisco. The result was, I think, that we were there before we really were quite ready, and I believe that Captain Baker was professionally penalized to some degree, at least, because it took us a time to really catch up to these other old hands in the way we were to operate. I'll tell you more about that as we move along.

Q: Yes. Mitscher was a little impatient about this sort of thing.

Adm. M.: Well, actually we were directly under Radford. He was the task-group commander at first and then Bogan. In our first operational experience, we were slow in launching, slow in recovering, and Radford was terribly impatient with us. We were the last ones holding up turning into the wind and turning out of the wind. After our first operational sortie, Radford sent over one of the air officers from one of the operating carriers to ride us for a couple of days. While the other ships were resting, we were still operating because they wanted to see what it was that was keeping us from being quite as good as they. They gave us a lot of advice. I have to say the story has a somewhat happy ending because within a month or two we were right up there with the first team. We always launched first and recovered first. We were proud of it and we had an operating team, but I'll tell you it took a little time to get that degree of skill in operations. It took some doing.

Q: When you joined the fast carriers, your first operation was Iwo Jima, was it?

Adm. M.: Yes - no, the first carrier raid was on Tokyo and, as I say, we were operating - I can remember when we were first told what the target was, we were operating 100 to 150 miles off Tokyo, and this was a rather interesting experience for people to be in combat for their first time that close to the Japanese homeland.

Q: Had you gone by way of Pearl?

Adm. M.: Oh, yes, we went by Pearl and actually we had another thing that made it a little more difficult than might have been the case otherwise. We operated with one air group during shakedown and thought this was the group we were going to take out with us, and it takes a little time for the ship's company and the air group to really meld together as a team.

We got to Pearl and Charlie Crommelin, one of the famous Crommelin brothers, was an air group commander there without a ship. I've never known exactly how it was done, but Crommelin somehow was able to swing it so that his air group came aboard and the other air group was left behind.

Q: Yes. He felt the same as your skipper did.

Adm. M.: He certainly did. He wanted to be there, be part of it. He had really a veteran group and they were well qualified in almost every respect. It was simply the fact that the group and the ship as a team hadn't been able to work together enough to have the smooth-working operation that you really like to see.

As you may or may not know, Charlie Crommelin was killed tragically in a mid-air collision during our deployment. Right after we got hit by a kamikaze in March, he was detached and went to Admiral Clark's staff for a short time. He was simply flying a routine flight and was killed in a mid-air collision, a very tragic loss.

In that air group, incidentally, were some people who went on to bigger things. Noel Gayler was one of the fighter pilots. He had one of the fighter squadrons in Charlie Crommelin's air group and already had picked up, I think, his third Navy Cross by this time. So we had some hard-hitting and very capable people in the group.

But the growing pains of the ship's company learning to operate with the group and operate smoothly with the group took some doing.

Q: That can't be short-circuited, can it?

Adm. M.: No, it can't, and the ship's company always feels - not always, but frequently - that they have all the dirty jobs to do and the air group are the glamour boys, and it's awfully difficult to get around this feeling that the air group are the elite and the ship's company are just a bunch of guys named Joe. I will say I think we were successful in combatting this feeling. As the assistant air officer, I had a lot of the administrative details to work out with the air group, their berthing, their messing, their ship routine, and I think we got a fairly high degree of acceptance of operating as a team. I got them to realize that they didn't get very far if we didn't do it for them and I think in a relatively short period of time we developed a relationship that I believe was somewhat unique between the carriers and the air groups.

I've been aboard other carriers to observe. For example, during the time that we were shaking down out of Norfolk for our first operating experience, I rode the Ticonderoga from Norfolk down to the canal, just as an observer. I watched to see how the air group functioned and I watched to see how the ship's company and the air group operated together, and I must say, in all fairness, I think we worked out a better operating arrangement, eventually at least, than I observed in

Minter, Jr. #3 - 133

the <u>Ticonderoga</u>. I had occasion to talk to many others about this. It's one of those touchy things that it's always a little difficult to resolve, but you've got to have understanding on both sides. I think Charlie Crommelin had a full appreciation of how important it was for his air group to work well with us and I think between him and Roy Simpler, our air officer, we worked out a fine working relationship, and I think the air group appreciated it.

Q: Inevitably, the pilots get certain privileges.

Adm. M.: And they should. There's no question about that, but it's a little difficult for the ship's officers, particularly of the Air Department. They frequently had to stay up most of the night respotting the deck or preparing for emergency launch or landing and some had the feeling that that sort of sacrifice wasn't fully appreciated, that they weren't recognized as being as much a part of the team as they would like to have been, but these things were overcome and I believe that a very fine relationship eventually developed.

Q: Incidentally, were there any bugs in the ship? You say that ordinarily they go back to the yard after the shakedown. Were there any bugs that it turned out you had to take care of otherwise?

Adm. M.: No, nothing of a major nature, and in this respect we were blessed with some very, very capable people. For example, the arresting-gear and catapult officer aboard the ship was a man who had spent his entire life with the Otis Elevator Company. He was thoroughly conversant with hydraulics and machinery of that nature. He was an absolutely superb individual and the arresting gear and catapult, as you well know, is an extremely important part of an aircraft carrier.

Q: Indeed it is.

Adm. M.: And in those days, of course, our carriers were axial-deck. We didn't have the angled deck that we enjoy now. So such things as the barrier were maybe even more important in some respects than is the case today. If you miss a wire now, you can go around again. Then, if you missed a wire, you were going to land right in the midst of everything forward unless that barrier came up.

We had exceptionally high-caliber talent. I mentioned the catapult officer, but I also recall our engineering officer who was a former enlisted man, a mustang, who'd lived all his Navy life in engine rooms and, here again, we had a man superbly qualified for his job. So we didn't have - or, at least, we hadn't uncovered - major problems that had to be redone back in the yard. The ship had been well built by Newport News, and what we had to have done we got done at Hunter's Point in San Francisco because the ship had to go there, anyway, to get her 40-mm sponsons installed. You couldn't get through the canal with those sponsons aboard. So we had to go there and have that work done and, while we were there for I guess it was about two and a half weeks, we had other repairs that normally would have been done in the building yard. But it wasn't considered important enough for us to have to go back. Captain Baker was pushing hard to get us out in the Pacific and convinced the powers that be in Washington that we should be allowed to proceed without returning to the yard.

Of course, we had inspection teams that flew down from Norfolk to watch us in an ORI at the time we completed our training in the Trinidad area, and they had experts aboard to look at every aspect of our operation to see if there was anything that really required yard work, and I think they were convinced that we were ready to go, materielwise, and they allowed us to.

Q: Shall we return to the raids on Tokyo, then?

Adm. M.: Yes. This was an exciting time for a green crew. It was our first combat experience. Actually, the raids were somewhat of a surprise, certainly to the Japanese, and were quite successful.

Q: Were these the fire bombings?

Adm. M.: Yes.

Our strikes were primarily against their airfields. We were hitting the airfields and industrial plants in the Tokyo area. Of course, I wasn't on any of the strikes, so I can only tell you the results that we got as the air group came back to the ship. We lost some planes, but not a large number, in those raids, primarily because of the surprise the Japanese felt at finding U.S. carriers operating less than one hundred miles from Tokyo and also because by this time we had air superiority. They hadn't actually been hit by aircraft from carriers since Doolittle had been in in 1942. Our air group also hit Iwo Jima and ChiChi Jima on our retirement to Ulithi.

The Randolph was slated for the Okinawa campaign and, while we were at anchor in Ulithi with the rest of the fleet in the middle of March - incidentally, Okinawa was to be kicked off on the 1st of April - we were loading cargo aft around 2000 on 11 March. We felt fairly secure because there'd been no enemy aircraft in that area previously, but we were hit by a kamikaze. A Frances hit us, apparently attracted by the cargo lights aft. Fortunately, most of the crew was forward at the movies on the hangar deck. It was eight o'clock at night, we were at anchor, and there'd been no alert until just minutes before three kamikazes came into the area. The pilot released his bombs just before the plane itself hit the flight deck on the starboard quarter. The bombs went through onto the hangar deck below, through the emergency radio station aft, and did a tremendous amount of damage. He couldn't have done much more damage, I think, with the bombs he had. And so we had our first real combat casualties then. The fires were pretty intense. We fought fires most of the rest of the night. In spite of the fact that most of the crew were forward on the hangar deck, we had a sizable number who were badly burned and injured, over 100, and twenty-eight or twenty-nine were killed.

The explosion was such that it wiped out our aviation repair shops in the after area of the hangar deck and destroyed a huge amount of our aviation supplies in that area, tires and things of that nature, wiped out a number of aircraft, of course, that were in the hangar bays for repairs, as well as planes spotted aft on the first deck. But, further than that, it blew up the flight deck aft. By the time morning came we'd gotten the fires out and inspection parties, including Admiral Spruance, came aboard to see just how serious the damage was. If you had seen it at that time, it would never have occurred to you, at least it never occurred to me, that the ship could possibly be repaired in the forward area. I thought we'd have to go to a navy yard. I simply didn't see any alternative, but that was because I was green and inexperienced and didn't realize the enormous talent that we had in repair facilities in the forward area.

Admiral Spruance, in consultation with our captain and with the repair experts in the area, decided we could be repaired at least temporarily in the forward area, enough so we'd be an operational carrier. They brought a repair ship alongside -

Q: In Ulithi?

Adm. M.: Right there in Ulithi and we were never moved. The rest of the fleet sailed - this was the 11th of March, and the repair crews worked round the clock, eight-hour shifts. They cut that flight deck down and replaced it. They couldn't replace all our shops, of course, but they did repair the spaces. They made the after end of our ship light tight so that at night we wouldn't have great holes in her where light could escape. And this catapult and arresting-gear officer whom I mentioned to you earlier, and his crew physically removed one of the catapult arresting-gear engines, they're huge things, and moved it forward so that we only lost one of the twelve arresting-gear wires after these repairs were completed. Between his crew and the repair-ship crew, the ship was ready to sail early in the first week in April.

Q: That's incredible.

Adm. M.: It was incredible to me because I'd never seen anything like it. It's the only carrier that I've ever known about that had not been returned to a yard for repairs after a kamikaze.

Q: It's simply illustrative of the great advances, the leaps forward, that the navy had achieved.

Adm. M.: Oh, no question about it.

Q: In the fueling and everything else.

Adm. M.: American sailors, and particularly the petty officers, are awfully good at adapting to a situation like that and so, though our aviation maintenance was impaired to some degree, it went right on. Really, in a couple of weeks' time you'd hardly have known that we'd had any difficulty of any kind because the air group was able to fly, our maintenance kept pace with the operations, and it was just a remarkable achievement all the way around.

Of course, the hangar deck itself absorbed a large part of the shock of the explosion and below decks very little damage was actually done.

Q: How many bombs did it drop?

Adm. M.: Two, I think. At least, that was the best estimate we could make.

We could actually see the next morning the indentations where the landing gear struts had hit the edge of the flight deck. He released his bombs just before those struts hit the flight deck.

Incidentally, his body was catapulted completely across the flight deck and landed in the port catwalk, and while we were fighting fire on the flight deck one of the airmen came up to me and said, "There's a body over here in the catwalk," and it was the Japanese pilot. We took him out and the intelligence people took over. They found in his flight coveralls a chart that we assumed indicated where he had actually come from. He'd come from Formosa, down to Yap, and from Yap across to Ulithi, in company with two other planes and had not been picked up by our radar until just about the time they were over Ulithi.

As I mentioned earlier, we hadn't had any air activity in that area before and so it came as quite a surprise to us that they could penetrate that far.

The kamikazes towards the end of the war, well, probably from Okinawa on, many of them I know for a fact were given very minimal flight training. They were just able to get the airplanes in the air and headed out in the direction of the fleet. The one who hit us had to have been a much more experienced pilot. A green pea would never have made that flight and never been able to do what he did. There were two others with him and one of them dove into the island right next to a building that was lit up. Apparently, he thought he'd hit an enormous carrier but he just burned a hole in the ground and that's all. The third one simply disappeared from the radar screen. So the only one that actually attacked any ships was the one that hit us, and we know, from the time the alert was sounded, that he'd actually been picked up as a bogey in the area just minutes before we were hit. He hedgehopped over several carriers and we always assumed that he hit us because we had cargo lights on aft and they gave him a good aiming point. He could see it was a carrier without any question and he made the most of it. But, as I say, I'm convinced that this fellow was certainly far from a green hand in an airplane because he never would have made that long a flight, been able to, if he'd been as poorly trained as the kamikazes were later.

Q: As a footnote, how was the body disposed of? Was he given a burial at sea or anything?

Adm. M.: Yes. You know, I'm sorry I can't remember that. I remember we carried him up to flight deck control. The body wasn't badly mangled, oddly enough. I remember that his head wasn't cut up or anything. He was turned over to the intelligence people and I just don't recall what disposition was made of the body, and I don't know that we ever identified him as an individual. I remember that the aircraft charts in his coverall were about the only thing that gave away the way he had come, but he as an individual I don't think was ever identified.

Q: It would be interesting to speculate for a moment on the ability of the navy, the way they developed these techniques in wartime. I wonder if there would be any contrast with land-based units, which had more resources to draw upon, or whether the fact that a naval ship is a unit unto itself at sea and has to develop some of these techniques, in contrast to land-based units that have other resources.

Adm. M.: I'm not sure I follow you. I do think that the problem is significantly different in the case of the navy because, as you indicate, a ship is a unit, and I was more than amazed at what capability we actually had to repair. But we learned so much during the war. So many of the carriers were hit and so many experiences of repair personnel had been utilized and finally brought to bear on things just like this that I think we were the first one that did not have to return because the repair capability was so significant.

Q: It was almost an instant application of the knowledge that had been gained.

Adm. M.: No question.

Q: And this was in contrast with earlier, with the torpedoes, for instance.

Adm. M.: Oh, yes.

Q: It took quite a long time to apply the knowledge that was being learned.

Adm. M.: That, coupled with the fact that earlier in the war the aircraft carriers were just besieged by difficulties with their fueling system when they'd get hit. The gasoline fires were just enormous. We had learned tremendously from the experience at Midway, with the Yorktown and other carriers that had been lost because we didn't have - well, our systems were not designed as well, nor did we have the knowledge of how to handle it. But this wartime learning curve was a pretty significant one and we benefited from the experience of those that had gone before us in combat in action like this.

Q: I suppose you'd say under duress!

Adm. M.: Yes, indeed.

Q: Well, having recovered from that near disaster, you then -

Adm. M.: We went to Okinawa.

Q: You weren't involved in the raids on Iwo Jima?

Adm. M.: Yes, we were. The first raids on Iwo Jima occurred before we got hit, and we were in those raids also.

Q: You might tell me about them.

Adm. M.: Well, I can tell you we weren't as involved in the Iwo Jima campaign. We were a member, as I think I mentioned, of Admiral Radford's task group -

Q: Approximately what time were you - ?

Adm. M.: This was late February or early March.

Q: That was after we had begun to land?

Adm. M.: That's right, and our air group made a number of raids on Iwo Jima. I should have the Iwo Jima time down here.

Q: Your log indicates that you spent three days with strikes against Iwo, and they began on the 18th of February which, I think was D-day minus 1.

Adm. M.: Yes, that's right.

Q: What kind of opposition were they offering to air strikes?

Adm. M.: Heavy, very heavy.

Q: They were using their airfields then?

Adm. M.: Yes, they were, but actually the island itself was heavily fortified, as you know, and the antiaircraft fire from the island itself was extremely heavy against the strikes that were coming in. I just don't have a feel for the number of aircraft that we lost during that time but we certainly lost some of our fighters particularly, during the strafing, the low strafing, of the fields and of the caves. They were firing rockets against some of the caves where we thought the Japs were actually holed up on Iwo Jima.

Q: And by that time certain of their fortifications had been revealed?

Adm. M.: Oh, yes, by this time it was becoming apparent that this was going to be an extremely bloody fight for the marines, particularly, so we were throwing everything we had in. But our own task group was there only for the three-day operation that I've mentioned to you. We weren't there longer than that.

Q: Did you take extra precautions against the possibility of kaiten attacks, because they had them there?

Adm. M.: Yes. Actually, this was the first time during the Iwo Jima operations that we had any air opposition against our own carrier. We fired our antiaircraft guns for the first time because during the Tokyo raids we hadn't had any bogeys that actually came out to attack the ship. But during Iwo Jima we did have some and during the night actions, as a matter of fact, we fired our guns for the first time. We did not get hit and just drove off the aircraft that were coming out, but that was the first time our guns had been fired in anger since the ship was in commission.

Q: I was referring especially to those little one-man submarines or whatever they were.

Adm. M.: Actually, we saw no indications of them there but we were always concerned about the possibilities of submarine attacks. When you're steaming back and forth in a single area for any appreciable period of time the danger of getting hit by a submarine is obviously increased. But we saw no indications of the kaitens in there.

Then, as I say, we went back to Ulithi. I told you about the kamikaze action there, and then we went to Okinawa and that was the longest single operating period that we experienced.

Q: And one of the most intense times?

Adm. M.: Really, it was the most intense fighting during the war, and this was the time when the kamikazes were in full flower. It was the last gasp, practically, of the Japanese. The number of kamikaze aircraft that appeared over the fleet during the Okinawa campaign was almost incredible. The number of ships that got hit was pretty significant, too.

We didn't get it, but we almost did. We shot down one just over the ship that was diving on us. Oddly enough, I always heard that kamikaze pilots had no parachutes, but this fellow did. We shot a wing off his airplane and he bailed out and was picked up by a destroyer aft of us. We never got the fellow.

Q: He was rescued?

Adm. M.: Oh, yes, he was rescued. He wasn't even injured. The story was that the Japanese simply put these fellows in the airplane and sent them out, never expecting to see them again.

Q: It was a suicide mission!

Adm. M.: A suicide mission, and I just didn't think that they'd provide them with parachutes.

Whether it's actually true or not, when I later had command of a squadron, which I'll mention later on, based in Japan, one of the employees in the hotel told me one night that he had been a kamikaze pilot. I always questioned whether that was really true.

Q: Tell me about your operations there at Okinawa,

your particular mission.

Adm. M.: This was the most intense period of the war for our carrier. We operated fifty-one days, I think it was, unbroken days at sea. I think the thing that I, as an individual, remember most about it was the continuity of that concentrated operation. I don't recall ever having very much sleep because the operations were so intense during the day and so much work had to be done at night in preparation for the next day that the air department was just going round the clock, practically.

Q: Was there any decline in efficiency?

Adm. M.: I think towards the end there was. Normal operating procedure would be that we would have strikes for, I think it would be, four or possibly five days, and then you'd withdraw and replenish. Of course, the standdown time was great for the air group but the replenishment period was twice as difficult for the ship's company because of the heavy demands for working parties. Loading ammunition, taking aboard fuel, taking aboard supplies, all required lots of manpower. The minute we got through with that, we were right back on the line and operating aircraft again.

Q: How far were you removed from the battle area?

Adm. M.: Not a tremendous distance because at this time it was pretty apparent that the danger to the fleet really was not going to be from an opposing fleet or from opposing aircraft carriers. It was going to be from kamikazes. There was obviously no danger coming from Okinawa itself to the ships. So the distance removed was not all that great. We'd spend about a day replenishing, and then be right back on the line again.

The dangers, of course, from the kamikazes were just round the clock. These fellows weren't just a danger in the daytime. They were a danger at night as well. One of the things that made for real difficulties for the carriers was the fact that you might be spotted, for example, for recovery, when you were the assigned ready deck carrier. A particular carrier in the group had to be ready to take aboard an aircraft at any time. To do that, you had to have all your aircraft forward and aircraft spotted on the hangar deck.

If, then, the decision was made that you had to launch aircraft, for some reason - say, a combat air patrol was needed instantly - then the respotting of the deck in the middle of the night, moving all the aircraft aft so planes could be catapulted was a really time-consuming and difficult process.

Q: It took some light, too, didn't it?

Adm. M.: Yes, but we got to be pretty expert in handling that. I simply say it was the most intense operational period that I have ever experienced, and our ship's company really worked like dogs during that entire time.

Our situation was exacerbated somewhat by the fact that we had a flag aboard. Admiral Bogan flew his flag in Randolph, but during the course of this operation, during Okinawa, Admiral Mitscher got kamikazed off of two carriers in a row. We were operating with the Bunker Hill in the daytime when she took two kamikazes. All the ships were at flank speed when this happened, and Admiral Mitscher was aboard. He and his staff then moved over to the Enterprise, and then the Enterprise got hit by a kamikaze, her forward flight deck was hit, and then Admiral Mitscher had to move over to Randolph.

Meanwhile, we had picked up another flag officer and his staff. He was waiting to take command of one of the task groups, so we had three flags aboard at the end of Okinawa, including Admiral Mitscher and his staff, and you can probably imagine the crowded conditions we lived under in that ship.

Q: You certainly were a suitable target for several kamikazes!

Adm. M.: Oh! Well, as I say, they got Admiral Mitscher's flagship twice.

So, at the end of Okinawa, we actually had three flags and staffs aboard. The wardroom was desperately crowded. But during this time, the ship really became an extremely efficient operating unit. I've really been proud of being associated with a group that did its job as well as this. The air group and the ship were working beautifully together. I can say with a certain degree of pride that we were always first on the launches, we were always the first to recover, and we were the ones waiting for others to turn into the wind or turn out of the wind by this time. We had a first-rate organization, and the reason I'm thinking about that so nostalgically now is that subsequently I became the air officer of this carrier, after the war, after we had lost all of that talent. It was just like starting from scratch when you take over a ship like this that had been so superb in its operations during the war, and then suddenly all that talent's gone, people have left the service, your experts are gone and all of a sudden you're just back to the growing pains again -

Q: What a cycle!

Adm. M.: Oh, yes.

Q: Could you provide any adequate opportunity for rest for the pilots under this? It seems to me essential that they have it.

Adm. M.: Yes. Maybe all the pilots wouldn't agree but, compared to those of us on the ship, they certainly did have time for standdown, particularly on those days when we were replenishing. They were totally off-days for the pilots, except maybe for combat air patrol. The ship would keep planes up for that but that took such a very small number that the bulk of the pilots could get a lot of rest.

The cycle was pretty intense. We did very little in the way of night operations, mostly day operations, and so when we actually closed shop at the end of the day the pilots then got a nice rest.

Q: By that time, night operations were assigned to particular ships?

Adm. M.: Yes, that's right. We had particular ships that specialized in night operations, and the actual Okinawa operation didn't require that much night activity. The close-air-support type thing is normally done in the daytime because you need visibility for your operations. So most of the pilots' operation was a daytime affair.

Q: Any particular examples of notable success in your operations?

Adm. M.: There's nothing that really stands out because it was just a continuous-type operation throughout this period. No, I can't offer you a specific example that would stand out above all the rest during this particular time.

Q: Was crew morale sustained during -

Adm. M.: It was remarkable. You seem to learn during operations something that we tend to forget sometimes in peacetime. It seemed that the harder you actually worked, the better your morale seemed to get. I don't recall, really, any drop in morale during all those miserable turns of the weather, sometimes cold and rainy up on the flight deck in the middle of the night pushing airplanes around. In those days, of course, we had plane-handling crews who had to physically push the airplanes forward and pull them back, when they couldn't be taxied or towed, and it was tough, unpleasant work. I was down there many, many nights, working with the crew and, during those circumstances, other than hearing the usual kind of expected sailor humor, I really can honestly say I didn't see anyone who was dogging it, or hear moaning about what a terrible life this

Minter, Jr. #3 - 155

was. It just was one of those things. It's sort of remarkable now when you think back on it, and maybe it was because everybody was totally convinced that what we were doing was important. I think they all realized that the sooner we got on with it, the harder we worked at it, the sooner the thing might be over. We were all there in the same situation, nobody was getting favored treatment, and all those things combined to get the morale where it was, coupled with the fact, as I mentioned earlier, that I think Captain Felix Baker was highly regarded by his crew and by his officers as an extremely fair, just kind of an individual who had a real interest in what we were doing. All these things combined to give us what I thought was an extremely high state of morale on that ship.

Q: Did you have an adequate medical crew on board?

Adm. M.: Yes, we did, we had some exceptionally fine doctors and the medical department, really, when the chips were down, were tremendous. When we got our kamikaze, of course, we did get immediate medical assistance from other ships because our doctors were totally swamped. With the number of injured and dying from the kamikaze and the fires, it would have been almost impossible for our own ship's doctors alone to have handled a catastrophe of that size, but doctors from other ships were immediately available to us. These were a seasoned group of people and they gained invaluable experience in that baptism of fire with the kamikaze. When we later in the summer had the misfortune to be hit by a flat-heading air corps pilot, while we were at anchor in Leyte Gulf, they had another opportunity to demonstrate their skill in a major emergency.

This was the second experience that we had with major casualties and, once again, our medical corps was superb, I thought, in the way they handled these things and took care of us. Nobody, I think, had any reason to be concerned about a lack of medical attention. These fellows were just as dedicated as the rest of the ship's company was.

Q: What about the work of the chaplains?

Adm. M.: Chaplains get a lot more attention in war, I think, than they do in peacetime. I was not personally as favorably impressed with the senior chaplain we had aboard as I have been with other chaplains later, but I think his work was adequate. In fairness, I would normally see him only at general quarters because he would be up in primary fire control with me frequently. He was a good friend of mine, I just never had a strong conviction about what a great chaplain he was. But, in fairness, I didn't really see him in operation enough to form a valid judgment about how well he handled his job.

Services were held at sort of odd hours, catch as catch can, and, frankly, I was so exhausted most of the time that I didn't attend his services very regularly.

Q: Did you have any contact at all with Admiral Mitscher?

Adm. M.: No, I did not. I saw Admiral Mitscher, of course, several times -

Q: He was in very poor health at that point.

Adm. M.: He was and he spent a large part of his time in flag plot. Flag plot was directly below primary fire control, where I normally had my station, and so just on my way up and back to the flight deck from my primary fire-control center I would see him occasionally.

I think I mentioned the tremendously crowded condition we had aboard with three flags, and I think I could move on now to -

Q: The Victor cruise?

Adm. M.: Yes. Towards the end here, we had a shift of air groups. Air Group 12, which had been Charlie

Crommelin's group, was detached and I can't recall exactly when, but Air Group 16 came aboard and we had them aboard -

Q: Was that a seasoned group?

Adm. M.: Oh, yes, quite a capable air group. One of the young pilots in that group was Mike Michaelis, who got to be a great personal friend of mine, and eventually became a four star admiral. He was one of the fighter pilots in the group. This group was aboard for the remainder of the summer.

Would you like me to make reference to that P-38 pilot incident?

Q: Yes, why don't you do that?

Adm. M.: Why don't I just simply mention this one episode -

Q: Because it was a U.S. kamikaze, really.

Adm. M.: It was a U.S. kamikaze.

We were at anchor in Leyte and a P-38 was circling overhead. It was the middle of the day and a number of our people were sunbathing on the flight deck forward and we had a number of aircraft forward. Of course, since this was a P-38 nobody paid much attention to him, except we noticed that he was doing more and more in the way of sort of flat-heading around the ship. We tried to contact him by radio to suggest that he was getting much too close and was much too active, but were unable to contact him and finally he started to dive on the ship. Once again, since it was a P-38, nobody was concerned about it. But he miscalculated and instead of pulling out at a reasonable altitude he started to pull out too late and squashed into the flight deck and started tremendous fires forward because we had aircraft forward, and some of the fuel from his own aircraft, I suppose, got this well started. He was killed and he killed fourteen men that were sunbathing forward.

I happened to be on the hangar deck, just below, when this hit and got up there with the fire-fighting parties. I can still recall how some of those poor fellows died just starting to push up from the deck to get up. They knew something was going to happen. I can remember one burned body there with the hand against the deck in a halfway raised position, and he was gone just like that.

It was a tragic, senseless waste of life -

Q: What was his problem?

Adm. M.: In the first place, we had a difficult time finding out who he was or where he was from. We asked the shore commands, the army, particularly since he was an army pilot. At first, they denied having any pilots in the area, then it subsequently developed that he was a pilot being transferred. He had orders back to the States, and he was ferrying this aircraft I think into Leyte from somewhere and that was to be his last flight mission and, as it turned out, it really was his last flight mission. He was to have been returned to the United States and we could only assume that he was just exuberant about leaving the war zone, the war being over for him, and so on, and he simply got carried away with it, but it was a tragic and senseless sort of an action, and, of course, once again we had a ship that was damaged. In this particular case, since no bomb was involved, it was really just fire damage and the loss of those lives. Otherwise, the damage to the ship was fairly inconsequential.

Q: Sort of cosmetic?

Adm. M.: That's right. We had to repair the flight deck, replace some burned-out planking, and a few things like that, but nothing that would have kept the ship from operating almost immediately, had we had to do so. But, as I say, it was such a senseless thing, and we were kind of trigger-happy, having been hit once before by a kamikaze, but this time it was an American pilot, which just made it all the more tragic and difficult to accept.

We were not one of the carriers sent up to Tokyo Bay at the end of the war. We kind of hoped we would be, but we weren't.

Q: Having had all that recognition from flag officers, you'd think you might have.

Adm. M.: Yes. Well, we might have. Now that the war was over, I can recall very well the ship's radio telling us about the bomb drops on Hiroshima and Nagasaki, but of course none of us had the slightest idea of what this portended. All we knew was that this had been identified as a super weapon of some kind, but the thought that it was an atomic weapon as we know them today never crossed most of our minds. We were told that it was the equivalent of 20,000 tons of TNT and, having labored to put 500-pound bombs and 1,000-pound bombs, trying to translate that into 20,000 tons, you began to realize the magnitude of the weapon they were talking about. But you still had a feeling there was something a little bit phony about this. They might have had a super weapon of some kind but the implications of it just didn't strike home. The fact that the war ended right after that was the thing of the most immediate importance to us, and I recall that once the word had been received that the Japanese had actually surrendered the tremendous elation there was in the ship.

We had a strike on the way in to Japan at this particular time. We had launched a strike. Rumors had been floating around for two or three days that the Japanese were about to surrender, but nothing concrete had come until this announcement. And Halsey, who was fleet commander at this particular time, word went out from his staff to the fleet that the Japanese had surrendered but we were still to be on guard because no one knew just what this meant as far as the opposition forces were concerned. We had no way of knowing whether the emperor's orders were going to be fully obeyed, and so Halsey's famous order to shoot down any bogeys in a friendly way was the order of the day.

A couple of days later, it was apparent that the order was going to be carried out and arrangements were being made to have people actually go ashore in Japan, and we began, along with the other carriers, to fly missions to the prisoner-of-war camps to drop supplies. I flew in a TBF with one of our ship's pilots on one of the drops.

Q: Had you had prior knowledge of their location?

Adm. M.: We had pretty good indications about where they were, yes, and we found a number of them without much difficulty. The intelligence people had gotten this information and so the entire fleet started flying these supply-drop missions to the prisoner-of-war camps.

An interesting sideline on this - one of the camps that we dropped supplies on turns out to have been a camp that housed Americans, Australians, and British primarily, and they took a panel of the parachute that was used to drop the supplies and wrote a thank-you letter because it was identified as the Randolph's air group that had dropped the supplies. How they did this, I'll never know, but they took that panel and printed in black ink a letter of thanks to the commanding officer of the Randolph.

Q: They must have had a stencil, too!

Adm. M.: It wasn't a stencil. This was something that was done with either a brush or some sort of a pen, and they listed the names of the prisoners of war in that camp. It must have been a tremendous job, and the captain of the ship received that flag - I've forgotten but at least a month later - but it was something that was kept in the Randolph's wardroom thereafter as a memento of this prisoner-of-war camp. It was a very significant piece of work. The Japanese are awfully good at this sort of thing, so possibly they helped them, I don't know. We never saw those individuals.

Q: Ink and brush?

Adm. M.: Yes.

I haven't mentioned, and I will now, one other experience that is worthy of note. It was not a combat experience but it was one that those of us that were aboard won't forget, and this was the typhoon that we went through. Halsey, you know, had a kind of a bad track record with his fleet in typhoons.

Q: Yes.

Adm. M.: We actually lost three destroyers in the typhoon in 1944. We caught one in '45, in the summer of '45, which was something that I won't soon forget because it was so difficult to turn the aircraft carrier in those enormous waves and with that tremendous wind and, although we had everything buttoned down as well as we thought we possibly could have, I can recall a couple of SB2Cs that were located on the after hangar deck, in the engine-shop area, which broke the fittings for the side mounts, and were actually swinging every time the ship rolled. They were tethered by the bow tie-down fitting and they swung just like a huge pendulum. They'd swing back and forth, and we had a couple of engines that got loose, so we had really pretty much of a shambles in the after flight deck area, and there was no way, once those things started swinging, that the crew could get them and stop them, they were swinging so madly.

Q: Was there any danger of capsizing under those circumstances?

Adm. M.: No, I never thought we were in any danger of capsizing, but what did happen and what led to subsequent carrier redesign, was forward flight deck damage during heavy weather because the old Essex-class carriers didn't have an enclosed bow. The flight deck forward had a large open area underneath and when the ship ploughed into a heavy sea, as we did in this case, you would take green water aboard. Many of the carriers had that droop snoot appearance once they got through because the flight deck would be lifted up physically by the waves and then just dropped back down and you'd lose the whole section of your flight deck forward.

Q: I've seen pictures of that.

Adm. M.: Yes. Well, that didn't actually happen to Randolph but there was great concern that it would and, as I say, it eventually led to enclosing those bows so that you could take a sea without physically losing your flight deck.

This was the storm in which the Pittsburgh lost her bow −

Q: That's the one that Jocko was in?

Adm. M.: That's right. A tremendous amount of damage was done and, for the first time, I saw what can actually happen in a storm of that magnitude. I'd been through heavy weather before, many of us had, but never a typhoon and never in an aircraft carrier. It's something that you have to experience to appreciate.

I never really quite understood. I thought that our weather intelligence was getting to be reasonably good at this time but I simply − I know I'm going to sound critical of Admiral Halsey and I don't mean it this way, it's simply that I never understood why we didn't know better the track of that storm. I thought there were enough indications that we might have gotten out of the track of it, but we didn't, and, as I say, Admiral Halsey was criticized −

Q: Well, he has been and it was only because he was

Halsey that he escaped.

Adm. M.: That's right. Isn't that remarkable, though? Halsey and Spruance couldn't have been more different individuals. I knew them both a little bit, as a junior officer. Halsey was a flamboyant type that could somehow get away with what appeared to be murder. If the same things had happened to Spruance under the same circumstances, I'm satisfied that Spruance would never have gotten any further.

Q: Yes.

Adm. M.: But Halsey somehow had a way of surmounting those things. That famous controversial operation of his when he left the fleet and the jeep carriers, you know, if they'd been wiped out, and they should have been, the Japanese should have gotten them all, what Halsey's name would have been like in history I don't know, but he got away with it and he ends up as a five-star admiral.

Q: Yes! In contrast to Spruance.

Adm. M.: That's right. In spite of what Nimitz tried to do for Spruance.

Q: Well, you were going to tell me something about your new skipper?

Adm. M.: Yes. Right after Okinawa, as I recall, Captain Jack Tate came aboard. He was a remarkable individual in many ways. He was an old-time fighter pilot. As a matter of fact, he has a son, Hugh Tate, who followed in his father's footsteps, became a navy captain and was a really superb pilot himself, in fighters also. But Captain Tate had a rather remarkable background. He used to brag to me that he had grown up in aircraft carriers and had had every job that a pilot could have in an aircraft carrier. This in itself makes for certain difficulties because if one considers himself still an expert at flight-deck control and hangar-deck control and all those other things, it's great to have that background, but it's difficult if the individual concerned still believes he's just as current as the guy who holds the job now.

Q: It's hard to keep abreast.

Adm. M.: That's right, particularly when you have difficulties on the flight deck, with your flight-deck bosun trying to clear away a crash, and you have a captain looking over your shoulder because he thinks he knows more than you and the flight-deck bosun combined. This happened to me later on. I'll tell you about it at some later time, but this can make for some difficulties.

He was a knowledgeable man, though, certainly, and recognized as one of the superior fighter pilots. He'd been a member of the old Top Hat fighter team, the grandfather of the Blue Angels, I suppose you'd say.

Q: Tomlinson's outfit?

Adm. M.: Yes.

Q: Davis and Tomlinson.

Adm. M.: He was one of those who went back to the early days of aviation. He was a fascinating fellow to talk to, about the development of arresting gear and catapults, some of the early experiences that the Navy had in attempting to get the aircraft on and off the ships. He had a fund of knowledge in this area and he had recently come from Moscow, where he had been on the ambassador's staff, so he was quite knowledgeable about what the Russians were doing in the war. He was a totally different type individual from Captain Baker, but in some respects I have a feeling that the air group people felt a closer kinship to him than perhaps they did to Captain Baker because Tate's flying background was a little more colorful than Captain Baker's.

Therefore, he had maybe a little closer rapport with the pilots themselves than Captain Baker, who had had a different background.

Captain Tate handled the ship well. Captain Baker did, also, I might mention. Tate was really quite good in giving on the job shiphandling training to his department heads allowing them to make the approaches and do the conning after coming alongside during replenishment. He took command late in the game and I always personally felt, as I think I've mentioned earlier, that Captain Baker may have harmed himself more than he helped himself by trying to push the ship to get there too early, but I thought he should have been allowed to complete his tour. He had command of the ship less than a year and was detached right at the time that the war was just about over, and I felt that he deserved to take the ship through the last few days. But I suppose in those days they were looking for opportunities to give commands to people who had had no chance to have them before, and maybe this was the reason why Captain Tate was given a shot at the command job. For whatever reason, he was an effective skipper and handled the job quite well.

Q: Did you have any other duties in and around Japan other than supplying the prisoner-of-war camps?

Adm. M.: No. We were detached very shortly after the war was over, and we got the first taste of the Magic Carpet duty that we got involved in later on. We took 1,000 passengers back from Pearl on our way back to the United States and it made for a very crowded condition, but no one really minded since we were on our way home.

Q: Was it affecting your own crew also?

Adm. M.: Well, of course, by this time, the war was over and the point system was being used for processing personnel out of the services, so we knew that we had a number of our ship's company who were going to leave as soon as they possibly could. I'll tell you at a subsequent period, if you like, about our real Magic Carpet cruise as it took place later on.

Q: Yes. A very precipitate kind of demobilization.

Adm. M.: Yes, it really was.

Interview #4 with Vice Admiral Charles S. Minter, Jr.
U.S. Navy (Retired)

Place: His residence in Providence; Annapolis, Maryland

Date: Tuesday morning, 14 August 1979

Subject: Biography

By: John T. Mason, Jr.

Q: Well, today we resume with an account of your tour of duty in the Randolph. You were beginning to get involved in the Magic Carpet.

Adm. M.: Right. I'll just make a few comments about the end of the war activity in WesPac. I did tell you that we dropped some supplies on prisoner-of-war camps and, just before we were detached to return to the United States, we sent a detachment of marines ashore and three of our ship's officers were also included in the group that were among the very first to go ashore in Japan. They served as sort of occupation troops in the initial efforts to get our personnel ashore. We didn't see them again. They stayed on, certainly until the ship returned to the United States.

We were detached on the 5th of September, somewhat to our surprise because the rumors had been that we might take part in the surrender ceremonies in Tokyo Bay, but that didn't eventuate and we were returned to Pearl Harbor. In Pearl, our 40-millimeter sponsons were removed to enable us to go through the canal and we took aboard a large number of personnel for shipment back to the United States, about 1,000 as a matter of fact. They slept on cots just about any place we could put them on the ship because we still had our air group aboard and our ship's company, so this was a pretty crowded situation.

Q: What did it do to the food schedule and that sort of thing?

Adm. M.: We had to eat in shifts, of course, but the ship had gotten to the point during combat where this really didn't present a great problem. They just cooked right around the clock, practically. It was pretty good training, as I'll tell you in a few minutes, for how we had to work in the Magic Carpet business.

As a matter of interest, when we were in Pearl Harbor, the ship was repainted in preparation for her return and there were a lot of people who felt this was a mistake. They would like to have had the people at home see her just the way she really looked in combat, pretty well beat up, the rust spots showing, all the warts, but it was decided that she ought to look spick and span, so she was dressed up.

Q: It detracted somewhat from the hero concept!

Adm. M.: Of course, it did, but it did give us a chance to put the air group's record up and have that spick and span. Our two air groups - we had two, we had Air Group 12 and, the last part of the war, Air Group 16 - their combined record was pretty impressive. They were credited with over 150 airplanes shot down and over 160 destroyed on the ground. They were given credit for about 90,000 tons of enemy merchant shipping sunk. They'd also done considerable damage to some enemy naval vessels during the last few weeks of the war when they were strafing and bombing.

Q: The few that were left.

Adm. M.: Yes, ultimately there were very few.
    Another small thing that never came to very much. Our captain had gotten concerned about topside weight in an aircraft carrier. I conducted an informal sort of a survey on the trip home for him to see what we could propose to the Bureau of Ships in the way of reduction in heavy topside weight.

Q: Was this inspired perhaps by the typhoon?

Adm. M.: It had a part to play, all right, but BuShips was getting concerned with the number of radars installed, splinter shielding, all the armor-plating, and so on above the hangar-deck level.

Q: The original design was sound but then all this ordnance is added!

Adm. M.: That's right, you just keep adding, so we did a little informal survey. As I say, it didn't really amount to very much. The results of our survey, I think, were sent in to BuShips for study but I never saw anything that came of it. It was something to keep us occupied on the way home.

The trip home was fairly uneventful. I mentioned the fact that we had 1,000 extra passengers aboard but the crowding was nothing particularly new to us.

Q: Well, now, just cruising, how were they occupied? What did you do for the passengers - anything?

Adm. M.: Volleyball, exercise, just about everything. There wasn't much really that you could do to pass the time. It was sort of a normal letdown after all the combat time. It was just like a pleasant cruise. The weather was good. We went through the canal zone in mid-October, and we were then told that the ship was going to be in Baltimore for Navy Day. This was the first time, and I believe the last time, that a combat carrier has ever been in the port of Baltimore. We had to make some special preparations for this which I'll mention in a moment.

We actually got home, in to Norfolk that is, on the 21st of October and we spent five days there, and then we sailed for Baltimore. We offloaded most of the air group. We had to remove ammunition and we had to offload some oil because the ship's draft was about 30 feet and the Baltimore Harbor at that time was just 30 feet. We got the ship down to 28-foot draft. The captain had about two feet to play with.

Q: That wasn't much.

Adm. M.: Well, we kicked up mud every time we turned the screws in Baltimore Harbor. But we made it with no real trouble and we had some display aircraft aboard - representatives types - for the public to look at. It's just hard to imagine now the excitement that was displayed by the people who came aboard the ship. We estimated 50,000 people a day came aboard. We had to be very careful, we had to have guards around the planes because we found the first day that some souvenir-hunters were tearing bits of fabric off the airplanes, just to say they had a piece of one of the planes that had been in combat.

It was really an interesting experience. The City of Baltimore turned itself over to us, and the crew and the officers were given carte blanche. We were given entree to all the clubs. It was a marvelous experience and, as I say, I've never seen anything quite like it since. I'm not sure anything like that has happened since.

Q: Pent-up excitement had been generated through the war years.

Adm. M.: Absolutely. They were so wonderful. We were very restricted in the area we were located in in Baltimore and people stood in line literally for an hour or two just to work their way up aboard the ship. We had arranged so they'd come aboard the hangar deck forward, get to the flight deck via the forward elevators, proceed aft past the display aircraft, down No. 3 elevator, and then off the ship. They never got below the hangar-deck level. We just couldn't accommodate them down below. So the hangar deck and the flight deck - I don't think we let them in the island either, it would have been just impossible to have taken them up in the island because of the vast numbers.

Q: Did the skipper entertain the VIPs at dinner or

anything?

Adm. M.: Yes, we had the mayor of the city and one of the senators, I've forgotten which one now, was aboard. They wouldn't miss an opportunity like this.

Q: No!

Adm. M.: I didn't personally participate in any of the dinners that the captain had but he did have some.

Right after the time in Baltimore, the ship went to the navy yard in Norfolk to prepare for Magic Carpet, and these preparations were rather interesting. I'm always a little bit amazed at how quickly BuShips was able to come up with a design - it wasn't that complicated, I guess, but I'm not sure I would have thought of it this way. They put 5,000 bunks on the hangar deck, A-frames that were five tiers high, to provide for 5,000 people to sleep on the hangar deck. All the aircraft were taken off, of course. This was purely an effort to transport personnel.

Huge galley equipment was also installed on the hangar deck because we were going to bring back 6,600 troops and we had our own ship's company, cut almost in half, by the way, just enough to steam the ship and to do essential -

Q: Not arbitrarily cut in half, but half the crew had gone, hadn't they?

Adm. M.: We were losing a lot. They hadn't all been mustered out at this time. We had lost quite a few, but we cut down the engineering gang, for example, to just a normal steaming watch. We knew that we wouldn't have the emergencies that you normally experience in combat, and almost every department was just about halved. Twelve hundred was the size of the crew that we actually had aboard and normally the ship's company was twenty-five hundred.

I'd become the air officer, by the way and, as the air officer, I then became the transportation officer. I was responsible for the housing and the berthing and the messing of this -

Q: You didn't have any planes to deal with!

Adm. M.: The planes were gone and so the spaces became mine. In the navy yard, in addition to the bunks that were put aboard and the galley equipment that was put aboard, they put ge-dunk stands all around the hangar deck, little places where you could get ice cream, books, and things like that. This was in anticipation of these troops that would be coming back not having had ice cream and so on for a while, and I tell you what that meant.

Q: Of course, BuShips had had a chance to plan all of this.

Adm. M.: Oh, yes.

Q: There had been advance planning in all areas for demobilization.

Adm. M.: Well, of course, it was really an emotional issue. People whose time was up were fighting to get home, the Congress was being besieged by people saying, "Why must my boy still stay overseas when the war is over?" Any number of navy ships were turned over to this type thing, but the aircraft carrier lends itself because of the huge size and the numbers it can accommodate.

I was assigned thankfully an army captain and six army technical sergeants. They were all fluent in Italian and the reason that they were assigned to me was because we took back to Italy several hundred Italian ex-prisoners of war, who had been doing hospital duty and various things in this country. They were to serve as a work force to augment my gang in getting the ship ready to take aboard these 6,600 troops in Naples. There were thirteen Italian officers, and I must tell you that, without any doubt, they were the worst officers I have ever seen in any service anywhere. They were totally useless. I may be being unkind but I had little difficulty understanding why the Italians didn't do any better if that was the caliber of leadership they were supposed to have. They didn't do one thing for their men, they didn't participate in any way on the trip over. They simply lay in their bunks the entire time and I, with my army captain and petty officers, worked their men.

Q: Maybe they were spoiled by being in prisoner-of-war camps?

Adm. M.: I think they had been. They were sort of considered less than - I think the term was cobelligerents. They were accorded the proper treatment of prisoners of war, but the Italians had a sort of strange relationship towards the end of the war.

Q: They certainly did!

Adm. M.: The U.S. Army had outfitted these Italians in World War I army outfits and they were a strange sight indeed when they came out for formation. They had those old army overcoats that came right down to the ankles and these fellows were fairly short to begin with. Their overcoats practically were on their shoe-tops. They were really a ragtag outfit that the army had simply put into something khaki to make them look like a military force.

Q: That in itself would be demoralizing, I would think.

Adm. M.: It was.

We had a lot of work to do in the week that we had at sea to get ready to take our troops aboard. The navy yard had installed the bunks, galley equipment and other things, but we had to number the bunks, put a mattress on each bunk, and plan on how we would break out the blankets, physically handle 6,600 unorganized troops. Of course we had to test the galley equipment, and other equipment that had been put aboard. I used those 770 Italians along with my air department personnel to do these jobs.

The first day out of Norfolk they worked quite well. The second day we ran into a little weather and they did get seasick, they were horribly seasick, and so that day I just worked my own ship's company. The next day the sea was calm and everything was great, but they had apparently found that if they acted as though they were sick no work was involved. So when I called the work detail, I had the army captain announce that I needed 300 of these Italians.

Very few rolled out of their bunks. So I told the army captain to call them once more and we got very few additional volunteers. So I simply gave mess cards to the fifty or sixty who showed up, and old Dr. Minter decided if they were too sick to work they were too sick to eat, and so, at noon, only the fifty to sixty who had worked got lunch. At 1300 I had all 700 of them ready to go, and we had no trouble the rest of the time!

Q: That was an inspiration.

Adm. M.: But we did get the ship ready, as ready as a ship can be for a totally new experience, taking aboard 6,600 troops and transporting them is no small chore, I can tell you.

An interesting sidelight. We got in to Naples and the ship had to go alongside, of course, to be able to load aboard these troops. Didn't have to, but it was preferable to do that. And the captain had to take aboard an Italian pilot who spoke no English, and he was giving orders in Italian to the tugs, and the captain was left just sort of guessing what was happening to the ship. He was nervous as a cat on a hot tin roof. I was on the bridge and I said:

"Maybe you'd like to have our army captain come up and translate for you?"

Well, that was a godsend for the captain because the army captain, as I mentioned, was fluent in Italian and he could tell what the Italian pilot was saying and relay it to our captain, and things smoothed down a little bit.

Q: What an awkward situation!

Adm. M.: It really was because, you know, he's still responsible and it's tricky getting into Naples Harbor with an aircraft carrier. There's nothing simple about it. There's a lot of shipping.

Q: And that harbor was littered, wasn't it, with all the - ?

Adm. M.: It was, indeed, and so it was no small operation, and the captain was understandably nervous about it.

An amusing thing, also. Cigarettes were the equivalent of gold, American cigarettes, in Naples at that time. There was a flourishing black market in cigarettes. You could buy anything with cigarettes. In hotels and bars, any place you went, a cigarette was a marvelous tip. You didn't have to think about money. And it was interesting to me because our captain was a chain-smoker and the Italian pilot -

I'm not sure he was a chain-smoker - but he certainly understood the value of a cigarette and every time the captain would flip up a cigarette for himself he'd offer one to the pilot, and the pilot would take three or four! He'd light one and put two or three in his pocket. He practically robbed the Old Man of a pack of cigarettes before he got the ship in.

We eventually did get in, though, and we had two or three days in port and then the influx of these army troops came. It's really hard to describe how this went because these, you realize, were not homogeneous units of any type, they were simply people who had their points, they were all tossed together, along with officers who had their points, and while there was some effort at organization - they were assigned certain companies and they had commands - it was just like a bunch of cattle coming aboard, and understandably. There were 5,000 who were going to sleep on the hangar deck and another thousand below decks and so on.

Q: Had they all been involved in the Italian campaign?

Adm. M.: They'd been all over Europe. They'd been everywhere. These were people who were going out on points. They identified those who had been overseas the longest and those were the first ones to go home, which was as fair a system, I guess, as you could have had. We did have some fairly senior officers. There were no generals in that group. The most senior officer was a colonel. I worked directly with them and I must say that they did the best they could to keep these troops reasonably well organized.

We had, as I mentioned, a total of 6,600 on board and we had 13 army nurses, who had to be given kind of special treatment. We had them up in the forecastle of the ship, in some of those rooms up there.

The loading aboard was really quite orderly. We had prepared instruction sheets, the bunks were numbered just like you number seats in a football stadium, so when a man came aboard he had a bunk number. We had ship's company assigned to guide them and lead them around until they got the feel of the ship. The moment we got the officers aboard, I got together with the senior army colonel to discuss the organizational structure and what we were going to require of them during the trip home. It went, I think, as well as things could have.

The captain, once we got them all aboard and we cast off all lines and headed for home, announced over the loudspeaker system that we were going to get them home by - I've forgotten what the date was, but he told them - one week's steaming time from Naples. That meant the ship was going to crank up to about 30 knots and we were really going to hightail it for home. Loud cheers went up when he announced we'd be in Staten Island on a certain day, and then the routine started.

Well, you don't really get yourself fully prepared for something like this, if you've never experienced it. So many things crop up that maybe we should have anticipated but didn't. It was amusing, looking back on it now, but it wasn't all that funny at the time.

I began to be worried about the safety of these troops. They'd been aboard ship, maybe transports, but I recall one day going up in the forecastle when we had some really heavy weather, I simply was up looking to see if the forecastle was all secure, and here were about ten of them up there just watching the waves break and come in over the ship and they could easily have been lost overboard. And mustering those people every day got to be a real chore. They weren't well organized and we could have missed two or three of them, I suppose, and never known the difference. I guess we would have known the difference, but in any event we were constantly having to alert them not to walk on the catwalks, not to get out on the open decks during heavy weather. But the real problems came in things that we simply hadn't even considered.

When our crew went through the messline, normally they would take one or two slices of bread. These fellows would take eight and ten slices of bread each. They hadn't had light bread to eat in two years, in some cases, and they couldn't get enough of it. We got to the point where we really had to ration bread.

In the ge-dunk stands that I told you we had around the hangar-deck area and a fellow would come up and want a dish of ice cream, ten cents, and could pay for it only with one of the big bills he had been paid off with. We eventually had to just give it away because there was no way that we could continue to make change.

The feeding overall really went pretty well. I thought the supply department did a superb job. But the routine was pretty dull. We would feed them and then we would darken the hangar deck and show a movie, we'd feed them and we'd show another movie. When the weather was good, they could get up on the flight deck - we had the entire flight deck that they could use for exercise. We had some touch-football games on the flight deck, and back in the after part of the ship, the hangar deck, where our kamikaze had wiped out our shops, we had actually blocked off those spaces back there and didn't use them for anything, but these fellows found a way to use them. I went aft one afternoon. The chief master-at-arms came up to me and told me that there was the biggest gambling game that he had ever seen in his life going on back there. I went back and walked in and, sure enough, a bunch of soldiers had a pile of money on a blanket that was staggering.

Q: Well, they had all that money.

Adm. M.: They had it all and they had a week to spend it in. It was boring in the ship, there was not much for them to do and these fellows really had a whale of a gambling game going on.

We had brought aboard games, we had chess sets, we had cards, we had everything you could think of to try to amuse them, books, paperbacks by the gallon, but when that ship reached Staten Island I wish you could have seen that hangar deck. We policed it every day and tried to clean it up, but when they finally left the ship it was just as though you'd had a herd of cattle aboard. Of course, some of them got seasick. We hit a bad storm on the way back and for one day we really were slowed down, and a lot of them got seasick, and that hangar deck was closed in, the roller curtains were down to keep the sea from coming in, and the smell in that place got pretty raunchy.

Q: You salvation, actually, was in the captain's desire to speed?

Adm. M.: Exactly. Well, unfortunately the payoff wasn't quite as good as we'd hoped. We did get them back, the captain got them in the day he said he would, but I've never understood yet what happened in the exchange of communications. We got in on a Sunday afternoon and word was given to me that the troops were to be fed their last meal at noon on Sunday because we'd be offloading them on Staten Island and the army would pick them up and take them down to Fort Dix for processing out on Sunday afternoon.

So, no preparations had been made for a Sunday evening meal. We got in to port and there was no transport for them. Nobody from the army was there to meet them, and the captain and our communicators swore that the messages had gone and were receipted for that we would arrive at this time. I guess the confusion arose over the fact that we did have that one day of a heavy storm, we were slowed down and it looked as though we weren't going to make it. But the Old Man cranked her right back up to 30 knots the second the weather abated and we did make it.

Well, we had 6,600 troops on our hands. We couldn't offload them. They were home, they were back in America, and here they were, right next to the beach and we couldn't let them off. There was nowhere for them to go. I tell you, they were a mad bunch of people on that ship and, to make things worse, we hadn't prepared an evening meal for them and they were starting to get hungry. Our ship's company, I must say, some of them, capitalized on this. They were selling sandwiches that they'd gotten from their own mess for a buck fifty a throw or something like that.

The army finally did crank around. Some poor flustered major came aboard and he was the subject of more abuse than you can imagine.

Meanwhile, our captain had gone on the loudspeaker, the ship's system, and he told the troops:

"I told you I'd get you here today and I did. It's your own army that's failed to get you ashore."

But, by nine o'clock at night - oh, meanwhile, the Red Cross did show up and they had doughnuts and hot coffee - the army showed up with transportation to get these fellows down to Fort Dix or wherever. We saw the last of them around 10:00 or 10:30 that night.

Q: What about their facilities on board ship? I mean it wasn't constructed with that in mind.

Adm. M.: No, but in addition to the ge-dunk stands, there were any number of urinals and temporary heads all around.

Q: They'd been installed?

Adm. M.: Oh, yes, they were installed at Norfolk.

As a result of our experience on that one trip - the ship made two trips, I didn't make the second trip, I went on leave -

Q: You were happy!

Adm. M.: I'm afraid so.

But the ship bought 30,000 pounds of bread and baked all the way over, getting ready for this onslaught of people who wanted bread. The paymaster took aboard an awful lot of silver because, as I mentioned, the soldier came aboard with nothing but bills in huge denominations to pay for the most minor purchase.

So we learned an awful lot on that first trip, and the second trip, although I wasn't aboard, I heard later went much smoother.

Q: Naturally it would.

Adm. M.: And those fellows were willing to put up with an awful lot, I can tell you, to get home, and they were happy to make it.

Q: Tell me a little bit about the Italian debarkation.

Adm. M.: Oh, I'll tell you about that. I forgot to mention it.

We got in to Naples and the Italians, of course, as a country were just horribly disorganized.

Q: There was really no government.

Adm. M.: No, there was really nothing. Those troops went off the ship with those thirteen worthless officers. They walked down the pier, they were dismissed, and, as far as I know, that constituted their total demobilization from the army. I talked to some of our army MPs in Naples during the few days we were there and they were really concerned because so many Italians were being brought in and were being dismissed and they were on their own. Many of them formed gangs there in Naples. There were pretty dangerous parts of Naples at night.

Naples was getting to be a real tinderbox at that time. The army was terribly concerned. With all the Italian ex-POWs who were just turned loose there in the city and, of course, there was a huge influx of our own troops coming into the area. It was seething cauldron, I can assure you.

Q: You went on leave when you came back?

Adm. M.: I went on leave over Christmas, and then I returned to the ship and, after its second Magic Carpet trip, the ship then went to the navy yard in Boston, where we had some very extensive repairs that had to be done, to get the ship ready to be an operating carrier again.

Q: She had to be reconverted?

Adm. M.: Reconverted, and she also had to reactivate those shop spaces that had been burned out and that we just sort of jury-rigged for the rest of the voyage. They had to be replaced with normal operating spaces. So we had a fairly extensive stay in the navy yard in Boston.

As I mentioned, I'd become the air officer and since we had not actually operated aircraft since the flyoff of the air group back in October and since we had a tremendous turnover of personnel and an influx of totally green people, this was one of the lowest spots for me. After having seen a flight deck that operated just like clockwork and a fueling gang and a dearming gang and an engineering group, the whole ticking like a watch, to suddenly tear it all apart and try to put it together again with just makeshirt parts was a difficult thing to do.

Q: Without the pressure of a war.

Adm. M.: That's right. Those who were still in and were wanting to get out, of course, they were eager to leave. We had so few experienced petty officers. We had some, certainly, that were going to stay in the navy and make the navy a career, but that drive that existed before was lacking now. It was a peacetime atmosphere and we had then to go back and be terribly concerned about the safety of our aircraft. Not that we weren't concerned before, but as an operating team, as good as we were, we knew we could handle that.

I can recall our first air group operation after we got out of the navy yard. AirLant used us for a carrier qualification carrier for a time, before we got an air group assigned to us, and we operated out of Norfolk, and we were used, as I say for qualification work. The Lexington, which is down at Pensacola, isn't always available to do the qualifying, so a new air group frequently had to come aboard and you had to have individual landings for individual pilots to be qualified and, normally, one of the operating periods was used for this.

This served a useful purpose for us because it gave us a chance, without the pressure of a full air group aboard, to slowly work ourselves back up because if you had any difficulties with your arresting gear or catapults, you could always send the pilots back to the beach. You were close enough that it was no great problem. It would be if you were far at sea and had no divert field, but I'll mention that in a moment, too.

Q: What did you do familywise?

Adm. M.: The families all stayed where they were. My wife had moved to Norfolk and the whole ship's company had because that was our home port.

Q: She wasn't in Boston when you were up there?

Adm. M.: No, she wasn't. Some of the people probably had their wives up there, but most did not. We were in Boston, as I recall, about six weeks. Something like that. It wasn't a lengthy stay.

But we slowly began to get our personnel back and we experienced again the buildup of the ship and started to operate. Eventually, we got an air group assigned to us, headed by a classmate of mine, and then we were told that the ship was going to participate in the midshipmen's cruise - I'm certain we were the first aircraft carrier to take midshipmen and actually fly them in air group airplanes. When the midshipmen came aboard in June -

Q: This was aviation summer?

Adm. M.: It was aviation summer. I don't believe those who came aboard the carrier went down to Pensacola. I'm sure that their aviation was simply what we gave them, and my recollection is that we planned two hours per midshipman in an aircraft, some deck launched, some catapuled, but the purpose was to familiarize them with aviation. We had an air group that had the same sort of growing pains we had, they had new pilots so we had to qualify the air group before we got ready for the midshipmen.

Q: Yes. Well, the midshipmen really got proper attention, something they don't always do on cruises.

Adm. M.: That's right. In recent years, when I was the commandant and the superintendent and even now it's really discouraging to see how difficult it is to have a summer cruise anything like - well, it can never be anything like it was when I was a midshipman. As I told you before, when I was a midshipman we had ships set up as a training squadron just for the midshipmen. That could never happen again.

Q: But maybe should?

Adm. M.: Well, you hate to see the midshipmen not really exposed to a proper summer cruise that combines the thrill for a youngster of going abroad for his first time. Also, it was combined with some real practical work. I've seen it so many times, and it can't be helped I guess, but when you assign a large number of them to an aircraft carrier, for example, alongside the pier for six weeks, they're stumbling over each other and the ship's company just doesn't have the time to offer much in the way of training. It can be demotivating.

Q: Yes, it is, indeed.

Adm. M.: Rather than a motivating thing.

Q: Perhaps it should be called summer training, as Draper said, rather than a cruise.

Adm. M.: That's right, that's correct. Well, in our particular case, with those midshipmen, we didn't go abroad. We cruised up and down the east coast and they weren't aboard more than approximately a month. At any rate, I think they got a pretty good look at air operations. Then, of course, here was a ship that still had a lot of people aboard who'd been through combat, and it gave them a chance to talk to people who had experienced it and gave them a little better insight into what operating a carrier was like.

Q: Yes. I can see, from your point of view, it must have been an awfully difficult period, but at the same time it was a challenge, if I might use that word.

Adm. M.: It was, and I can say we didn't lose an airplane, or any personnel. We had one really difficult experience, though, that I think I mentioned to you earlier. Our captain was still Captain Tate, Blackjack Tate, who had boasted to me that he had had every job aboard an aircraft carrier that a pilot could possibly have and I'm afraid he allowed this to sway his better judgment on occasion, and this occasion was one.

An airplane came aboard, a TBF, landed off-center and got over in the catwalk on the starboard side of the flight deck aft. Randolph was still an axial-deck carrier, so with that airplane in that position, the entire flight deck was tied up. Nothing could be done until we got that airplane clear. It had gone over in a very awkward way. No injury to the pilot, but the starboard landing gear was in the catwalk and the port gear was still on deck. She was canted over and she was still hooked to the arresting wire with a tail hook.

Well, the first thing you do is release that tailhook pressure. Then you get what the aviators call Tilly, that's a Le Tourneau crane, that huge crane that lifts aircraft -

Q: Tilly?

Adm. M.: Tilly is short for Le Tourneau. We got the crane out and I have to emphasize now we had an air bosun who was pretty new to this business. He normally handled the crashes and that sort of thing on the flight deck, but I could tell he was getting in trouble, so I went down from primary fly to assist in the operation. The plane was at a very awkward angle for the crane. The crane couldn't get far enough out to get a direct purchase on the end and pull it directly up, so it was pulling at an angle and it tended to cant up the after part of the Le Tourneau crane. The crane was as close to the catwalk as we could get it. We had it chocked. But those huge wheels were really within inches of going on the catwalk itself, so it had to be very carefully done.

Well, we had just gotten things all set and all of a sudden I heard orders being given to the crane operator from the other side. Somebody was telling the guy to do something different from what I had said, and it really made me furious, but I shouted to the operator to cancel the other order right then because he was just about to go into the catwalk. The order that had been given was going to move him a little closer. If he ever got the Le Tourneau crane in the catwalk, that's the end of it. You're really stuck then, and we were at sea with the air group circling overhead and trying to come aboard and there was no place for them to go except this deck.

Well, the voice was the captain's. I went around and here was the captain giving instructions and I really was furious. When he saw how mad I was he sort of backed away.

We eventually got the plane out of the catwalk and operations went back to normal. I said nothing to him, he said nothing to me at the time, but we discussed it later and he agreed to let me run emergencies from then on, and he did.

I remained as air officer until the middle of that summer, then I was detached to go to Patuxent River.

Q: Did this come as a surprise, or did you want it?

Adm. M.: I wanted Patuxent very much. The surprise came when I went to Op-54 - that's the aviation detailing unit that used to be separate from BuPers. It dealt just with aviation detailing. The aviators did their own detailing at that time, before they became absorbed in BuPers. A classmate of mine was my detailer and when I went in to call on him to see where I might go I found that he had lined me up to be his relief. My goal was Patuxent and I protested his proposal so vigorously that I finally got a set of orders to the Naval Air Station, Patuxent. My hope was to move to the Test Center when an opening became available.

Q: Why did you want it so badly?

Adm. M.: Patuxent was just really getting underway. It was very obvious to me and to others that it was going to be the focal point of naval aviation development. There was just no question about it. The purchase of that land down there, nearly 7,000 acres, and the location was certainly one of the wisest things that's ever been done, in my judgment. It's just proved itself time and time again.

Q: Who engineered that? Radford?

Adm. M.: Radford had a big part to play in it. Yes, indeed he did. You know, at this time, it was obvious that we were going to start getting jets, jet aircraft, in the navy, and you had to have an isolated area and you had to have a big area, and you had to be off the airways. There were so many things that required that you would have a space like this. There was real excitement in going to Patuxent because the newest developments in naval aviation were certainly going to take place there, and so every aviator had that kind of as his goal in those days, getting there, if he possibly could.

So I accepted an assignment - I say "I accepted," I was given an assignment and -

Q: On the administrative staff?

Adm. M.: On the administrative side. Captain Abe Vosseller was the commanding officer of the air station at that time, this was in 1946, and the station was really only about three years old. In addition to the test center, where the new aircraft were testing, the air station also served as host for three VR squadrons, transport squadrons, that were stationed there at the time. So the station was really pretty active.

Q: Was Vosseller also commander of the fleet air unit there?

Adm. M.: It wasn't started.

Q: That didn't exist?

Adm. M.: No, that was separate. Vosseller had just the air station. It was interesting, the parallel, just having come from an aircraft carrier and seeing the relationship that had to exist between the air group and the parent carrier. There's a strong parallel between the air station and the naval air test center, because they're tenants aboard the air station. The air station is responsible for the logistic support of tenant units and, while they are competitive in so many ways, their relationship had to be compatible. It was interesting to me to watch how the relationship between the senior officers developed there. It wasn't always the happiest one. The commanding officer of the air station occasionally had his difficulties with some of the test-division directors who were of comparable rank.

Q: But he was senior, wasn't he?

Adm. M.: No, he was not. The director of the flight test division, for example, was a classmate of his, senior to him, and they were not the closest professionally. I can't really say whether a certain jealousy existed. There was a glamour about the test division that wasn't given to the air station. The air station was the workhorse and the test division were the fellows who got all the -

Q: They were the prima donnas.

Adm. M.: They were, and with some justification. After all, they were charged with the responsibility for test flying these brand-new aircraft we were getting in the navy, so they had the best people assigned to them. Top pilots in the test division and top personnel running the test division.

But, to get back to my keen desire to get there, I just felt that if I could ever get there, eventually a slot might open up in one of the test divisions and I could move into it, which is just what happened in my case.

Q: What did you do as an administrator?

Adm. M.: Well, I tell you, that was not the happiest assignment I ever had. I was given the title, and I don't think it existed anywhere else and maybe it was just because of the curious relationship between the air station and the test center, I was given the title of management coordinator. The best thing I can say for that job is - not the best thing, but one of the things I will say about it is - it really sort of in one shop encompassed all the unpleasant things an executive officer normally has to contend with.

I suddenly found that the personnel division was under me, housing was under me, the athletic program was under me, and at one time, facetiously, not completely, I said to the captain:

"What does the exec do on this station? I've got everything that I've ever seen an exec do before?

Housing! Housing was an absolute shambles. Patuxent was so new that there hadn't been time for commercial housing to be developed anywhere near to the extent it was required. People, I knew, were commuting from as far away as Waldorf, which was forty-some miles away, daily, and the jumble of housing we had on the station in itself was a curious hodgepodge. We had quonset huts that were divided in two, two families to one quonset hut.

Q: No privacy there!

Adm. M.: You accepted that. But occupancy cost you your housing allowance, the same as if you were living in one of our brand-new lovely two- and three-bedroom apartments.

The curious thing was I learned that the postgraduate school up here at the Naval Academy had quonset huts also for its personnel and they were only paying thirty dollars a month, which was about twice what you should have paid because they were miserable places to live. So I came up to Annapolis to find out how they could do that when my public works man told me we had to take the housing allowance from people. Well, it was a quirk in the construction law. These quonset huts up here were built with funds that allowed them to be rented whereas at Patuxent all housing could be occupied only with loss of housing allowance because of the nature of the appropriation bill under which they were funded.

Construction was going on at a very, very rapid rate, I will say, and by the time I left most of our people were very well housed.

Q: Why couldn't the rules have been changed to make the quonset hut living just a first step?

Adm. M.: Some people accepted it on that basis. They could get themselves on the list. Housing is always a problem. You always have to concern yourself with whether the station policy should be one that seniority alone determines the type of housing you get, but when you do that you end up sometimes with senior people with no children occupying a four-bedroom place and people with six children trying to crowd into a two-bedroom place. So there's always that argument about which way you should go. Should you pay more attention to the size of the family and simply ignore seniority? The other argument, of course, is that people say, "I've been in this Navy all these years, why shouldn't I live reasonably well?" We just had a constant battle over all these things.

Fortunately, eventually we got housing such that we didn't have to continue quonset huts, but when I first went there, they were certainly a part of the housing program, and some people were so desperate that they would take them, complain like crazy, but once they were in they at least had a roof over their head and some place that they could hang their hat.

Q: In some quarters, I can see, you weren't very popular!

Adm. M.: Oh, indeed I wasn't. There were constant complaints about housing and there was no way around it at the time, until things could be improved.

An amusing sidelight. Later on, I mentioned that the athletic department came under my sponsorship, and we had some pretty good athletic teams down there and a very widespread intramural program. I found out years later, when I was ordered to the Naval Academy my first time as the executive officer to the Director of Athletics, the commandant had selected me for that job by looking at my record. He didn't know me. He looked at my record in BuPers and somehow had come to the conclusion that I had actually run this enormous athletic program down there and therefore knew intramural athletics and I'd be the kind of guy they wanted here at the Naval Academy! The truth of the matter was I had athletic specialists, I had officers who ran the thing, and it was simply a facet of my department. So I got my foot in the door at the Naval Academy purely by mistake, as a result of that experience at Patuxent River.

Q: Well, the base had to be self-contained because the community offered nothing?

Adm. M.: Oh, nothing, absolutely nothing. Lexington Park at that time had a few enterprising people who certainly saw the handwriting on the wall. A few pilots and enlisted men also realized the economic possibilities of the area. When they got out, they started restaurants, bars, stores, et cetera. Incidentally, in those days, in St. Mary's County slot machines just abounded. You couldn't go into a grocery store without finding people pulling at a twenty-five-cent or fifty-cent slot machine.

As a matter of fact, our officers' club ran on slot machine revenues. We had ten slot machines in the club and we took in three thousand dollars a month on those things, and they were pegged to pay the highest return you could possibly pay. They paid something like 91 or 92 percent. In Las Vegas, I think they pay about 70 percent, or something like that. Anyway, we were just rolling in money in the officers' club. The result was you could practically give away your drinks, you could have your food for practically nothing. But the minute that the Department of Defense came out and banned slot machines everywhere in the United States and eventually overseas as well, we suddenly found a loss of three thousand dollars a month in our take there at Patuxent, and it resulted in some real soul-searching about how to keep the officers' club going. People were accustomed to martinis for fifteen cents, then suddenly they were having to pay for them.

Patuxent is so large that the officers' club is six miles from the main gate and, when people found that they could go outside the gate, just outside, and have dinner, drinks, and slot machines there, they wouldn't come to the club when we lost the machines. So we had to see how to make that club attractive. We put movies in, we even went to the extent of setting up a bowling alley, but I tell you, when you lose three thousand dollars of your income it makes a real dent in your operations. The club was another part of my responsibility, not totally, but it came under me so I was pretty conscious of the kind of club we'd operate as well.

Q: What kind of living quarters did you get?

Adm. M.: I had good quarters. I was a reasonably senior Commander and Mary and I were in a very good, four-bedroom apartment. It made it even more difficult to be sitting there in that apartment and telling somebody that he had to go into a quonset hut. In fairness, it was the more junior people who were hit hardest in the housing squeeze.

I wasn't really awfully happy in that management coordinator assignment. As I say, it had no counterpart that I knew of in the navy. It eventually became what's known as the administrative officer. All our stations now have an administrative officer, there's no such thing as a management coordinator. But, because of the interrelationships with the test center, it was felt that it really was a coordinating job, and it was. You had to deal daily with the test center personnel, and I enjoyed the people I worked with. Captain Vosseller was an extremely sharp, competent man, and I got along quite well with him. The executive officer of the station was an old friend of mine. We'd flown together in Iceland. As a matter of fact, he's retired and lives down there at Patuxent now.

The whole time I was in that job I kept looking for the time when I could move to one of the test centers, and eventually that opportunity opened up.

Q: How did you keep up your flying prowess?

Adm. M.: It wasn't all that difficult because there were aircraft available. The operations department of the air station was really responsible for those of us who were on the station staff. They had a pool of aircraft, mostly multi-engine types, SNBs and things like that, and you could get your flight time in. Of course, everybody was just champing at the bit to get in the new airplanes. The new jets were just starting to come in. The F9F, the Grumman fighter, and the Banshee, the McDonnell aircraft, were our first jets, and, of course every aviator wanted to get his hands on one of those.

It got to be a little bit of a problem that was eventually solved when a visiting pilot from BuAir came out. He had been a fighter pilot, but only prop aviation, and he somehow was able to convince the test center people that in his job he needed to know something about jets, so they let him check out in a Banshee. He got so excited flying the plane that he neglected to see where he was and we almost lost the airplane. He just barely got it back to Patuxent, on the deck, before it ran out of fuel.

That did it. From then on, if you were not attached to the test center and were not in a particular test division, it didn't matter who you were, you were not going to fly one of those airplanes. So the air station people were not about to get their hands on the planes that were used for test work, neither were the visiting firemen who'd come down and make every effort to fly. It was understandable. Everybody wanted to get into the act. We had some experimental jets there that were never going to be used for actual operations.

I flew my first jet there, and it was just a little single-engine developmental airplane that the air force would use more for developmental purposes than anything else. But, as I mentioned, I eventually did get to one of the test divisions and then I found life much more interesting because I was then back in an active aviation activity. I was attached to the tactical test division.

Q: In June of 1948?

Adm. M.: Yes, that's right, and the director at that time was a very well-known pilot during World War II, Bill Martin. Bill had a superb combat record. He was a night fighter pilot and did extensive night-fighter developmental work after he left Patuxent River, as a matter of fact. He had been in one of the night fighter squadrons during the war and was a top-notch aviator and a wonderful friend of mine, and I went to be his exec.

He didn't stay long after I arrived. He was relieved by a totally different type character, Gus Widhelm. Every aviator in the navy knew Gus Widhelm. Gus was really what could be termed a character. He had done it all. He'd been a dive-bomber pilot during the war. He had tried to join the Flying Tigers before we actually got into the war, and had talked three of the young aviation cadets in his air group into going with the Flying Tigers, only to find that he wasn't allowed to go with them. He was regular navy and they were naval aviation cadets and were allowed to go.

One of them subsequently became a brigadier general in the air force. After their Flying Tiger experience, they put those fellows in the army air corps and, then, when the air force was formed, they became Air Force officers.

Gus had had a raft of experience in World War II in combat. He had been shot down, I can't recall what the operation was, but he got out, he and his wing man. Gus had been in a big poker game the night before and his flightsuit was just filled with money. Why he took it with him I'll never know, but he did. They got in the life raft and they were three days in the raft.

Q: That money wouldn't buy much!

Adm. M.: The point was it was all waterlogged and so he took it out on a still day and spread it around to dry out and a breeze blew up and these twenty-dollar bills were all dropped into the drink and Gus was fighting to get them back until he capsized the raft. The fellow just lived that kind of a life.

The third day, the last leg of a search, a plane spotted his raft. They were going to call the search off that day, but his raft was spotted and he was rescued. He was a character just hard to describe. I've often wondered what might have happened to Gus because he's one of those individuals that the war was just made for. It was just his cup of tea. He loved it, and I think peacetime operations were not really quite -

Q: Pretty dull!

Adm. M.: He was killed in a strange aviation accident while he was still a captain, before he'd ever come up for admiral, and so I wouldn't speculate on what his chances might have been.

Q: Was he still at the test center?

Adm. M.: No, he wasn't. He was commanding officer of Beeville Air Station in Texas. This happened several years later and the accident has never been fully explained. He and a marine major were flying in an SNJ, a very modest little training aircraft, and went in on a day of very clear weather.

In any event, I got to the test center, to the tactical test division. It no longer exists now. Its functions have been absorbed by others, but at that time -

Q: Test and evaluation now, isn't it?

Adm. M.: That's right, yes.

It was an exciting time because, as I mentioned, we were just starting to get the new jet aircraft in, and I became a test pilot, not in the jets, but I was doing the test work on the P2V. My background, as I mentioned to you, was in patrol planes and so I was assigned to the test project on the P2V. This was going to be the coming fleet patrol plane and was the forerunner of what we have now, the P-3C. It's a Lockheed airplane and a very good one.

During the time I was there, the P2V set the long-distance record. A specially rigged P2V flew from

Australia to Washington, 11,000 miles, a twin-engine airplane with a crew of four aboard. Three of them were classmates of mine, and they were given the Distinguished Flying Cross by President Truman.

Q: I remember the publicity on that!

Adm. M.: Truculent Turtle was the name of the airplane. It's still on display down at Norfolk.

In any event, this was a very versatile patrol plane. It was starting to go into the fleet when I eventually got command of a squadron. I thought I'd been very wise in choosing one that was to be the first to get the P2Vs, but the Korean War came along and changed that. I'll tell you about that a little bit later.

Q: How many different types of planes were under testing?

Adm. M.: At Patuxent?

Q: Yes.

Adm. M.: Well, let's see. We had the F-9-F, we had the FH in the fighter category, we had ADs, F3Us, we had A-3Js, we had P2Vs. Of course, we had a number of aircraft that were actually in the fleet and were back getting special tests, these were already operational. I guess we had, total aircraft in Patuxent test divisions at one time, we might have had as many as twenty or thirty different types. And, as I mentioned before, we had some really top-notch pilots.

Q: You had to have quite a staff of pilots?

Adm. M.: Oh, yes, we did. One of the junior pilots in those days has just retired as the deputy chief of naval operations for air, Admiral Turner. I remember him as a JG. During his time, incidentally, he did a rather interesting and exciting thing. The FH was able to get to about 50,000 feet and he got some wonderful photographs taken of New York City and Long Island on a beautifully clear day. The photography was really superb. I have somewhere in my files copies of those pictures. They were the first really good high-altitude photographs I ever saw.

But a more interesting project and one that he planned for and worked at and one that got the navy a lot of very favorable publicity related to a Life magazine feature article on developments in the, I think, their first half of the twentieth century - the things that had happened between 1900 and 1950. A highlight was to be an article they wanted to do on the way transportation had changed, the speed of transportation, and they took 1900 as a benchmark and then 1950 as the point we had reached.

We at Patuxent River figured out the latest time in the day a jet aircraft could take off from the East Coast, and still get to the West Coast prior to sunset. Freddie Turner took off in late afternoon from Jacksonville in an FH, and we had two refueling stops and crews available to expedite the operation. He had camera equipment aboard with which he took color photographs of every phase of the flight. The sun was getting low when he left Jacksonville, and the last picture he took was of the sun setting over the Pacific from 40,000 feet. *Life* ran this as a feature article. As I say, it took a lot of doing, but it gave the navy a lot of very good publicity, showing the capability of the jet aircraft and the type of aircraft we were flying.

Q: Did you have any foreign plane types that you were testing at the test center?

Adm. M.: No, we didn't in tactical test. As I recall, the flight test division had a couple. I'm quite sure they did, but we didn't in the tactical test division.

Interestingly, though, the Tactical Test Division, had a section that dealt with instrument flying, and with the use of airborne fire control radar. That's what the division was designed to do, to fly the test aircraft as they would be used in combat. This was at the time that the so-called revolt of the admirals was taking place, the enormous fight over the B-36, and what role the air force was going to play. Captain Arleigh Burke was Op-23 at this time. The air force people had just claimed almost everything for the B-36. It was touted to be totally invulnerable, nobody could get to it, fighters couldn't even reach the altitude the plane was flying, according to the Air Force.

We in the navy, of course, knew the claims were wild exaggerations and were determined to prove it. And we did. We ran special tests, the tactical test division, out in the desert in California, using F-9Fs - I'd have to check my figures to see the altitude, but let's say 40,000 feet - the B-36 people claimed that they were operating at that altitude but that nobody could get to them. We had test results to show that we'd locked on and actually could have shot down anything at 40,000 feet. We were funneling this stuff in to Arleigh Burke and his gang in Washington just as fast as we got it. The flight would hardly have completed and the pilot would call us and we'd shoot it up to Op-23.

It was tremendously beneficial to Arleigh Burke's operation there because we were able to show him a jet fighter intercept capability that invalidated the Air Force claims. These results had a significant effect on the service budgets, particularly Navy and Air Force.

Q: In California - this was China Lake?

Adm. M.: Yes, our pilots were flying there.

We had another interesting sidelight to this thing. Idlewild was going to be commissioned and President Truman was to be present. Once again, to get some favorable publicity for the navy, it was decided to have three admirals fly jet aircraft from Patuxent to Idlewild and do a flyby. Dan Gallery, Bat Cruise and Apollo Soucek, who at that time was commander of the naval air test center, were assigned to the flight. All three had had extensive aviation backgrounds though Apollo Soucek was the only one with any significant jet time.

Of course, Apollo Soucek had been checked out in the planes they were going to use. These were FHs. Dan Gallery came down and checked out in the Flight Test Division. We checked out Bat Cruise in the tactical test division, both ground and Flight check including a thorough check of the fuel system. He did a test flight and all went well.

The day came when Idlewild was to be officially commissioned. 100,000 people were there including the president, and the three jet admirals were flying in from Patuxent River. They were supposed to make a high speed fly by in front of the stands, then pull up and land in formation. Gallery was leading the flight and on the way to New York he lost his radio and he turned over the lead to Apollo Soucek. Apollo took the lead and he checked in with the ground controller who was timing it so that they'd make their fly by on schedule. It was a hazy day, and they started their run-in only to find at the last minute they were going behind the stands instead of in front. It was too late to change so they pulled up and the second time they went in front of the stands. Then they pulled up to land and Cruise lost both engines. He had neglected to shift his tanks. He didn't know the fuel system that well. He made a deadstick landing and got away with it. It was beautiful. He pulled up, dropped his gear, dropped right in and nobody ever knew the difference in the stands. They thought it was part of the show and naval aviation got a lot of favorable publicity for having three admirals flying the latest jet fighters.

I was in Admiral Soucek's office the following Monday and I heard him talking to the chief of the Bureau of Aeronautics. They were discussing what a close call Bat Cruise had had and I remember Admiral Soucek saying:

"I don't know, if Bat had lost that airplane, I guess the only thing we could have said would have been it was just youth and inexperience."

Q: This was in the days before you had a coordinator for all the test centers throughout the country. How did you cooperate with them at that point? Were they in existence?

Adm. M.: They were in existence, and our relationships were sort of casual. They weren't formal. They weren't established in such a way that the commander of the naval air test center would do more than have a sort of liaison with the China Lake and the other areas. He didn't control them. It was actually controlled through BuAir, and our functions were really quite separate and distinct. There wasn't that tie that maybe should have existed.

Q: Well, it took a number of years before it did come into being.

Adm. M.: Oh, yes. We had some really wonderful people heading that organization out at Patuxent. Soucek I mentioned a moment ago, but it was interesting in a way, the man I had the highest respect for and still have, as head of the test center and was the coordinator of tests when I first arrived, was Fred Trapnell. He was really an unusual blend of talent.

Q: Quite a war record, too.

Adm. M.: A superb aviator, but he was also top flight engineer. He knew more about what made an airplane tick than anybody I have ever known. He was a bachelor at the time, he was divorced, and his idea of a good time was to call the flight test division at ten o'clock at night and say:

"Crank up an F-7 for me. I'm going to go out and fly for an hour or two. Don't know when I'll be back."

He'd go out in the middle of the night and fly it.

I can remember on one occasion, Patuxent River served as a host for all of the squadron commanders and air group commanders - I guess it was just the East Coast, it might have been the West Coast as well, but there was a large number of air group and squadron commanders, and the idea was to show them the newest airplanes we had at Patuxent, what they might expect to be getting in their squadrons. Johnnie Hyland and Trapnell were flying F-9Fs and part of the demonstration was a high-speed low flyby across the field. They came in fast, and Johnnie hit a bird with his vertical stabilizer, one of those ospreys, fish hawks. At that high speed, it simply took the stabilizer right off the airplane. Although, fortunately, he hadn't started to roll or anything, he pulled up to about 10,000 feet and Trap went with him.

The pilot tube for the air-speed indicator was located in the vertical stabilizer in those airplanes, so when he lost his vertical stabilizer he had no longer had an air-speed indicator. He didn't know how fast he was going. He didn't know at what speed he was going to stall without the stabilizer. They were anxious to save the airplane, of course, and the question was could he get it back aboard the field without that stabilizer. So Trap flew alongside and they slowed down and Trap kept telling him what speed they were at and kept asking him if he had good control. Johnnie said, "Yes, as long as I keep straight and level, I'm all right." Trap said:

"In a minute I want you to drop your landing gear and we'll see if you can still control it with your gear down. But, Johnnie, something to remember, when that gear goes down, if one gear goes ahead of the other, it might tend to slew you because you don't have the vertical stabilizer."

That's exactly what happened. They got down to, oh, a fair amount above the stall speed, but when Johnnie dropped his gear the airplane immediately went into a spin. Johnnie was over the bay at the time, and he started into a violent spin without the stabilizer and he couldn't get it out. We didn't have ejection seats in those days. He said that he wrestled the airplane down to about 3,000 feet and he heard Trap say:

"Johnnie, get out, get out!"

Johnnie by this time realized that he wasn't going to be able to pull his airplane out. He was able to get out of the airplane - just, but when he got out in his parachute, he was in such a violent spin that his body was oscillating back and forth under the chute just before he hit the water. Fortunately he was a superb swimmer, otherwise this story would have a tragic ending. He hit the water and the chute folded over him and he was just smothering under that chute, but he finally got out.

John told me later, "You know, Trap knew exactly what was going to happen to that airplane. It was astonishing because I would not have thought of that, but Trap said, 'Watch out because when that gear starts down it's apt to throw you into a spin,' and that's exactly what happened."

As I say, he knew more about airplanes and what made them work than anybody I've ever seen, and he was an absolute bear for the regular reports that went out from the test center. He simply did not allow sloppy English. You had to write with precision -

Q: Isn't that curious?

Adm. M.: It is curious because it's unusual for a really good test pilot to be able to express really clearly what he's seen and experienced. I've talked to the Grumman people, I've talked to other aircraft companies, and it's an unusual thing. Many test pilots can tell you what happened, but have difficulty writing it down. You might take it down and maybe if you're an engineer you can put it together. But it's not something that the average test pilot did well. It used to be a joke in a way at the test center. We would send up a finished report on a project that we had completed. It would have been proofread, of course, and while every effort would be made to stick to the test pilot's language, usually the report had to be edited. The report would go up, and frequently it would come back with Trap's red pencil pointing out split infinitive, dangling participle, things like that. I mean, the substance could be there, but he was not going to send something out over his signature from that test center that wasn't letter perfect, or as near as you could make it.

Q: Admirable!

Adm. M.: It was admirable, and it became a large part of my job as exec for Gus Widhelm to do all the editing for our pilots. It turned out to be a real wrestling match sometimes because I wanted to be sure I kept the flavor of what they wanted to say, but they would say it, many times, in a clumsy way. It was a red-letter day for all of us when a report would go up and didn't come back. We would just hold our breath when a report went forward and then a cheer would go up if it didn't come back.

But, I tell you, Trapnell had the respect and the admiration of the people at that test center, and in the aviation industry. He was a superb fellow, and he did something I'd never seen before. He got orders to fleet up to Commander of the Naval Air Test Center from the Coordinator of Tests assignment, a promotion richly deserved. He served in that capacity only a short time when Soucek got orders to relieve him. But it was recognized that he had so much to offer the test program at this critical time that he was asked to step down to his former billet of Coordinator of Tests and stay on under a new Commander of the Naval Air Test Center.

Q: He couldn't stay on as commander?

Adm. M.: He couldn't stay on as commander because Soucek had orders in, but he agreed to the demotion. No, in fairness, they knew that he was going to get command of an aircraft carrier, and he did, so maybe they just said, "Well, Trap, if you'll just stay a few more months, then you'll get command - "

Q: An interim appointment.

Adm. M.: And he eventually got command of Coral Sea.

He asked me, when he got command of the Coral Sea, if I'd like to come as his executive officer. I can't tell you how flattered I was because I was very, very junior and I was certain that BuPers would never approve my assignment.

Furthermore, I was right in the middle of a project that I was very interested in there and had some hopes of getting a command myself when I left Patuxent River, so I told him I didn't think it would work in my case. But I just can't tell you the admiration I had for the man.

He flew across country with me one time. Gus Widhelm and I took a P-2V out to the factory at Lockheed, and Trap, who had not flown a P-2V but had a world of curiosity about what made everything tick, spent the entire flight out going over the manual for the P-2V and checking out the plane and by the time we got to the West Coast, I think he knew as much about the airplane as I did and I'd been flying it over a year. He had a remarkable combination of talent and background.

I mentioned that I was doing the test work on the P-2V, and there was a thought of trying to take a P-2V aboard an aircraft carrier. The P-2V had reverse-pitch propellers and it could actually land at a very low speed, and if you reversed pitch, under certain circumstances, you could stop the airplane in between 400 and 500 feet. The plane was very versatile, and it was also being considered as an aircraft to be used in the Antarctic, operating on skis. Skis were to be mounted on the airplane so you could either land on wheels or on the skis. We got the first plane at Patuxent to do test work on. The skis had been designed by a company in Minneapolis, I forget its name now, and I took the first airplane out to Bemidji, Minnesota, looking for a place with suitable snow conditions for our tests. The night before our arrival it had been 40 degrees below in Bemidji. The airport at Bemidji is a very flat, level area, and we had plenty of snow off the runways, and permission to use the area for our ski tests.

By the time we got out to try to take off on skis, the temperature had warmed up to about 15° Farenheit, very dry and cold, and the snow was beautifully packed. I remember telling the copilot to keep his eye on the air-speed indicator, as I was controlling the airplane, but we never could get it above 40 knots. With full power, the drag on those skis was still such that we couldn't get it above 40 knots. We tried all of that morning and never were able to take off in the snow, so we had to come back to Patuxent River and write up our report. We were sure that the skis, in the first place, were too large. We thought that they were too broad, created too much drag, and something had to be done to streamline them. They went back to the drawing board and modified them. The airplane did eventually get off, but not with me at the controls because I had turned the project over to another pilot. He took the airplane out with the new skis and, in taking off from Bemidji the forward ski support wire parted and the ski dug in, jamming the after end of the ski into his gas tank. He had gotten airborne but was spewing gas from the ruptured tank and had a real emergency on his hands. He came around immediately and landed and fortunately, no fire ensued.

But we then had the problem of what we were going to do with the airplane. It was able to fly on back to Patuxent River but we could not do the repairs there. We had to fly it out to Lockheed. We had to fly it the entire way across country with our landing gear and our skis in the down position, a curious-looking bird, and we had to cruise at something like 120 knots, and it's a long time getting to the West Coast cruising at that speed. I remember

I flew the airplane to the West Coast, and I remember coming in to El Paso, Texas, and I reported in the landing pattern, reported my gear down and locked and I still remember the tower saying - I've forgotten my number now - but:

"There's something hanging under your wheels," they said.

"Yes, they're skis," and there was the longest pause from the tower and then he said:

"What did you say?"

I said, "They're skis."

It seemed an interminable time. I was on instruments from Patuxent River to Roanoke, Virginia, and, of course, when you're on instruments, you check in with each reporting point and the ground controller states what your ground speed is. Of course, they're accustomed to a P-2V breezing along at a pretty good rate of speed, and when they had me logged in between Roanoke and Pulaski, I think, they came up on the air and said, "What kind of aircraft?" I said P-2V, and he said:

"You're only doing 110 knots," and I said, "Yes, that's about right." Well, we had the landing gear down and we had the skis down and your ground speed isn't going to be very impressive under those conditions.

Q: Would you talk about weather conditions and how

you sought different weather conditions in the testing process?

Adm. M.: Yes. I'll go back to that particular test just for the moment, the test for use of this airplane in the Antarctic. I was given a flight profile to fly, simulating the maximum expected of the plane. It was supposed to be capable of thirty-one hours of flying, about six hours of which was to be at 15,000 feet. I took off from Patuxent River and I had special clearance to parallel the airways down the east coast of the United States, around Key West, up the gulf coast and around almost to Houston, and then reverse track. The mid-portion of the flight was at 15,000 feet, with the beginning and end done at 15,000 feet. Of course, you had to have very careful setting of your speed and anticipate, of course, the weather during this flight. As it turned out, we didn't really get that much weather.

I flew the airplane and I stayed in the seat for twenty-seven hours. We got back to Patuxent River –

Q: Lindbergh!

Adm. M.: Well, yes, and I still had fuel enough that, extrapolated, I knew I could have done the other four hours, but it just seemed kind of pointless. We had established the fact that the profile could be flown.

To get back to the other test we did. Our instrument test section of tactical test was a very active one and we were trying at that time to improve our instrument capabilities in the fleet for bringing aircraft aboard in very heavy instrument weather. At Patuxent River you'd occasionally get some very dense fog and we would launch on those nights and actually use our GCI equipment to get the planes back aboard. Our fighters were involved in this operation.

We were also interested in attempting to see when and if you could predict icing on an airplane and how serious a problem it might be. We'd had, of course, some experience with icing, but you never could be sure when it was actually going to happen. Bill Martin, whom I mentioned earlier, took a P-2V and actually looked for the worst weather conditions he could fly in to see if he could make the airplane ice up and see in what weather conditions this would actually happen.

Q: What about hurricanes? Did you attempt to fly any of the test planes near a hurricane or into one?

Adm. M.: Yes, we did. We had a hurricane project, and one of our pilots actually flew through the eye of a hurricane and established the fact that it was a feasible operation, nothing that you would really care to do on a daily basis with an average airplane, but, as you know, we now have hurricane-hunter aircraft and these have been very helpful in recent years in spotting and projecting the path of a hurricane and so on.

Q: Later on, I know, you had down there an oceanographic squadron. Did you have anything of that sort at that point?

Adm. M.: No, we didn't. As a matter of fact, just last month I went down to attend a change of command at Patuxent and the pilot taking over that squadron was a former aide of mine. His squadron is heavily involved in oceanographic projects for the Navy around the world. The oceanographer of the navy was there and I talked to him a little bit about the squadron.

Q: Did you have a school for test pilots?

Adm. M.: Yes. I'm glad you asked that. That started during the time I was at Patuxent River and that was one of the direct results of Trapnell's influence. He recognized the fact that just bringing fleet pilots in, however experienced they were or however good pilots they might be, was not going to be enough in the coming days, and you have to have people who have the kind of qualifications he had and know what made an airplane fly.

Q: Basic training?

Adm. M.: Decidedly. An officer named Sid Sherby, who was an aeronautical engineer, an AEDO, actually took over and started the school with Trapnell's full backing and support. This was at the time that I was attached to the air station and I attended the classes as frequently as I could. That was the forerunner of the test pilots' school we have there now. I think it's one of the real fine technical schools anywhere in the world. It does a superb job in qualifying these fellows for test pilot assignments. They have their own aircraft for the test pilot program, and this took some doing because you're always short particularly of new aircraft and BuAir found difficulty, I'm sure, in getting an allowance of aircraft just for the test work, because people were saying, you've got all the test divisions and they have the pilots there, why do you have to have aircraft just for these fellows. But anything like that to work really has to have its own planes. The test divisions couldn't be expected to provide project aircraft for Test Pilot School pilots.

Q: And conform to another schedule?

Adm. M.: That's right. They had to have their own and this was recognized. Once again, I give Trapnell full credit because he was so good, he knew so well what was required, and he was able to kibbitz the effort and he was able to apply the horsepower to get BuAir to come around. He was very persuasive, and I think the test center is indebted to Trapnell for this test pilots' school. It's a fine school and the top pilots in the navy now go to this school.

Q: At the beginning, did they have foreign pilots come, too?

Adm. M.: No, not originally. We had no foreign pilots.
I can't honestly tell you what their procedure is now. When I was at Patuxent about a month ago I didn't have time to go by the school. I saw the location of the school, but I didn't get a chance to do more than talk briefly with the test center commander, so I don't know what they do right now.

Q: Were you using in-flight fueling at that point?

Adm. M.: It was just starting. It was a brand-new type of operation. We were just beginning to get into that.

Q: What about the use of computers? Did you have anything of that sort?

Adm. M.: No, that was in its infancy completely then. We didn't really have computers at Patuxent at that time.

Q: I think they were being tried out at Dahlgren. Did you have any connection with Dahlgren?

Adm. M.: No, we didn't, we had no real ties with Dahlgren.

Q: What about relations with the air force? They were bad at that time!

Adm. M.: They were bad and yet we got some cooperation from the air force. I can think of one specific incident. The navy was able to get a B-29 from the air force and it was used to see if there was any reason to believe that a B-29 would have any value as a navy airplane. We ran a project in the tactical test division. We had one B-29 and we attempted to see whether the airplane was really feasible at all for use an an ASW aircraft and, of course, it really came to nothing. The airplane just wasn't designed for that. It was much too big to be very maneuverable down near the water where you almost have to be. So the P-2V was going to be our real ASW plane. I don't remember the precise circumstances under which we got it but we must have made some arrangements with the air force.

We also had other air force jets. We had some of the early air force training jets, I recall.

I think our relationships perhaps at that level with the air force were far better than they were at the upper levels, where strategy was really being fought out. We didn't have that much difficulty. I can't really speak with any great authority about how Trapnell worked with his counterparts in the air force. We also, as I recall, were able to use the air force climatic hangar down at Eglin Field. I don't know whether you know about that, but in those days they had a hangar that they could simulate almost any weather conditions. For example, they could lower the temperature in that hangar to forty degrees below zero, and you'd let an airplane cold soak for a day or two then see what troubles you had starting it or what equipment would fail. It worked in such a way that the airplane didn't exhaust into the hangar, but into pipes that ran outside.

It was a pretty remarkable hangar, and they were doing all their climatic tests in there. They could simulate desert conditions, antarctic conditions, almost any kind of weather, as I mentioned.

Q: That certainly was a time-saver!

Adm. M.: Indeed it was. We didn't have anything remotely like that at Patuxent. I recall that usually we had three or four navy aircraft with the air force, space available, down at Eglin, and they'd be there for as long as a month, maybe, for a series of tests and then we'd bring them back.

Certainly in those days our relationships at the test level were probably better than they were in the upper echelons, where the fight was over funds.

Q: Well, in that billet, you must have received as much as you gave in terms of learning?

Adm. M.: Oh, yes, it was a wonderful experience for me.

You know, naval aviation really is divided into roughly two parts. There are the carrier pilots and there's everybody else, and there's just not getting around it, the carrier tail-hook aviators have always considered themselves really the first team. Of course, when the jets came along, the jet tail-hook guys were the super first team. But the distinction between an aviator aboard an aircraft carrier and all the others is well drawn. Aviators don't talk about it a lot but it's really there. I had a foot in each camp.

Q: Class distinction!

Adm. M.: It really is. The only reason for mentioning it is that I had toyed with the idea, having been in patrol aviation as a pilot and having been aboard carriers as a ship's officer, and wondered whether I was making a mistake by not attempting after the war to shift over to carrier aviation as a pilot. And, you know, I came to the conclusion, and I'm satisfied now that it was the right one, that it was too late. I have a classmate who did this, but he was never really accepted because they all knew that he didn't have the combat background in fighters. He took a fighter squadron and I've heard some of these pilots joke about him because they knew he simply wasn't that good.

Q: He just hadn't grown up in it?

Adm. M.: He hadn't grown up in it and if you try to

get there when you're a commander time has passed you by. But the distinction is so clear and, frankly, it really has a serious bearing on your career. In my case, I can say without any hesitancy that if I hadn't had a few sort of lucky breaks along the way, with my background I would not have gotten command of an aircraft carrier. It just happened that the man who was actually making assignments in those days, I think, had a reasonably high regard for me. In any event, I got the command. In normal routine scheduling, if I'd got command of an aircraft carrier it would have been an ASW carrier and not an attack carrier, as I got. And I've thought many times by having a foot in each camp, a patrol-plane pilot with a lot of background in carriers, stood me in reasonably good stead, because your chances of selection for flag really are enhanced materially if you get command of an aircraft carrier. They were less enhanced if you got command, in those days, of an ASW carrier.

Q: Personal attributes are also thrown into the scale, aren't they? I know they are.

Adm. M.: I'm sure they are. Well, I've sat on flag selection boards and I've seen how we work this. I'm not taking exception to it but, as I say, there are two breeds of aviators, two distinct camps. I will say this, I think in recent years the distinction has been less because I think there is appreciation in the aviation community of the tremendous job that the more sophisticated patrol planes are able to do, these P-3Cs particularly. So I think it's less pronounced than it was, but the tail hook boys have always considered themselves the first team and I think they rate that designation.

Q: And beyond that, you didn't rank in the navy!

Adm. M.: Exactly right. You could go back to those days and look at the flag selection boards every year, and roughly 50 percent of those selected were aviators, and of that 50 percent only a few with ASW backgrounds were going to be included and the rest were going to be your former air group commanders and skippers of CVAs and so on. That's just the way it worked.

Interview #5 with Vice Admiral Charles S. Minter, Jr.
U.S. Navy (Retired)

Place: His residence in Providence; Annapolis, Maryland
Date: Wednesday afternoon, 3 October 1979
Subject: Biography
By: John T. Mason, Jr.

Q: Well, today, Sir, we're about to be heavily engaged in the Korean War, which broke out on the 25th of June 1950 and I think you were en route immediately, weren't you?

Adm. M.: Yes. I had just been detached from Patuxent River and was en route to take command of Patrol Squadron 28 based in Honolulu, and was actually driving across country with my two boys at the time the Korean War actually broke out. My wife had preceded me with the baby daughter and was out in California. So I stepped up production and got to the West Coast as quickly as I could. I had a brief period of schooling in the San Diego area, electronics school and a couple of other minor schools, then I went straight to Honolulu.

Q: Where had it been intended that you would operate

with 28, before the Korean War broke out?

Adm. M.: I would still have taken command at Barber's Point. The squadron was homeported at Barber's Point and the squadron had just returned from a deployment to Okinawa at the time I took command. But when I arrived in August of 1950 there was much speculation about what the future of the squadron was going to be. There was talk that it might be turned right around and sent right back out to WesPac, although it had just returned from deployment.

I might mention at this point that the squadron was supposed to get P-2V aircraft, which was a type airplane that I had been flying at Patuxent River and I got the squadron in anticipation of having a P-2Vs. The planes that the squadron actually had at the time were PB-4Y2s, Liberators, and because the war required such a shifting of assets, it was decided that the squadron would not get P-2Vs and would retain the PB-4Ys and we would redeploy with those aircraft. Well, I had never flown a PB-4Y, so it required a complete check-out for me as commanding officer.

In any event, we did not deploy as early as first indications were that we might and actually I had the squadron in training at Barber's Point from September 1950 until the squadron deployed in the spring of 1951. During that time, we, of course, received a number of new pilots and one thing that might be worthy of mention is that the training command at Whidby had turned out a very sizable number of ensigns who were qualified for patrol-plane squadrons and there was no place for them to go, and all of a sudden I found the squadron receiving orders for fifteen brand-new ensigns when we were well over midway through our training cycle. This would have presented a tremendous load on the squadron, particularly one that's about to deploy. Fifteen ensigns who knew nothing about the squadron or the operations, would have been a severe burden.

I went to my wing commander in Honolulu and protested this and asked if he couldn't get ComAirPac to cancel the orders. I didn't need those fifteen ensigns. I had the entire complement of my officers and frankly could do better with less than with more than my complement of personnel.

Q: Yes, that's the navy's option.

Adm. M.: That's right and it's true. It's very true. There's nothing worse than having too many people falling over each other with nothing to do.

Well, I protested to the wing and the wing sent a message to AirPac to see if these orders for these ensigns could be cancelled, and AirPac came back and said no. So I protested again to the wing and got permission to fly back and make my own case at AirPac headquarters. This had some rather interesting consequences. The wing commander of Fleet Air Wing 4, the training wing, was required to come down to this conference with me and with the chief of staff of AirPac to thrash out this matter. I was a commander and, of course, he was a captain, the wing commander, and he was making a very forceful case for the fact that they had no place to use these ensigns and why couldn't an operational squadron take them aboard, and so on. I was just as vehement in my protest that we simply were so far along in our training program that we couldn't use fifteen brand-new officers, and that it would be a disservice to them and to the squadron. I made as strong a case against taking them as I possibly could. We couldn't get anywhere with the operations people on the AirPac staff and we ended up in the office of the chief of staff of AirPac who was at that time Captain T.B. Williamson, who later became my boss as Admiral T.B. Williamson.

The interesting thing was I won the fight but I began to think I'd lost the war because while we were arguing this issue before the chief of staff, and I could tell that he was sympathetic to my position -

Q: As an operational man, he should have been.

Adm. M.: Oh, yes - a telephone call came in from Washington and Captain H.J. Dyson, who was the wing commander of Fleet Air Wing 4, was called to the telephone. He came back a moment later just beaming and announced that he had just been told that he was going to be commander of Fleet Air Wing 6 in Japan, which was to be my operational commander as soon as I reported out there.

Well, I did win the fight and Captain Dyson and I shared an airplane going back to San Francisco. On the way up, I remember very well, he said to me:

"Well, Commander, I guess that will teach you not to fight with your new wing commander."

I said: "Captain Dyson, you're going to be the happiest guy you ever saw that I won that fight because I'm going to bring you a well-trained squadron, a lot better than it would have been - "

Q: That's right.

Adm. M.: It did actually work out that way.

Q: Let me ask. Those ensigns entered training after the outbreak of the Korean War?

Adm. M.: No, these were ensigns who had completed flight training, they had their wings, but they went to our specialized patrol-type training at Whidbey Island and after completion they were farmed out to the various patrol squadrons. I can't tell you why they suddenly felt that VP-28 needed a large influx. I was never able to see why they couldn't have been spread out more evenly, but, in any event, I got such a large input that I simply couldn't have handled it. I just couldn't take them.

Q: The reason I asked that question was because you intimated that they were in the nature of surplus and I wondered how there could be surplus at that point when we heard so much about Johnson cutting down on everything.

Adm. M.: That's correct, but they had - as I say, they got their wings and this was to be a stepped-up training program to qualify them for patrol flight operations but I don't quite know why VP-28 was to take the brunt. Perhaps it was just the fact that we were at that time a Barber's Point-based squadron. They weren't going to send them out forward and saddle people out there with them, and so they decided they'd put them in the squadron at Barber's Point.

Well, as I mentioned, the squadron did get orders to deploy and we left in early March of 1951 for Japan.

I'd better mention a couple of things about that. The air station at Atsugi, outside Tokyo, was being completed at that time and we originally were told that we could be operating from Atsugi. Atsugi was also the location of fleet air wing headquarters, and I can't tell you how delighted I became later on not to have to work directly under the sponsorship of the fleet air wing. I was sent to Itami, Japan.

Q: Where is Itami?

Adm. M.: Itami is a field that the Japanese used as a fighter field during World War II. It's just outside of Osaka. It wasn't the best field I ever saw, the runways needed a lot of work and they were really very short for our patrol plane fully loaded. In weather it could be a little bit difficult. About 5,000-foot runways and, as I say, not in good shape. But our orders were originally for Atsugi and all our squadron gear was packed and ready to be sent there, and, all of a sudden, the order came that we were to operate from Itami. That threw things into a kind of an uproar because you can't imagine the amount of gear that a patrol squadron has to take when it goes to operate from a field that's not actually set up for patrol-plane operations. That's something that I really thought an awful lot about. I tried to think of some way that you could cut back on that tremendous lot of gear because most of it had to go by ship, you know. Some of it could go by air, we'd take squadron tools and things like that, but many of the heavy maintenance items had to go by ship and it would take a couple of weeks before it could get out to WesPac.

Q: The only way to circumvent it would be to have depots in —

Adm. M.: That's the problem. That's what you always face when you're operating from a land base and that's one of the reasons that a carrier is such a mobile instrument, because it carries all those things. But that's one of the reasons why this change from Atsugi, which did have good shops and good spaces and good supply systems created some problems. We could operate much better from Atsugi but here we were going to a base that had practically nothing. The base was used at the time we first occupied it by the Marines for a lot of maintenance work on the Marine aircraft from Japan.

Q: It was kind of an auxiliary base?

Adm. M.: It was, so we had to practically set it up from scratch as far as patrol-plane operations were concerned.

I might mention at this time also that when Korea broke reserve squadrons were being called back pretty quickly and I remember a friend of mine who had a reserve squadron that was based in the San Diego area came through Barber's Point on his way to WesPac, and he was pretty unhappy because he felt that his squadron should have been delayed certainly longer than mine. We were a regular squadron and we really did, in all fairness, get better-trained personnel because the reserves hadn't been flying that much and my friend was a little bit bitter about being pulled into action as quickly as he was. He felt there were regular squadrons that should have been deployed first. I had to be sympathetic with him, I must say. We deployed about two months after he did, but whether it was because they weren't trained adequately or what, and I think that was the answer, they had some difficulties. They lost a couple of airplanes in weather, and it showed the necessity for keeping the reserve squadrons on a ready basis. These were pretty much businessmen, fellows who flew on the weekend, suddenly they were pulled together and deployed to Japan during the bad-weather season. It was a little more, I think, than should have been expected.

Q: It also raises the question of reserves and up-to-date equipment, doesn't it?

Adm. M.: It certainly does. Their airplanes were about the same as ours. I can't say that we had any great advantage over them, but we had the major advantage of operating from a base that was fully stocked and had all the spare parts we needed, and they were a little bit shy of this sort of thing. But they were primarily shy of the training.

Q: You can't get that from a depot, can you?

Adm. M.: That's right, so I did feel that they were short-changed a little bit on that. As I said, we ended up at Itami, a base that the Marines were using for a major logistics support and also an air base for their airplanes in Korea. It was also an R & R base for the Marines who were getting out of Korea.

Q: Oh, is that so?

Adm. M.: Yes. All the officers lived in the Takoraska Hotel, a Japanese hotel that had been taken over by the U.S. Air Force and was being operated by the Air Force for our people, both our squadrons and the Marines.

Of course, it was an unpleasant situation for a little while. Our people were doing primary reconnaissance flights over the Sea of Japan. We weren't in any real danger of any kind and here were the Marines who had come right out of combat in Korea and they were inclined to look down on our fellows who had not faced any real danger. It was an unhappy experience at first, until we got into the flare-drop missions, flying with them in Korea. I'll tell you about that in a little bit. That changed the whole flavor of the operations and the relationships.

Q: And simultaneously, men on rest and relaxation –

Adm. M.: That's right. They were back and they couldn't believe that we were really fighting much war. We were doing very routine operations.

Q: I can see that!

Adm. M.: These were fighter pilots and attack pilots, they were back to have some fun. So, as I say –

Q: There wasn't a golf course there, was there?

Adm. M.: Well, there was one not too far away, not a

very good one. You could play a little golf.

When we arrived in Japan I made a tactical error, I must admit. We had a long-range forecast, that the weather was going to be good in the Itami area for our arrival and I wanted to fly the entire squadron in, nine planes, you know, make it very impressive coming in. It's roughly a ten-hour flight from Guam in these PB-4Ys to Itami, and the closer we got to Itami the worse the weather got, and by the time we were within less than 100 miles of Itami it was solid overcast and heavy rain. Here we were, a nine-plane squadron and we had to suddenly break up and make our individual approaches to the field. It was the stupidest thing, I think, I've ever done. I never ever tried to do something like that again. In any event, our pilots were really very well trained and there was no question about our instrument capability. The real question was whether we'd be able to break into the air-control corridors properly with nine planes coming in. Although they'd been advised we were coming, you still had to worry about the north-south pattern on these Japanese air ways and getting ourselves into the base at Itami.

It worked out and, as I say, I learned a real good lesson out of it.

Q: I would ascribe that to a lack of proper weather intelligence rather than error on your part.

Adm. M.: It was, but, you know, in the springtime, in early spring, In Japan you can get some pretty bad weather conditions and, after all, this was eleven hours after our takeoff. Weather can change pretty drastically and it did. We did not get any warning that the weather had changed that much. We came in with a very low overcast and heavy rain, but even so, it wasn't a very smart thing to do. I just wanted to make a little impression on the town, nine planes arriving, we were going to look pretty good, you know, the Minter Air Circus arriving in town.

I might tell you a little bit about the operations.

Q: Yes, indeed, I want you to.

Adm. M.: When we got there, we were given a day or two to really familiarize ourselves with the area. They allowed us to make several instrument flights around the area, and then we numerically relieved a squadron that had been based up in Atsugi and it was allowed to go home. We then took over the missions that they'd been flying.

Primarily and initially, our missions were out over the Sea of Japan. We did weather-reconnaissance flights, we did shipping-reconnaissance flights because there was a blockade of Korea and we were watching everything that was going in and out of Korea. But

Minter, Jr. #5 - 257

I think one of the best things we did, or one of the things that was most important perhaps, was weather-reconnaissance because we were able to give weather information to our forces, our carrier forces particularly, about what the weather was like and they'd be able to make their forecasts based on the weather flights we were doing.

Q: And they were operating up around Wonson?

Adm. M.: Wonson and that area, yes. The Seventh Fleet was in there then with the carriers.

Q: Was Clark still there in command?

Adm. M.: No - oh, you mean in Korea?

Q: Of the carriers, of the Seventh Fleet.

Adm. M.: Oh, yes, he was.

Of course, I checked in with the headquarters in Atsugi shortly after arrival and made myself known to the new wing commander. As I say, I was just so happy because they were 250 miles away, and they could send me my messages and tell me what to do but they weren't there to watch everything that I was doing. It was just a beautiful operation. I really enjoyed it. The people who operated directly under control of the wing up at Atsugi had nothing but my sympathy because they told me many times that the wing staff was constantly looking over their shoulders and kibitzing their every movement. There is nothing better than having your own operational command and being alone and just told what to do and allowed to do it.

Q: I suppose the other situation, though, is fairly typical, isn't it?

Adm. M.: Oh, yes. At a later point in my career, I had a similar situation when I had command of an aircraft carrier and did not have a CarDiv staff aboard, so I once again operated on my own and once again was the happiest guy you've ever seen.

We flew a lot. We flew a lot of hours, and we had a pretty good reputation. As I say, I thought a lot of my squadron and I was pretty proud of the way they were trained. They were fully capable. Every one of my patrol-plane commanders was fully capable of doing any job assigned to him.

Q: Tell me how the weather data that you got on your reconnaissance flights was incorporated into things.

Adm. M.: We would send direct weather reports. We

had a weather code that we would send out in the clear and could be picked up by the carriers and by the wing staff. We would debrief when we got back in, of course, and give information on the weather. But it was simply observation. We weren't given very sophisticated instruments but we could give the wind force and direction and the height of clouds and the precipitation, and that sort of thing, which was able to be picked up by the carriers and then they could use it for their own meteorological efforts. It saved them doing what they frequently would have to do, send out weather flights of their own to make decisions about whether to fly strikes or whether to fly at all.

Also, of course, we were continuously taking pictures of every ship that was in the area other than our own. There was very close surveillance of all the shipping in the Sea of Japan. We didn't spot any submarines but we were on the lookout for them -

Q: There weren't any really operating?

Adm. M.: No, but we thought there might be and as long as we had fleet ships operating there, we were obviously on the lookout for submarine activity.

Q: Since you did photo reconnaissance, this implies that the squadron had to be fairly indoctrinated in this?

Adm. M.: Oh, yes, at least the pilots had to be capable of operating an electric camera, the K-28 camera, which wasn't a very sophisticated piece of equipment, and it was pretty satisfactory for the purposes we used it for. You'd fly down within maybe 1,500 feet of a ship and you'd get three different views, identify her, and, of course log it, then when we got back this was all tied in to the intelligence people, shipping reconnaissance –

Q: You had to know something about photo interpretation, too?

Adm. M.: Yes, we did. Although, as I say, this really wasn't terribly sophisticated. It wasn't like the photo interpretation you do over a target, for example.

Q: No.

Adm. M.: It was purely ships and –

Q: But in order to have understanding in taking the right kind of photo.

Adm. M.: Oh, yes. As a matter of fact, there got to be quite a bit of competition among the crews to see who could get the best photos. We'd post the best photos of the week on the bulletin board so other crews could look, and you'd identify the crew that had done the best job. I think the fellows got to be pretty good.

The photos were sent to the wing and the wing then made disposition of them. They usually sent them back to CinCPac's headquarters. They eventually got back there. But daily, after a flight came in to debrief they gave the total number of ships they'd seen, where they were, and so on. So we had a very, very good picture of what was going on in the Sea of Japan the entire time we were operating there.

Q: Was there any possibility of observing mines and that sort of thing, because that was a big problem?

Adm. M.: Yes. Off the coast of Korea a number of the squadrons - they'd had more activity along that line actually before we got there. The PBM squadrons did a lot of mine-spotting. Our squadron didn't really have that much in the way of mine-spotting but that was part of the mission, certainly, to look for any particular activity in that connection.

We didn't actually begin to operate in Korea proper until Admiral Radford came out on an inspection trip, and this was the most interesting part of our entire deployment in my way of thinking, and the thing that did more for the squadron's morale and for the relationships with the Marines than anything else did.

Admiral Radford came out on an inspection trip and he went to Korea. He talked to the commanding general of the Marine air wing. The Marines at this time were attempting to do night-interdiction work against the truck convoys coming down from North Korea.

Q: Coastal convoys?

Adm. M.: Well, no, not all of them. They were inland as well. From Wonson down, they were working the roads and bringing in supplies. The Marines were dropping flares but they were using DC-3s, which is really the clumsiest sort of an aircraft to try to drop flares from. It wasn't designed for that sort of thing. The results were not very satisfactory because a lot of trucks were getting through without the Marines being able to hit them.

So the air wing commander apparently made a plea to Admiral Radford to see if he could get him something that could drop flares in a much better fashion than this. Admiral Radford decided that they would try the PB-4Y, our airplane. They weren't designed for this but we did have a bomb bay and we did have means of providing flare drops. So we sent one plane over from that reserve squadron - I think that was the first one that went over - and it did work. As a consequence, I took the first detachment of four aircraft from my squadron over and we started operating in Korea. My chief ordnanceman worked up a flare-drop rig that allowed the flares to be dropped through a chute. We worked as a team with the Marine night fighters. We took off, fully loaded, from the Marine base and the patrol plane would get up over the area we wanted to work in. We'd pull up to about 3,000 feet on clear nights where we could spot the truck convoys coming in. They ran down these roads with very dim lights, but you could see them. We worked with a Marine night fighter who came up fully loaded with rockets and machine guns, the works, and we'd make rendezvous in the area. When he said he was ready, the patrol plane would drop down to about 2,000 feet and drop these high-intensity flares over the road. By the time that flare went off, it lit up the whole landscape, and the Marine was right in under it and started strafing before the trucks could get off the road.

It was an interesting thing to watch. It was like ants running from an anthill. The minute the flare burst, these fellows all started pulling off and trying to get under trees or whatever, but we had them many times. This was a very successful operation. The number of trucks, and I can't begin to tell you what the total number was, that the Marines racked up under these circumstances was impressive. It was pretty sporty business for the Marines, too, steaming down at tree-top level practically, to try to strafe these trucks and try to knock them off, but they lost some -

Q: Well, in the first place, your planes were pretty vulnerable, weren't they?

Adm. M.: We were. If we'd ever been hit by these things, we'd have made the biggest, brightest star in the sky. We weren't, we -

Q: The caravans didn't have any AA?

Adm. M.: They normally didn't have, although in areas we flew over frequently we'd get flak, but it was not very accurate. There were times when we came very close to being hit, but the greatest danger that we were exposed to up there was the possibility of a midair collision. Planes flying around, totally darkened ships, no lights on, no running lights. One night I came closer to getting it than I ever have in my life. It was a Marine F-7 coming right head-on for me. I saw him at the last second and he saw me, and fortunately, we each did the reverse thing, I dove and he climbed. We missed by feet, literally feet.

When you're going north, although you don't have air-control procedures up in the combat area like that, you attempted to maintain an odd altitude and going south you'd have an even altitude, but once you're up in the combat area you're maneuvering around and looking for these trucks at all sorts of altitudes, and it's just one of those things, the luck of the draw, when you aren't flying around up there with lights on to disclose your position -

Q: No, and your focus is the caravan?

Adm. M.: That's right, exactly.

Overall, I thought it was a very successful operation. Typical. You'd take off at, say, six o'clock in the evening and get up over the area by the time it was good and dark. Normally we had range enough and clearance enough to operate with four Marine fighter planes during the time we were on the station. We'd be in the area for about four hours and each plane would check in with you - we had a predetermined general locale where we were going to be operating - the Marine would check in with you and when you were both ready, you'd start the flare drop, then he was good for maybe twenty-five or thirty minutes. Then you'd just wait for the next one, and you'd have four before midnight, say, and then turn around and go home.

And then we'd have another flight on station for the rest of the night and he would operate for roughly four hours.

Q: And home was where, South Korea?

Adm. M.: Home was South Korea. The First Marine Air Wing at the time we started this was based at K-9, which was right near Pusan. We operated out of that field the whole time that I was in Korea.

Q: Was this kind of operation also translated to the coastal area with the trains?

Adm. M.: No, we never got any trains. We didn't do that during my time. It may have been done later because when my squadron was detached I was required to leave behind four airplanes with a detachment commander for another two months before they got another squadron out to relieve, and they may have copperated on trains. Incidentally, we carried a couple of bombs, also. Our bomb bay was just about totally taken up with the flares but we carried a couple of bombs along and it was always great fun for the guys to release a couple of bombs on the road on their way home.

Q: How large were these flares, since they were special?

Adm. M.: I think they were about 50-pound flares with, I think, 3,000,000 candle power. They really lit up the landscape. When one of those things went off, you could see everything down below. Of course, you had to gauge your wind, you had to gauge your altitude, so that you gave the pilot the maximum amount of benefit of the illumination, and you had to drop it high enough so that he could get under it so he wouldn't be blinded by it on his runs in. So it took a little maneuvering, but after a flight or two everybody did pretty well. We always talked to the Marines. As soon as we got back, we would talk to the pilots we'd worked with and talked to the intelligence people to see how we could improve the technique and how it went.

Q: Those flares must have been relatively new. They weren't in World War II, were they?

Adm. M.: Oh, I think we had the concept in World War II.

Q: Did you have big ones in World War II?

Adm. M.: Yes, I think we did. I don't recall, actually though, come to think about it, we may not have, certainly in the operations in the fleet, in the carrier fleet, weren't operating with them then. They may have had them in England. I just don't know. I don't remember them being all that new, though, at the time. It was a new technique to carry these, about a ton and a half or two tons.

Q: Well, that was born at that time, wasn't it?

Adm. M.: That's right, only this was a totally new technique that we were using there, as I say, but it served a very useful purpose. It really did. In the first place, the kids in my squadron, just like all the others, they were bored stiff with just flying out over the water. They felt they were really in part of the combat operation in Korea when they did this and, living with the Marines, as we did, in their tent villages down there - messing with them. Well, it was just part of a whole team effort and it changed the relationship totally when the Marines would come back to the little hotel over in Tokoraska. After that they were great buddies of our fellows.

Q: What time of year was this, when you were doing this?

Adm. M.: I think we started in August. I believe it was August of '51. The squadron got out in -

Q: You went out there in the wintertime?

Adm. M.: No. We arrived in Japan in early March of '51 and we stayed until October of '51, then I left a detachment behind that continued to work with the Marines until December, as I recall. But the weather, by and large, was pretty good. We didn't have a lot of heavy weather and, of course, if it was really bad there was no point in going up because the fighters wouldn't be able to get in under heavy clouds and that sort of thing. We always got a good weather report before we took off.

There were times, I remember a couple of times, when we got up there and the weather was unsuitable and we couldn't do anything and had to fly back. But generally we had very clear nights and very good weather conditions.

Q: It's very interesting that you were flying this contingent over there over land and your own squadron probably was contributing the information on the weather.

Adm. M.: Yes. Of course, we had to reduce somewhat our flights that we had been doing from Itami because we took four aircraft over and that was about half the squadron. We had nine planes in the squadron and when we had a detachment in Korea, it reduced our other flights to some degree but not that much.

We saw and we could hear the carrier operations off the coast frequently up in the area above the 38th parallel, but we operated totally with the Marines. We did not operate with our own carrier aircraft in this operation. They were doing a totally different type operation.

Interestingly enough, later on, Admiral Radford decided that we ought to transfer some of these aircraft to the Chinese on Taiwan and some of that took place after I left the squadron and became part of the wing establishment, a nice job, and I'll mention that a little bit later. Radford came out there not regularly but he certainly came out frequently enough to keep himself personally advised of what was going on in the area. During the time we were in Japan, of course, this was the time that MacArthur was finally fired and this, as you can imagine, created great consternation, though not at our level. We didn't feel the repercussions operationally down that far, but it was interesting to me the reaction of the Japanese. I had a Japanese interpreter, who was an interpreter for the port of Osaka, for the army, come to the hotel two nights a week to try to teach our officers who were interested in learning something about the Japanese language. He tried to teach us a little Japanese. We didn't flatter ourselves that we were going to learn the language, but we thought we might learn enough to get by in the stores, trains, and everything. He was a very interesting young fellow, very fluent in English, and he was quite helpful to us in teaching us a little Japanese, but frequently the sessions turned out to be more questions about what the Japanese thought about various things - this was all conducted in English, of course - than learning the Japanese language. I remember the lesson right after the announcement had been made that MacArthur had been fired, and some of the young fellows in the squadron said to me:

"Let's find out how he feels about this."

Well, I asked him. I said:

"Would you mind telling us what you think about General MacArthur being fired?"

I think my question was phrased rather badly because the young fellow, I think, felt very awkward about trying to explain his feelings about this. I tried to put him at ease. I said:

"You know, really it's up to you whether you answer or not, but we'd really be interested in knowing what your thoughts are."

And finally he said:

"My mother and father are just shocked. They can hardly understand this or take it in. It's a tremendous shock to them. But the younger Japanese don't find it so difficult. If we understand your democracy as we've been told, no soldier is in a position to defy the commander in chief. We understand it. We hate to see MacArthur leave Japan, but if we understand what happened, we can accept it, but the older people, the older Japanese, find it a tremendous shock."

It was almost the equivalent, I suppose, of what they experienced when the emperor had to tell them that they had lost the war.

Q: Well, MacArthur, in a sense, was a quasi emperor, too?

Adm. M.: Yes, he had really filled a vacuum. He was all-powerful in Japan. He did a lot for the Japanese, he really did, including practically writing their constitution and I'm sure that there were those to whom it looked like the whole world was collapsing when MacArthur was going to be pulled out.

Q: Were there any repercussions in your area, within your group and so forth, on what he wanted to achieve?

Adm. M.: No, no. We really, as I said, were so far down the operational chain that it didn't affect us at all. We were too far removed from that for it to ever have any bearing on us.

Q: Well, after that stint over the land with the flares,

what was your next endeavor?

Adm. M.: That was pretty much it. We were just about winding down our operations when this first started. As I say, I'm quite sure it was late in the summer when we started the flare-drop missions. We rotated most of the crews through it, and I was in Korea for - I've forgotten the total time, but I was there a couple of times with detachments, and about this time we had just about wrapped up our operations. We were scheduled to go home in early October and we stuck to that schedule.

Q: And that's when some of the planes were flown to Taiwan?

Adm. M.: No, oh, no, this was a little bit later. I came back out as the operations officer for Fleet Air Wing 2 and that's when the planes were actually transferred to Taiwan.

Q: So you brought the squadron back to Pearl?

Adm. M.: I brought the squadron back to Barber's Point and shortly after I got back Admiral Williamson called me and asked if I'd be the operations officer on his staff. I said I would be delighted and very shortly after that I got a call from CinCPac headquarters asking if I'd be interested in being Admiral Radford's flag secretary.

Q: Had you known him before?

Adm. M.: I had, but I don't think this originated with Admiral Radford - it came from farther down the line - but I had known Admiral Radford at Patuxent River. He was a great friend of Trapnell. He used to come down and sail with us, so I did see him at that time. I knew him slightly then. He didn't know me well.

But I'd just accepted the orders to be Fleet Air Wing 2's operations officer and I was in a kind of quandary. I went in to see Admiral Williamson and told him:

"I've just been asked to come up for an interview for Admiral Radford's flag secretary and, of course, I've accepted your offer to be your operations officer. I think I ought to tell you about this."

He said: "I want you to come and be my operations officer but I realize that this is an opportunity that you might not want to turn down, so I'll just have to leave it up to you."

I thought about it for a while. I've often wondered. I would love to have had that job. The fellow who had it was a very good friend of mine and in trying to convince me I should give it a try, said he'd never had a more interesting job. He was right next to Admiral Radford. He saw everything that Admiral Radford did and, of course, Radford was one of the really great figures of that time and became even greater. But I finally called up and said I'd rather not be considered and I went ahead with the operations job. It was something I knew pretty well and -

Q: You felt honor-bound?

Adm. M.: Well, I did. I'd said I would do this and I just kind of felt an obligation to Admiral Williamson. He was getting ready to deploy with his staff and, had I not gone, they would have had to go and find another operations officer somewhere. I don't mean to suggest that it would have created an insuperable difficulty because it wouldn't have, but -

Q: It seems to me that this is a variant on the application of the honor code, isn't it?

Adm. M.: After a fashion! In any event, I did not take it and this friend of mine who tried to get me to take the job later said he couldn't understand why I hadn't tried for it.

Q: Did he get any farther than you?

Adm. M.: No. No, he didn't, but later on this same fellow, oddly enough, became aide to the secretary of the navy and he called me and asked me to relieve him there and I said I'd just taken another job, and he said:

"We're going through this again, are we?" and I said:

"I am afraid so. I've got something I really want this time and I'm not prepared to make the move."

But just before going to that staff, I went back to Whidby Island and I ferried the first P-2V coming out to Barbers Point. It was supposed to be a VP-28 plane but once more VP-28 ended up deploying with the same old airplanes because some change in aircraft assignment caused another squadron to be outfitted with P-2Vs first.

Jack, I can't think of anything else to tell you about the squadron's operations in Korea. I might move on to Fleet Air Wing 2.

Q: All right. Where was that about to operate?

Adm. M.: The fleet air wing organization in the Pacific was a rather peculiar one. Fleet Air Wing 2 was based at Barber's Point and it was responsible for the training of the patrol squadrons that were based there and getting them ready for deployment to WesPac. When they got to WesPac they either operated under Fleet Air Wing 1 in Okinawa or Fleet Air Wing 6 at Atsugi. Admiral Williamson actually, at one time, was two-hatted. He had Fleet Air Wing 1 and Fleet Air Wing 2, under his Fleet Air Wing 1 hat, when he was deployed, became Commander, Task Force 72, the Formosa patrol force. So I became his operations officer in the spring of 1952 and deployed to Okinawa and operated primarily from the seaplane tender Pine Island, which was generally based in Buckner Bay. This was primarily a seaplane tender. It operated the P-5M type aircraft pretty much.

The interesting part of this particular tour was the fact that Commander, Task Force 72, was responsible for the briefing of all the incoming destroyer squadrons that were going to operate in the Formosa patrol force, in the straits themselves, and, as operations officer, I used to have to fly in to Taiwan to brief each incoming squadron commander. And, of course, I had to brief all the new aircraft squadrons coming in to our area.

But the interesting part about this particular tour was the fact that we were also responsible for the training of the Chinese Navy in Kaoshung, and Admiral Williamson, who was an extremely energetic man, decided to fly down and spend three weeks or more observing this training, leaving the main staff under the Chief of Staff. He was going to stay aboard the little seaplane tender that we operated out of Kaoshung. We had a little AVP, not an AV, an AVP, which is a small type seaplane tender. It's for advanced base operations, pretty much, and it was the unit that was primarily used for training the Chinese Navy in destroyer-type operations.

Well, the admiral decided to fly down and he told the chief of staff he wanted me to go with him. I went, and we were there for three weeks, and the chief of staff and the rest of the staff just sort of conducted the routine operations. Actually, the operations of the squadrons out of Okinawa were not that extensive. They did fly the Formosa patrol but it was a very routine type thing, just like an airline every day they'd crank around that track and touched base with the destroyers in the middle of the strait and so on.

Q: The Quemoy and Matsu business hadn't begun yet, had it?

Adm. M.: Not to that extent, although that was part of it. We were keeping close tabs on everything that was happening there.

Q: That dueling back and forth.

Adm. M.: That's right.

We had an experience here that clearly showed me, if I ever needed any proof, the difficulties you can get into when intelligence people get into the operations end of the game. We had a specially configured VP aircraft, a P-2V, that had special photographic capabilities and electronic gathering capabilities.

CinCPac intelligence headquarters had a keen desire to get as much information as they could about the coastal radar installations along the Chinese coast. So much so that this pilot was personally briefed at CinCPac's headquarters on what they were looking for and what they wanted. We would get from CinCPac a request for a reconnaissance flight covering a certain area of the Chinese coast, and the pilot on one occasion, a tragic occasion, was doing surveillance along the coast and actually went over the coast just a little way, not very far, maybe less than a mile, half a mile, something like that, to photograph a radar installation and he got hit with ground fire. Admiral Williamson and I were aboard the Suisun, this little AVP in Kaochung, monitoring the frequency that the plane was on and we got the May Day call. He'd been hit. At first he said he was pulling up into the overcast and hoped he'd be able to get back to base, but subsequently he announced he was going to have to ditch. He couldn't make it. He was losing power, and he went down near Swatow, off the Chinese coast.

Q: Over the water?

Adm. M.: Over the water and this was a land plane, a P-2V. All we knew was he was ditching. Of course, we got no further reports, he just gave us his location. Well, we immediately alerted the destroyers in the Formosa patrol force and headed one of them to the area. We got underway with the Suisun from Kaochung and headed out across the strait and we got aircraft in the area. We arrived on the scene around ten o'clock at night and one of our two destroyers from the Formosa patrol force, commanded by a classmate of mine, as a matter of fact, picked up the pilot with, I think, four of his crew in a life raft. We still had another life raft out there with men in it and we were unable to locate it in the hours of darkness, and a wind had sprung up and was blowing onshore, so we were pretty sure they were going to be beached very shortly.

We had earlier dispatched a search and rescue PBM from the Philippines to fly out, and this plane came in before dark, made a water landing, and got all except one man, as I remember - one fellow was killed in the crash - got them all aboard and started his takeoff and crashed on takeoff. Then we had two crews in the water. We had the rescue crew and the original P-2V crew. As many of them as could got out in the life raft, and the pilot of the P-2V and the pilot of the PBM, as I recall, were picked up by the destroyer, but another group of these fellows were in the life raft that was floating ashore. By the time we got there, it was ten or eleven o'clock at night.

Meanwhile, the British had sent us a couple of ships - frigates - from the Hong Kong area, and the next day we had a five-ship patrol sweeping the waters close to Swatow and being fired on by the shore batteries. We were actually straddled on one occasion and had to move out. By this time we had searched the area very carefully with aircraft and were determined that there was nobody still in a life raft out there, in any event. So we pulled out and returned to base because we'd done all the searching we possibly could, and we notified the Seventh Fleet, Jocko Clark. He shot off a blistering dispatch to CinCPacFlt about this affair, and, to make things really nice, when I got back to base, I went up to the Chinese Navy headquarters. They were very curious about the way this had happened, what had happened and the follow up, so I had to brief them on the operation. I was showing them where we'd done our search and the Chinese operations officer said:

"Oh, that was a minefield we had in there."

They hadn't told us anything about this previously. I didn't have the heart to tell the admiral we'd been searching a minefield all night! That would have been just all we needed.

But the point of this whole thing is the minute this airplane was shot down intelligence no longer had anything to do with it. All of a sudden, it was an operational matter, and, in all fairness, Admiral Williamson's career ended at that time. It just finished him. I'm satisfied that he would have gone a long way in the navy, but the message that Clark sent was a blistering one to CinCPac headquarters, and our message explaining what had happened and what we'd done evidently was not fully accepted. Admiral Williamson asked me and told me directly because I was about to be detached from the staff, anyway, he sent me back to Pearl Harbor with a personal message for Admiral Radford. He wanted just Admiral Radford to see this. I was to give it to Admiral Radford alone.

Well, I never got to see Admiral Radford. I got up as high as one of the flag officers on the staff who I guess doesn't need to be named, but I knew that he and my boss really were at sword's points and he flatly refused me admission to Admiral Radford. He said:

"I'm sorry but Admiral Radford has told me to tell you to tell me what the circumstances were and what Admiral Williamson wants." I said:

"This message I have is for Admiral Radford alone and I'll have to get Admiral Williamson's clearance to give it to you, but I can tell you that he wanted to be sure that Admiral Radford understood the circumstances under which the loss of this airplane took place. He felt it was very important."

He said, "Well, I think we have all the information we need," and that was that.

I sent a personal message back to Admiral Williamson telling him the circumstances - of course, I've seen him several times since - and explained to him that the staff procedure was such they weren't going to let a commander in to see Admiral Radford and bring him up to date, after all the staff had its own priorities in intelligence operations and they were satisfied that they had all the information they wanted.

Q: But was it reasonable to put the responsibility on him? These operations were going on all the time, weren't they?

Adm. M.: They were going on all the time and the thing that made me really sore was the fact that this pilot told me personally that he'd gotten directions from the intelligence people on the CinCPac staff how desperately they needed this information. I'm sure they never put it in writing to him but they left no doubt in his mind that he had more latitude by far than we could ever authorize him and he was simply trying to do a job by going in a little way and when he got tagged the intelligence people all started running for cover right away. It wasn't their fault, you know.

I've always been irritated - more than irritated, really burned up about it because they were getting into our business and directing this pilot to do things that we weren't even fully aware of. Some of these flights were strictly for intelligence purposes, but it finished a rather promising navy career for Admiral Williamson who never went any further. He was reassigned and that was about the end of it.

Q: I want to ask you to comment on this, the fact that he was disabled and had to come down off the coast; the Red Chinese themselves weren't terribly alert, were they, or they would have been after him right away, after his ship - ?

Adm. M.: Yes. They didn't actually send anybody out to pick him up and we had a destroyer on the scene fairly quickly, and we also had the PBM. Of course, the PBM rescue plane wasn't armed or in a position to fight off anybody coming in. But they did pick up the survivors who floated ashore. The Chinese got those.

Q: Did they put them to death, or what?

Adm. M.: No, they didn't. They actually were paraded through the streets. I found out later that they were paraded through the streets of Swatow, tied together and paraded in front of these Chinese, but they were not executed. And I don't know when they were actually returned.

Q: Well, with that unfortunate incident, then you were detached?

Adm. M.: I was detached then, but not because of the incident. I was due for normal rotation.

Q: Did you return then out there after attempting to deliver the message to Radford?

Adm. M.: No, I didn't. Admiral Williamson personally

was deployed for an entire year out there. He went out in the summer of 1952 and stayed until the summer of 1953. I was there as the operations officer for nine months or something like that, then I came back, and I was under orders to come back to the Naval War College, as a matter of fact, but actually my orders were changed and I came to the Naval Academy for my first tour of duty there.

Q: You might, before you leave that theater out there, say something about the Taiwanese and how they responded to the training they were given by us.

Adm. M.: They were extremely enthusiastic. Of course, they were operating with really very, very antiquated equipment. The ships they had were old and beat up, but they were an enthusiastic group and their leadership was really quite young. Their commander in chief was an admiral named Ma - I think that's the way it was spelled. He was a man very little older than I. We were guests in his quarters for dinner at least a couple of times while we were there.

But I went aboard the Chinese ships. I actually went out with them once or twice to operate and watch their drills. I went down and watched them in various places, and they caught on rather quickly but, as I say, they were attempting to operate with such antiquated equipment it really wasn't a very impressive performance that they could put on.

The Marines' experience in training these people was pretty interesting also because I was in the field a couple of times with the Marines at Marine bases and observed their training techniques, and they again were impressed with the enthusiasm of the Chinese to take on these training tasks.

It was a curious time. Chiang Kai-chek had totally convinced those people - or, at least, they always said they were convinced - that they were going to go back to the mainland. Every time you went to a Chinese dinner or a Chinese party, there was always a toast "to our return to the mainland." You always heard that. It was just uppermost in their minds. Of course, from a practical standpoint, you knew they were never going back to the mainland.

Q: It's impossible for the Western mind to comprehend that.

Adm. M.: That's right, but Chiang kept them on their toes and they just assumed it would be just a matter of months until they were actually back on the mainland. They were determined to go.

We did do a lot for them. I guess one of the real sad things to me is the almost callous way in which we discarded those people. I couldn't believe the lack of class in the administration's dismissal of the Taiwanese. It's something that it's difficult to comprehend. All those years we'd promised them our protection and they had flourished in a way that very few others in that area had.

Interview #6 with Vice Admiral Charles S. Minter, Jr.
U.S. Navy (Retired)

Place: His residence in Annapolis, Maryland

Date: Tuesday morning, 16 October 1979

Subject: Biography

By: John T. Mason, Jr.

Q: So, today we come back to the States and to the Naval Academy, where you took a very interesting job.

Adm. M.: It was interesting in this sense. I'd been anticipating orders from Fleet Air Wing 2 and the first word I had was that I was to go to the Naval War College. I'd actually made a down payment on a house in Newport in anticipation of completing these orders, when suddenly I got a change of orders and was directed to report to the Naval Academy to be the executive officer to the director of athletics. This came as a total surprise, first, because I had no indication that my orders to the Naval War College were about to be canceled, and secondly because I hadn't the faintest notion of what the job consisted of.

Q: Who was the director of athletics?

Adm. M.: Captain Ian Eddy was the director at that time. Interestingly enough, I found out much later that my orders to the Naval Academy came as a result of the then commandant, Taylor Keith, going to the Bureau of Naval Personnel to look over the record of a number of officers who might be considered to relieve the then executive officer to the director of athletics. He wanted someone who had an extensive background in intramural athletics and, for some reason, my name fell out of the pot, and I really hadn't had that kind of background, but they went back to my days at Patuxent River when the athletic program was under me, in a sense, and apparently got the impression that I'd had a lot to do with a major intramural program there, which just wasn't the case. In any event, based on that information, I was ordered to the Naval Academy, and, in a curious way, that little mixup eventually led to my becoming the commandant because at the time I was acting as exec to the director of athletics the head of the English Department was Admiral Johnny Davidson. We got to know each other quite well and when he became the superintendent - and I'll talk about this at a later time - when he started looking for a commandant my name came up again and he knew me well enough at least to not want to turn me down.

So, through a curious mixup, I ended up at the Naval Academy. It was an interesting assignment, though, and I enjoyed it tremendously. I found myself involved with the athletic program, which I was tremendously interested in, but we had some interesting problems in those days.

The head football coach was Eddie Erdelatz, who had a national reputation as a coach, but was just like a little boy who never quite grew up. He was a good football coach, there was no question about that, and he commanded the loyalty of his troops but he had very little loyalty upward and when I arrived at the Naval Academy I found to my surprise that there was a tremendous cleavage between Erdelatz and the then director of athletics, Ian Eddy. They rarely spoke. They simply didn't communicate except through Rip Miller, the Assistant Director. It was a curious sort of a situation.

Q: Did Erdelatz have a military background at all?

Adm. M.: No, he did not, or at least very little, and that's an interesting point. Every coach that we've ever had at the Naval Academy who has not been a graduate has always come to grief eventually, partly I suppose because of the lack of real understanding of what is required here.

Erdelatz had gotten a pretty big name by the time he eventually left. He'd been a professional football player and he'd done some assistant coaching in the professional ranks, but Eddie had a sort of an exaggerated idea about where he stood in the athletic world and eventually began to feel that he was bigger than the institution here, and he eventually got fired.

Q: That's more or less the tradition with our athletes, isn't it?

Adm. M.: Yes.

Q: In every field.

Adm. M.: Yes, but the Naval Academy seems to have gotten an awful black eye over the years. I'll tell you later about when I was here and we had to fire the football coach. It always seems that after we lose to army the press immediately assumes that that's the reason the fellow is fired, and so many times the background goes so far back over such a period of time that it's impossible for them to sift out the -

Q: Well, of course, that's the end of the season, anyway.

Adm. M.: That's right. Half the time when I was here and first began to realize the extent of the cleavage between the director and the head football coach, I was naive enough to think that I could go down and sort of bridge that gap. I really felt perfectly confident to go down and talk to Erdelatz and make him understand that I'd be happy to sort of be the bridge between him and the director of athletics. But the minute I walked into Erdelatz's office to talk to him, it became apparent to me he was never going to listen to anybody in the front office.

Q: You were tainted!

Adm. M.: I'd just come back from Korea where, you know, people were dying, the war was on, and to come back here and find what appeared to me to be the petty jealousies and the petty little differences of opinion, it just struck me as ridiculous. I thought, well, I can go down and perhaps I'll be able to help the director and help the head football coach. It was a total flop. He wouldn't accept me any more than he would the director of athletics.

But in a year's time, Elliot Laughlin came in, and this is not to be derogatory at all to Ian Eddy, who was a wonderful man, but the point had been reached where he simply couldn't get along with the head football coach. Elliot Laughlin came in and did an absolutely superior job as the director of athletics.

I truly enjoyed my year with him and he was able to get to Erdelatz to a degree that nobody had before. He understood Erdelatz, I think, better than most, and actually that year was our most successful year. We went to the Sugar Bowl that year. George Welsh was our quarterback at the time and, for the first time in thirty years, the Naval Academy went to a bowl, the Sugar Bowl, and won. That did a tremendous amount for the football program, for all the athletics here at the Naval Academy. Recruiting stepped up tremendously because we were major underdogs in a major bowl and we won the thing 21-0, and everybody was talking navy all around the country all of a sudden.

I might just mention a little bit about that bowl game, some of the lessons we learned. We hadn't played in a bowl in thirty years, as I mentioned, and our acceptance of the bowl bid hinged on beating army, as it usually does. The army game wasn't played until late that year and the result was that the bowl people were just on edge, afraid if army won, you know, navy would not be available, and they could find themselves too late to line up another top team.

Q: Yes.

Adm. M.: Well, they gambled on us and we won, but the

consequence of that was that the actual planning for the bowl game, as far as the athletic association was concerned, was a terribly frantic effort to try to compress in just about two weeks' time all the countless details associated with a major endeavor like a bowl game. It just made for many, many mistakes, and we made several.

Q: And the media element made all of those arrangements.

Adm. M.: Oh, yes, exactly.

Well, here was the problem. I was sent down to New Orleans to meet with the Sugar Bowl people right after we had accepted the bowl bid.

Q: The opponent being who?

Adm. M.: Mississippi.

I got my first major shock when I was told that in an 82,000-seat stadium Navy was going to get 13,000 seats only, and 9,000 of those would be in the end zone.

Well, I knew Admiral Boone, who was the superintendent, was just going to have a fit when he heard about this, but what we didn't realize was that the stadium that the game was played in was largely built through bond issues and the people who bought bonds for the stadium got preferential seating. The result was that visiting teams had very little to pick from. Admiral Boone had gone on record as saying that any midshipman who wanted to go to the game would not only be guaranteed a seat but would be given a seat of the 50-yard line or as close to it as possible and also his way would be paid back to the Naval Academy out of the proceeds from the game.

Q: Ow! That was a rash promise!

Adm. M.: So we had a sizable number of midshipmen who were planning to end their Christmas leave in New Orleans at the expense of the athletic association.

I made arrangements for the football squad, where they were to stay, and this was no great problem. Tulane University was kind enough to allow us to have the squad stay there. It was during their Christmas vacation period.

As I say, I brought back the news that we were only going to get 13,000 seats. Our ticket man at that time was Morris Gilmore, a wonderful fellow who was with me on the trip and, of course, he was the one who actually had the problem of distributing the tickets.

But the real problem was that in the short time we had to make preparations, the athletic association decided to use the same procedure in issuing tickets as they did for army-navy games, just tailor it to this particular contest. But what they didn't realize was that this gave each individual member of Congress six tickets, and those who didn't want their tickets gave them to others. So, all of a sudden, there was a huge congressional block of tickets going out and we only had, as I mentioned, 4,000 seats on the sidelines, and this created some tremendous problems.

Eddie Hebert, who was the congressman from New Orleans, for example, had more than 300 tickets and still wasn't satisfied. He sent a request to the director of athletics for another 100 tickets.

Q: But he should have understood the situation?

Adm. M.: He did understand it. It was the most classic example of a politician's maneuver I've ever seen, and he admitted it himself.

We had a set deadline for ticket applications to be in by the 15th of December and we announced that any that we received later than that would not be honored. We received a letter from Eddie Hebert's office asking for 100 or 150 tickets and it was postmarked the 16th of December. So the athletic association just sent him a polite letter back saying they were sorry but they couldn't honor his request. We didn't have the tickets in the first place.

Well, the next thing that happened was a blistering three page telegram from Hebert to Superintendent Boone, saying he couldn't understand the athletic association's callous disregard of his request for tickets. He was the congressman from that area. He went on at great length. Admiral Boone was one who really took these things seriously, and he got terribly upset at that telegram. He sent for Elliot Laughlin and me to ask what we'd done about this. We explained that his request had come in late, we didn't have the tickets, and we had to tell him that.

Later on in the spring, long after the game was over, Eddie Hebert, who was a member of the Board of Visitors to the Naval Academy, came on a board visit and had lunch with Elliot and me at the Yacht Club. Elliot said to him:

"Mr. Hebert, you know that telegram you sent to us really didn't do us any good." And Hebert said:

"What telegram?"

"That one where you complained about the failure of the athletic association honoring your request for tickets."

"Oh," he said, "you didn't pay any attention to that?" One reason he had sent that wire was so that he could show the people asking for tickets, "I told the superintendent off," and that was the whole purpose of the thing!

Q: That's the old political ploy!

Adm. M.: Yes.

Q: Telephone calls and all that sort of thing.

Adm. M.: Well, it was an exciting time at the Naval Academy. As I say, the national television of that game and navy winning, being a big underdog, improved our image all around the country. It was a time that I remember well.

Actually, at that time, too, Erdelatz's first assistant then was Ben Martin, who was a Naval Academy graduate and who really aspired to eventually become the head football coach here. I would love to have seen him make it, but he left the Erdelatz staff and finally got the head coaching job at the University of Virginia. Every time the coaching vacancy came up at the Naval Academy in subsequent years, Ben had just taken another job. Even when I was here, I contacted him and he'd just taken an extension of his contract at the Air Force Academy, so he never came back.

That's why I think George Welsh is so successful here. He fully understands the Naval Academy, having been a graduate and having been an assistant coach here for a time. He has an appreciation for what he can and cannot do, what's expected of him, to a degree that the average civilian coach just never seems to be able to quite take aboard. Some are better at this than others.

Q: Do the other service academies have the same problem?

Adm. M.: They have the same problem but they've not solved it the way we have. Ben Martin was a longtime coach at the Air Force Academy and he certainly understood the problem better than, perhaps, his successor does. There has never been a graduate at West Point since Earl Blake was there, I don't think they've had a graduate at West Point, and last year, you know, the coach left under rather an unpleasant set of circumstances. They've got a new fellow in now who is not a West Pointer. The head coach at the Air Force Academy, as far as I know, is not an academy graduate.

All I say is that it's money in the bank if you can get somebody who is a good coach and who also understands why he can't have the football squad for four hours every afternoon the way you do in some schools. He has to understand the part that football plays here and how it has to tie in to the rest of the program for midshipmen. I think we're very lucky to have George Welsh here who has that sort of background on the thing.

Q: That must have occupied almost your full time for a few months?

Adm. M.: Oh, it did, yes. I don't know whether this has any particular bearing but Erdelatz could be, as I mentioned a moment ago, a difficult man to deal with. As long as things were going his way he'd be the friendliest, nicest guy, but he just never seemed quite to understand the limits of his authority. For example, he promised the football squad, after they won the Sugar Bowl game, sports jackets, civilian sports jackets. I remember they were $50 a piece. He made this promise without asking anybody in the front office where the money was going to come from, and we were suddenly confronted with this request for a sports jacket for each member of the football team. I've forgotten the total figure. It might have been $1,500 or something like that. Well, of course, the director couldn't approve that without getting the superintendent's approval, and when it went across the street to Admiral Boone he just about blew up. He said:

"This is a Naval Academy team. They've got their N blankets, they got Sugar Bowl watches, they got all these things, and I'm just not about to approve a request for civilian sports jackets."

Q: Where would they wear them, anyway?

Adm. M.: On leave. There was a fellow here in town who used to supply us with athletic equipment perfectly legitimately but he also had a sports goods shop and this was all to be bought through him. I don't mean to suggest that there was anything improper about it, but he was going to give a little better buy, I suppose, than they could have gotten elsewhere.

The only point of this whole story was that when Erdelatz was told that his request was denied, he refused to have anything to do with telling the football squad. He'd made the promise to them, but Elliot Laughlin and I were the ones who had to go down and call the squad together, and it was an unpleasant task because they thought they were going to get these jackets, and Elliot had to tell them that they weren't and the reasons why. I thought it was small of Eddie not to show up with us. But he was his own worst enemy in many, many ways.

I'd like to mention something else about that assignment. The most interesting thing other than my association with the sports teams, concerned our efforts to get the field house at the Naval Academy. We were having a terrible time convincing the Congress that we needed a field house, because the term "field house" to most congressmen denotes a major athletic enterprise, a Notre Dame type football factory, that sort of thing. But we were in desperate need of that facility.

Q: Were you somewhat handicapped, too, by the fact that the stadium monies had been raised privately?

Adm. M.: That's correct. Of course, the stadium money came after this. Smedberg came later.

Q: Oh, that's right.

Adm. M.: Yes, but we had a wonderful supporter and, as a matter of fact, as far as I'm concerned the man who really swung this thing for the Naval Academy was Dr. John Hanna, who, I think, had been the president of Michigan State. In any event, he was a strong supporter of the necessity of a field house for us and he was a great witness before the appropriations committees in support of this. He pointed out the Naval Academy's lack of athletic facilities, indoor facilities, was hampering the program here. He was much more persuasive than anybody in uniform could be. Anybody in uniform obviously was suspect, but a person who came from the outside who had a good name in academic circles, as Dr. Hanna did, was well received. We couldn't have done it without him, I don't believe.

I went up with the commandant to testify about what the plans were, about what the cost we'd estimated was going to be, and why we required it, and, as I say, Dr. Hanna was the one who really swung the pendulum in our favor and eventually we got it.

For a long time we weren't allowed to even call it a field house. We called it extra physical education facilities or something like that, some pseudonym to avoid the connotation that it was going to be a field house -

Q: That's rather small!

Adm. M.: Well, it is, but I got the assignment to go around to several universities that had field houses, once we heard we were going to get it. I went to Michigan State and I went to the University of Pittsburgh, to at least three or four major schools that had field houses to see what sort of problems they had in field houses, what their difficulties were.

We knew the size the building was going to be, the size it is today, and I contacted each one of our coaches to ask what he felt his sport would require. Not surprisingly, every one of them needed almost the entire building for his particular sport.

Q: Yes!

Adm. M.: Erdelatz wanted it to be one football field.

Q: A whole field, yes!

Adm. M.: So he could go inside and practice on a full football field on a rainy day. Other coaches were a bit less demanding but they all wanted an inordinate amount of space. Well, as you can imagine, we listened to all their ideas, then we went ahead and planned it the way it's finally come out.

We thought that was a major step forward at the Naval Academy. It was the first big new building the Naval Academy had had in a long time and certainly something that you sometimes wondered how we could ever have done without.

Q: How much money was appropriated for it?

Adm. M.: I think it was something like $4,500,000 or

$5,000,000.

Q: A bargain price!

Adm. M.: It was, oh, yes, and it served a variety of purposes ever since. It was just such a step forward for the Naval Academy and we were really pleased when we heard we were going to get it because for a long time it was a very questionable item. It took some real selling, and I repeat I think Dr. Hanna was the man who really swung it for us.

   I don't think, Jack, of anything else of any real significance.

Q: How did you function with intramural sports?

Adm. M.: Well, actually the Physical Education Department comes under the director of athletics and under me, and I did get very close to the intramural sports program here, of course, because it's such a large part of the midshipmen's daily routine. We had a highly competent staff down there in that department and, strangely enough, Tony Rubino, who is now the senior professor in the Physical Education Department, served as an athletic officer under me at Quonset Point in 1942, when I had my first squadron.

He was an athletic specialist. He was a boxing coach. He's just a wonderful fellow and we couldn't have done better than to have him here in this program. He's got more knowledge and background and understanding of that type program than anybody I know anywhere. So it was a delight to come back here and work with Tony again, and with all the coaches down there. I developed a pretty close relationship with all of them, and when I came back as commandant, of course, that paid dividends for me because I knew most all of them down there. I'd worked with them or been with them during my time here.

Q: In that particular period, were the revenues from football games sufficient to finance the whole program adequately?

Adm. M.: Yes. Well, there was always that worry about whether they were going to be adequate, but they were. We played about four big games, so-called big games, a year, and four that were less important. The army game was the big game and Notre Dame was a big game. Of course, that year at the Sugar Bowl we had a nice windfall there from television and from the Sugar Bowl receipts. So, yes, the football program was carrying that.

Q: You had a stellar team.

Adm. M.: Oh, yes, we had a very fine team that year.

Q: What would the proceeds be from, say, the Sugar Bowl, and that sort of thing?

Adm. M.: I'd have to go back and research that. It's been a long time back, but it seems to me, and this sounds like small potatoes these days, but it seems to me that our share of the Sugar Bowl was $200,000 or something in that neighborhood. That's small potatoes now compared with what money is like for the bowl games now.

Q: Yes, television rights and that sort of thing.

Adm. M.: Yes. Well, in those days, just like today, if we ever lost the television rights for the army-navy game, the athletic association would really be in trouble.

Q: Well, it was questionable two years ago, wasn't it?

Adm. M.: That's right. Oh, yes, it's been up in the air. But at that time the army-navy game was nationally recognized every year as the highlight of the season. It was the traditional rivalry. Now, the Army-Navy game has a lot of competition among the games people want to see. Notre Dame and Southern California, for example, is always a competitor for national audiences these days, and the army-navy game has frankly decreased in stature because, well, both of us have gone downhill as far as top football teams are concerned, and there's just less interest on the part of the general public. They want to see the big teams.

Q: They're more interested in professional football?

Adm. M.: That's right, and also the top ranked teams now like Alabama, Oklahoma, Southern Cal, and some of the other football powers just have more drawing power on television than army and navy.

Q: It would be interesting to have a comment from you at this point on the influence that the media have in the scheduling of games, the time of games, that sort of thing, because they almost dictate this now, do they not?

Adm. M.: They certainly do dictate the times and you're wise, I suppose, if you agree to them because your financial life is so dependent on them. They don't have anything, or very little at least, to do with the scheduling of games. I was quite surprised to find when I arrived here with the athletic association how far in advance these games are lined up. No superintendent ever comes in and is able to do anything about his schedule. It's already been made long before he arrives. They're looking ten years down the road, the athletic association, the director of athletics, and that makes for some interesting developments because it's awfully difficult to predict that far in advance just what caliber of team you're apt to be up against, and you have to plan these things hoping to get fairly sizable crowds at your games, but you simply don't know, in many instances, whether you're going to have a drawing card or it's going to be a turkey eight or ten years from now.

The navy scheduling process at the time I was here was pretty much that we would have certain set opponents every year. We always played Notre Dame, we almost always played Virginia, we almost always played William and Mary, we always played Army, and that left you a little bit of flexibility. The idea was to try to have the navy team seen around the country. We'd play in the far west one time and in the midwest some other time, and in the deep south sometimes. We'd play Georgia Tech, we'd play California, and we'd play a representative midwest team, frequently, of course, it would be the Notre Dame game in South Bend that would be the major game.

There's just no question about it, to get back to your original question a moment ago, the part the media play, the part television plays, in almost dictating the way a game is played these days is enormous.

Q: This has a tendency to play down the sport itself, as a sport, doesn't it?

Adm. M.: It does, yes. I don't know how you're going to lick it, though, because it finally gets down to the dollar and how much you're going to get. The teams that are good, good enough at least to be on television once or twice a year, have got things going pretty much their way. This year, for example, navy had the Illinois game on regional television and it's going to have the army-navy game on national television. I don't know what their income will be but it will be pretty substantial from those two games alone to carry the football program for this year. But who knows what's going to happen next year.

I think this is Bo Coppedge's last year as president of the NCAA television committee, and certainly he's been instrumental in seeing to it that navy gets its share of the television pie. But if you don't have a winning team or at least an exciting, competitive team, you're just not going to be looked at by the television people. They're not going to put on a team that has maybe a 2-4 record at midseason on national television.

Q: Well, it gets back to what is the philosophy back of the Congress's disinterest and failure to provide funds for the athletic program at the service academies?

Adm. M.: I think primarily it goes back to the early days of the academy, the early days of football. Football has always been self-supporting and Congress has never been disposed to provide funds for anything other than the intramural program, the program for the midshipmen, that has nothing to do with gate receipts.

I don't think you'll ever see Congress get in the position of subsidizing our money-making teams. I think the criticism would be that we were interested in bringing in football players just to play football and for no other reason. I don't see any sympathy at all for Congress to go that route.

You know there has been a suggestion made, though, and I don't think it has much hope of being realized, but there have been people who have suggested that to keep army, navy, and air force competitive with the other big schools around the country, consideration should be given to establishing special rules for highly qualified athletes. The only way you can be competitive, of course, is to get the talent, the players who are capable of playing the game as well as the other fellow and these, generally speaking, are people who have in mind at least the possibility of going into professional football after they've finished college –

Q: Now, they do, yes.

Adm. M.: And, of course, we can't be as competitive as the other schools because we can't give a young fellow any kind of a guarantee other than five years or four years of service time after he leaves here. The result is that we don't get the so-called blue-chip athlete, except once in a great while. Roger Staubach is a very rare exception to that rule.

Well, the suggestion has been made that, quite on the level, a young man who has that sort of talent or believes he has, come here and not be bound by the four-year rule after graduation. Allow him to play football here, allow him to go to the professional ranks, allow him to stay in the reserves, say, and do reserve duty in the off season from football. I don't think this has a prayer of ever being realized. I can see all sorts of administrative nightmares you'd run up against in trying to do something like that, but it has enough appeal that at least it's been proposed seriously by a couple of people as a means of keeping the service academies competitive in big-time football.

When you look back to the years when Army was a great football power, World War II days when Glen Davis and Doc Blanchard, Arnold Tucker, and that gang were such a great football aggregation, the old Army-Notre Dame series which were bitterly fought and were great and wonderful football games, the Army-Navy games of those days when the whole nation was interested in the Army and Navy game as they are in the world series of baseball, those were the glory days of the academies. In 1926 the national championship was shared when the Army-Navy game ended in a tie 21-21. Those days a lot of people look back on with a great deal of nostalgia and a sincere feeling that we ought to be that competitive again, but you can't be competitive unless you can get the talent, and the talent won't come to you if the talent sees all the money to be made in the pros and sees only a five-year tie to the service after graduation. So it's a difficult thing for -

Q: And you have that other major obstacle that has built up since then, I mean the professional circuit, which has really mushroomed.

Adm. M.: Oh, yes. Oh, tremendously.

Q: And they command the attention now, rather than the college teams.

Adm. M.: Exactly right. You know, sometimes it's a little hard to realize how recently, really, all that big money in the professional football ranks has come about.

Q: One additional question in this area. You mentioned just a little bit ago that the suggestion has been made from time to time that some of the rules be relaxed in order to get some of these very capable youngsters to play on the football team. It occurs to me that the rules have been bent somewhat in the case of Tom Hamilton, when he was coming back and forth from regular navy assignments, coming back to the Naval Academy to be director of navy athletics or head football coach or what have you. This happened three or four times during his active career.

Adm. M.: Tom was so closely identified with sports that his entire navy career was colored by his allegiance to the sports program. And I think from a purely navy career standpoint it unquestionably in my mind legislated against him going to a higher command. But I think Tom did this fully aware of the fact that he was perhaps reducing his chances for flag rank by taking repeated assignments in the athletic area, because he got to be identified with that.

Q: He is an example of the fact that -

Adm. M.: He is an example, and, you know, he was very instrumental - in World War II the athletic program that Tom ran then was terribly important.

Q: Yes, it was very important indeed for a pilot -

Adm. M.: Indeed it was, and Tony Rubino, the fellow I've been talking about, was one of Tom's fellows in that program during the war. Tom was instrumental in bringing Tony here to the Naval Academy. Tom had a great, great impact on navy sports and Naval Academy sports. He was a coach when I was here as a midshipman. Such a wonderful man, so highly regarded, and such a gifted athlete. Gosh, there was nothing he couldn't do in the athletic area.

But, you're right, they did bend the rules a bit there, but they bent them also for Joe Bellino. When Bellino graduated from the Naval Academy he had been signed by the Boston Patriots. Roger Staubach was also on the Dallas Cowboy's list. But Bellino was allowed to fly to Boston every weekend from Norfolk when he didn't have the duty. The Bureau of Naval Personnel authorized that. The Patriots paid his way up and back, for him to play with the Patriots on a Saturday or Sunday afternoon. Of course, he was a big drawing card up in the Boston area. He was from there. He was a Heisman Trophy winner, still in the navy, serving aboard ship out of Norfolk. But they did authorize him to do that, and I know they did it with some real trepidation. Smedberg was the chief of BuPers at that time and I know there was a certain amount of discussion about whether this was or wasn't a good idea. Bellino was really an exception. He was the first Heisman Trophy winner we'd ever had at the Naval Academy. He was not going to stay in the navy. He was doing his active duty during the week. He was not allowed to go on weekends when he had the duty or when the ship was at sea or whatever. So they convinced themselves that this was in the best interest of the Navy. He wasn't hurting anything, and in a way I suppose there was some feeling that it sort of carried on the navy name in big-time sports. Here was a fellow who was doing his active duty and was able to -

Q: Yes, it had its emphasis in recruiting, I suppose?

Adm. M.: Yes. That would never happen now. I mean it couldn't ever happen now. The professional football teams are so highly skilled and the time required is such that no one could just pop in for a weekend and play, then go back for five days, and go back the next weekend. So I don't think that problem will ever arise again if anybody had the opportunity.

Q: Well, your next assignment after the Naval Academy was in a really scholastic area. That was the National War College. It was quite an honor to be selected to go there. It was an indication that you were going on to higher rank.

Adm. M.: At that time, National War College selection was considered as a stepping-stone up. At that time also the National War College student body was composed primarily of people at the captain-colonel level. I had been selected for captain but had not actually made it at the time I went to the National War College. I hadn't made my number at that time, but I had been selected for captain, as my classmates who were there that year had.

It was a tremendously interesting year to me. It was such a break from anything I'd ever experienced before. For the first time, I knew what an 8-to-4:30 day really meant because that's the way it worked and sometimes much less time than that.

We had a succession of the most interesting speakers during that year, really top-flight people from every walk of life. Foreign dignitaries like Montgomery and Mountbatten came to speak to us and, of course, we had numerous national dignitaries such as Senators, Ambassadors, even the Vice President. The President didn't speak that year but he frequently did come over -

Q: This was Eisenhower?

Adm. M.: Yes, but he did not speak to us that year. We had, of course, all the top members of the Joint Chiefs of Staff, Arleigh Burke spoke, Curt LeMay was there, and it was certainly of tremendous interest to the student body to be able to see these people firsthand and be able to ask some questions, and frequently, then, to be able to sit in a seminar with them and have a much more intimate sort of a question-and-answer period.

Q: It was strictly off the record, too, was it not?

Adm. M.: It was, yes. There was no attribution whatsoever. They were told when they came that there would be no reporting of it, that the student body had been cautioned that they were not to make reference to it, other than among themselves, and this pledge was kept. They were very candid in their comments.

Q: I understand there has been a violation or two in recent years?

Adm. M.: There has been, and the minute that happens it makes a speaker very suspect. I mean he's very suspicious. He doesn't feel like he can really talk totally off the record and say precisely what he thinks.

Things just seemed to be different in those days. People did tend to respect that sort of thing more than I think they do now. I may be wrong about that, but it seems that way to me. I see more and more disclosures in the papers of things that previously people would not have considered making public.

Q: In that time, the sense of accountability was very pronounced?

Adm. M.: It was, indeed. Such things as the Pentagon Papers disclosure would never have occurred to anybody to do something like that. We were just brought up in a little different atmosphere, I think, we honored it more. Certainly, all those people who came to speak had no inhibitions. I remember General LeMay –

Q: He never had any inhibitions anyway.

Adm. M.: Anyway, he never did. In the question period, I'll never forget, I knew I'd been tagged to go to the P-6M program, which I'll talk about later, but somebody got up in the question period and said:

"General LeMay, what do you think about this jet seaplane the navy is building?"

He said: "I don't think anything about it. Give me the next question." Bang! That was all!

But there were some really top-flight speakers there and it was a fascinating year for me. It gave me a chance, and all of us a chance, to really stop and think about things other than our own service and the routine day-to-day experience.

Q: Where did you live at that time?

Adm. M.: I lived here in Annapolis. That might have been a mistake but we had been in quarters at the Naval Academy and when I got orders for the National War College, our three children were all in school here, were doing well, and we talked it over and decided it was better to keep them here and I commuted to Washington. I actually rented a house like Ike Kidd owned down on Market Street. It made for sort of a commuting problem. There wasn't all that much -

Q: Were you in a car pool?

Adm. M.: Yes.

Q: That had its value.

Adm. M.: Well, I was fortunate. I found that there were two people who were at the Industrial College, on the staff up there, and their hours were the same as mine and we went to the same place, Fort McNair, so it was great. We could drive back and forth and frequently, of course, discuss among ourselves the lecturers we had heard that day, because many times, almost always, when a speaker of real international repute was there, both colleges were cut in on the lecture and the question-and-answer period. So it was good from that standpoint. We could hash things over back and forth, and also I learned more about the Industrial College than I would have known otherwise. Although they were right next door, our programs were totally different, and I didn't know that much about what was going on there.

So it was an interesting sort of assignment and the car pool was fine. It saved us money and it made the trip back and forth much more enjoyable than driving by yourself.

Q: Yes. Well, other than the car pool, the association with other students from the State Department and so on must have been useful to you after that.

Adm. M.: Oh, it really was. The students in that War College class were very well screened and selected, and several of them went on to much higher positions. In the State Department, for example, I can think of at least four or five who became ambassadors. Marshall Green was a classmate of mine and became the head of the Far East section in the State Department. I think he still is, as a matter of fact.

And in the service group I frequently ran across in subsequent tours people that I had served with there who went on to general-officer rank in the air force, the army. So round the world, you did have occasion to see these fellows. It not only gave you an insight into the other services, but it also gave you entree. If you know someone and you can pick up the phone and call him, you can frequently get a lot more than if you go through normal channels, and I had this advantage in subsequent tours of duty in the Pentagon when I had occasion to call a classmate from the National War College to try to get information assisting me in deciding which way I should go with an inter-service problem. It had major benefits in that respect and I appreciated it.

I still run across many of them. There are many of them around the Washington area now and, of course, we're all retired, but during my service time I had several occasions when I ran across a classmate.

When I had command of the <u>Intrepid</u> and went in to Istanbul, a classmate of mine was the Number 2 man in the embassy there. He was very helpful. I had some sailor problems ashore. It was the first time I'd ever had any difficulties with the dope problem among sailors and this fellow was very helpful to me in giving me advice and assistance there when we were in port. So it serves a very useful purpose.

Q: What was your particular subject for investigation that year?

Adm. M.: Well, that was interesting. When we first arrived, they told us that we would have to do a thesis that was supposed to be the caliber of a product that normally would be used for a master's degree in a college. We were given a series of subjects. As I recall, there were 150 subjects that you could choose from, and if you didn't find a subject that really appealed to you, well, then, you could propose one and the faculty would decide whether it was a suitable subject for your paper.

I chose - looking back on it, it was about as far-reaching a subject as I possibly could have chosen - "The Future of Red China as a World Power." Just a modest little effort, you know! And I began to realize early in the game that I had really bitten off a pretty sizable chunk to chew on in the brief period of time that we had to do it in. The schools started in August, I think, and the papers were due in February. And I really had no background in this. I knew nothing about China to speak of. Of course, I'd had some time, as I mentioned earlier in Taiwan, so I got exposed to it. I guess that's what triggered my interest more than anything else.

Incidentally, the faculty advised you that you could either take a subject with which you were reasonably familiar but hadn't ever had time to go into in great depth, that was one route, or take something that you were totally unfamiliar with and just use this as a means of expanding your knowledge. I was somewhere in between, I guess, in this "Red China as a World Power" exercise of mine, but I did a lot of reading in Chinese history. I did a lot of reading of Russian history as well, and I had a faculty adviser, a former Marine officer, who was an academician and was a recognized expert on Communist China.

Q: In that day, China and Russia were friendly?

Adm. M.: Yes, that's right, and it was quite apparent that there was going to be a major split, at least I thought it was apparent.

I contacted people in the State Department who were supposed to be knowledgeable about this, and every time we had a lecturer who came to the school and had any sort of background, why, I would try to have lunch with him or quiz him, at least. But I had a real difficulty with my faculty adviser because when I was putting my paper together I told him what my conclusions were, essentially, and he claimed that I didn't have enough evidence to support my conclusions. My conclusions, essentially, were these: that from all I had read and all I could observe and all I had heard, historically when a new culture or a new idea or a new group of people somehow penetrated China, over a period of time that particular idea came out sort of Chinese in character and not the way it went in. I really had become convinced that communism was going to have the same sort of a fate in China. I really believed that it would be a Chinese form of communism and not necessarily the Russian type. I just couldn't believe that the Chinese were going to allow themselves to be subservient to the Russians in dictating the way the communist movement should go in China. That, essentially, was what I had come up with, and my faculty adviser said he didn't think I had the evidence to support my conclusions.

But I don't know how you get more evidence than Chinese history itself because historically that's what has happened in China.

That was my ultimate conclusion. I predicted there would be a major split between the Chinese and the Soviets. Well, as I say, I didn't get his endorsement of that conclusion because he didn't feel that I had enough evidence to support it, but it actually worked out about the way I had sort of anticipated. I don't mean to suggest that I was all that wise, but it certainly convinced me that the Chinese were going to go pretty much their own route and it just looked as though there had to be a confrontation between these two major communistic societies at some point down the road, and that's kind of the way it's gone.

Q: It was a very valid thesis!

Adm. M.: Well, as I say, it was interesting to me because he said that, in spite of all the references that I made to others who had come to conclusions like this, he felt that I just didn't have a sound enough case for it. Communism, according to him, was an ideology that was common to both peoples and I hadn't shown that the communist doctrine itself was going to be modified. He didn't believe I could show that because there was no evidence in his judgment at that time that supported this thesis.

It was interesting to speculate about, but, as I say, I was satisfied I was right and I haven't had much occasion to change my mind.

Q: Because he didn't approve of your thesis, did you have a chance to read it before the group?

Adm. M.: No, I didn't. The faculty had the job of choosing only two that were to be presented to the entire class. I made a presentation to my own seminar group. We all exchanged, synthesized, our findings in our papers. Then, of course, the paper was written up and it was kept on file there. It had to be secret, the classification of the paper, because I had a lot of excerpts from national intelligence estimates of China. It has long since, I'm sure, been declassified, but it was secret at the time it was presented, so it couldn't have had wide dissemination even if it was good enough to be disseminated.

My son just graduated from the National War College last year and there's a major difference now between the way the school is run and the way it was in my day, not the least of which is the fact that every year during my era the National War College made overseas tours. There were three areas: the European area, the Far East area, and South America. If you had had significent duty in one particular part of the world they would not, normally speaking allow you to go back there, just because you might want to go back. They purposely sent you to areas where you had little experience.

I really had had very little time in Europe and wanted the European trip, as most people did, but it turned out that I got a pretty good break. I was assigned to the South American trip and the president of the college at that time was Admiral Woolridge, who had been the head of the Pan American Defense Board, and he made the South American trip with our group. We had one airplane assigned to us for the entire trip. We never had to change planes or get baggage off, and anything you bought could go aboard the airplane. It was a top-flight trip.

We went to Havana first, and from Havana to Panama, then Panama to Peru, Peru to Chile, then across to Argentina, up to Rio, Caracas and home. It was a three-week trip, and at every stop we were given briefings by really top officials of the government. The fact that Admiral Woolridge was along and had so many ties to the South American countries made it an even more impressive show because they went all-out to do him honor and the result was -

Q: It really gave the delegation a status, didn't it?

Adm. M.: That's right. The student body benefited from the fallout from the fact that we had such a prestigious individual along with us.

It was a fine trip and one I've never forgotten. I remember specifically going to Rio, and being told at that time of plans to build Brasilia which was to be the national capital. Of course, Rio was serving as the national capital at that time. Later, when I had command of a task group that went into Rio, I flew up to Brasilia, and I'll talk about that at some later time, but I remember the planning that was going on even then for the construction of the city of Brasilia. A lot of the diplomatic corps even then were expressing regrets about leaving Rio to go 600 miles inland. It was not going to be all that happy an experience.

During that year at the National War College, I got a real shock. I think it was shortly before Christmas, I got a call from the Bureau of Naval Personnel and was told that my National War College assignment might be terminated to allow me to be sent to another job, a very urgent job. I was going to be coordinator of the P-6M program and, as I say, about December I was told that there was some move afoot in the Pentagon to get somebody over there right away. Admiral Burke was unhappy with the P-6M program or, at least, he wanted some individual in the Pentagon to monitor the program and I was afraid I was going to get pulled out before my year was over. That didn't happen but I was called over to the Pentagon and told that I'd have to come right after the completion of the school year, with no leave, because they were in such a hurry to get somebody in the job. But at least I was able to finish the year, which I was afraid I wasn't going to be able to do when this thing first came up.

I can't think of anything else of particular significance relating to the National War College year. It certainly was a year that I'll always remember as not only a pleasant one but also one that gave me an opportunity to read extensively and do some thinking and be exposed to different ideas, and to different branches of the services and government. There are those who, I think, considered it just as a holiday, and you could approach it that way. You could really spend very little time working at the job if you wanted to, but very few people did it that way and, altogether, I guess this is an indication that the students were carefully selected. People were serious about their careers and they recognized this as the opportunity it was to do something that you just never would have time to do in your normal assignment. You just couldn't read that much and spend as much time just in thought about the world and about the other services and about so many things that you would like to have had the time to do but never did.

Q: I suppose in that sense it's a contrast with the postgraduate school where you go as a routine thing?

Adm. M.: Oh, yes, it is. I never had any postgraduate training of any kind. That was the closest thing to it. At the time I was there, you could get a master's degree in international relations. Let me back up. You'd be given credit for a certain number of hours towards a master's degree in international relations, and then you could go to George Washington University or some other place and complete your requirements, if you did it within - I've forgotten, there was a time frame that you had to do it in. I would like to have done that but the job I went to really had me tied hand and foot, and I never had the time to accomplish it. I don't think it would have made that much difference, anyway. A lot of people did it, though.

Q: One other thing you might say a word or two about is the athletic program. There was one, was there not?

Adm. M.: Yes, not very extensive. We had a rivalry yearly between the National War College and the Industrial College in softball. Fort McNair had a little golf course, and some tennis courts. We didn't have a squash team, as such, but I played squash in the little squash courts we had at the school. But there wasn't really a very sizeable sports program. I'm not sure they don't have a bigger one now. When my son was there this last year he played on the softball team and he played on some other team, I think he told me. Really, it was an individual choice with us. There was no requirement that you take part in any intramural sports or anything like that. It was just if you liked it, do it, if you didn't, you didn't have to.

Q: So, you went to a very exciting program and a somewhat controversial program?

Adm. M.: Yes, it was.

Q: How much did you know about it in advance? I mean the particular plane that was being investigated.

Adm. M.: Well, when I was told that I was under

consideration to be the P6M program coordinator, I began to look into it. I had some friends over at the Bureau of Aeronautics and while I was still at the National War College I went by two or three times to get as much information about the airplane and about what the plan was as I could. So I went to the Pentagon with at least some foreknowledge of what was anticipated here.

I got my orders, as I said, with no leave, and then I found to my surprise that after all the talk about how urgent it was to get someone over there, I arrived to find that not only did they have no office for me, they didn't even know where I was going to be assigned. I reported in to the deputy chief of naval operations for air, a man whom I'd known at Patuxent River years before, and was told almost immediately that if I had any notions that because it was urgent for me to get there I was going to have a vast staff and have anything comparable to the Polaris program, well, I could dismiss that from my mind right away. He wanted to make it perfectly clear that this was no Polaris program.

Q: He being who?

Adm. M.: Vice Admiral William V. Davis.

In retrospect, I don't know that I could really

say what Admiral Davis's views on the P6M really were, but I don't believe that he was wildly enthusiastic about it. I'm not sure that he was ever completely sold on the basic premise on which the program was planned, and it was quite obvious that he could foresee, I feel certain, that eventually the P6M was going to be in competition dollarwise with other major aviation programs, specifically, carrier programs. The A-7 attack aircraft was one that was coming along about the same time. The P6M program was going to cost a lot of money, it was going to take a lot of the aviation resources, and I don't think he was of the view that he was going to get additional funds to support the P6M over and above his carrier program and these other programs.

I've never actually talked to him about this in this vein, but I can't escape the feeling that he, at that time, had a lot of reservations about it. But Admiral Burke was most enthusiastic about it, and it was a daring concept. It would be a major breakthrough, if it worked properly. It was a high-speed, jet seaplane that was supposed to be able to operate over the ocean, it was supposed to be able to land in protected harbors around the world, and be clandestinely fueled by a submarine, for example. It had very high-speed characteristics at low level for run-ins to the target area, whatever that might be.

It was actually identified as a minelayer and it did have that capability, certainly -

Q: Is that why the "M" designation?

Adm. M.: No, the "M" was for Martin.

But the airplane also was going to be capable of strategic use, and so it was going to be capable of doing an awful lot of things.

As I say, Admiral Burke had been really convinced that this was going to be a great airplane for the navy and because of this enthusiasm and his endorsement of it, I just have to believe that his senior aviators, although they weren't enthusiastic, to the best of my knowledge never tried to really seriously discourage him from proceeding with the program until it well advanced. And the reason, apparently, that I was assigned was because Admiral Burke wanted somebody in that building to whom he could go to find out what was happening to the P6M program at any time.

In those days we didn't have program coordinators, as such, for major programs. That's something that's come along in recent years, a very fine move because I just can't begin to tell you the frustrations I experienced in this job. It's incredible to me even to this day to think about the enormity of this program, what was actually planned, 108 airplanes, two major operating bases, one on each coast, one at San Diego and one at Harvey Point, North Carolina. There was to be an armada - that's not quite the right word, but certainly a minor fleet of supporting ships, submarines and tender types, and all this was just a sort of a dream. It wasn't really on paper as a program. The Martin Company did a marvelous job of selling this idea, with great graphic displays of the ships around the world and the P6M landing in these remote places and operating, never having to be dependent on bases other than its bases back home.

As I say, the idea would capture your imagination.

Q: Who dreamed up all the ramifications to that, then? Was that Burke?

Adm. M.: No, no. This was presented to Admiral Burke by the Martin Company, showing how the program might work. But we didn't have a single ship - I'm sorry, we had a seaplane tender that I later commanded, the Albemarle, that was actually assigned to this program that had installed a loading ramp for the airplane, and there was one submarine, the Guavina, that was used for practice refueling of P5M seaplanes in anticipation of later using this technique for the P6M.

But I was so surprised when I arrived and found that the P6M program was in bits and pieces all around the building. Op-05 has responsibility for aircraft purchases and planning for the airdromes. The Bureau of Aeronautics was responsible for the airplane development and for supporting equipment. The Bureau of Naval Personnel was ultimately going to be responsible for deciding who would fly the airplane, how they were to be trained, and at what time this all had to be done. But no one at that time was responsible for doing anything about planning for the ships that were going to support the program.

It's still astonishing to me that a program that had this sort of a start and had really been funded at least for a few airplanes didn't have more of a staffing job done and more of a staff that was dedicated to it.

Q: You, in fact, became the program manager?

Adm. M.: I was. I sat down and worked out a plan for the ships we might use for the program. I was trying to be as economical as I could. The possibility of using LSTs or LSDs, that type of ship, for support ships was considered. But the program wasn't pulled together, and I found that my first job was to try to get some kind of identifiable and acceptable overall program that you could plan on. Were we going to build a base at San Diego, really? Were we going to commit construction funds to it, or were we just going to talk about it? It was true that you didn't have to plan it - I mean, you had to plan it but you didn't have to commit funds until it was evident that you had a going concern with the airplane. This obviously required a testing program to be done to prove that the plane would do what the Martin Company claimed it would, that it would take off and land in heavy seas and that it would be able to operate like this, and that the plane was going to function in other respects in the way it was planned.

I finally got assigned as Head of the Aviation Ships Branch of Op-55. Admiral Dave MacDonald was the head of Op-55 at the time. And so I wound up in, I suppose, as logical place as I could have been in the building for the program because the aviation ships branch was responsible for the aviation input into the Ships' Characteristics Board for all ships relating to aviation, carriers and the rest of them. I've never been spread quite as thin with my meager talents in my life, trying to run an aviation ships program and trying to run this P6M program and trying to keep the program from foundering at every turn and realizing more and more as time went on that there was a heavy undercurrent of opposition to this program in aviation circles. It was definitely there. Many of the senior aviators never thought it was going to work and certainly were critical of the likelihood that it would be in serious competition for carrier aircraft funding.

In any event, I did sit down finally and I took the planning production of the aircraft and the basic plans for the bases, and I worked out a rough idea of what might be used really for support ships. I remember going up to see the deputy chief of naval operations for air with a program that was going to cose between a billion and a billion and a half dollars by my estimate, based on figures I had.

Q: That was an astounding figure for that time, was it not?

Adm. M.: For that time, oh, indeed it was, but, you see, that's what was so bad about this program. As long as you didn't actually have dollars attached to it and you weren't actually spending the money, the idea could go right along. It wasn't until you really had to start having to appropriate for it that it would begin to bite. I just can't tell you the frustrations I went through because I was aware, I became increasingly aware, that this was not the most popular program in the building. What it really needed, if it was going to go, was an admiral aviator and a staff to do this job. One captain trying to monitor such a major program was totally inadequate.

But I took this program up to Op-05, Admiral Nappy Kivette, and I told him - we had a little discussion, just the two of us - that:

"This program really hadn't been defined as well as it should be, but if we go according to present plans, it's going to cost between a billion or a billion and a half dollars."

And, I'll never forget, he said:

"Charlie, do you know how much a billion dollars is?" And I said, "Well, I have some idea."

"A billion dollars," he said, "you could stack up $100 bills and it would reach as high as the Washington Monument. That's what a billion dollars is."

I said:

"Admiral, I'm sorry, it may reach that high but this is what it's going to cost, if we know what we're talking about."

Well, without beating the thing to death -

Q: Let me ask, when did this knowledge reach the CNO? The cost?

Adm. M.: That particular estimate did not get to the CNO because it was my first rough cut after I got in the building.

Actually, the funds that were being expended were pretty much centered around the aircraft program itself at that time, and of course, the CNO was eventually going to have to approve everything that went into the total P6M program including support ships, bases, and personnel. And the fact that we had the Albemarle and we had the Guavina, identified as operating forces of the program at that time tended to obscure the need farther downstream. I kept on being told, well, you don't have to have those ships yet because the program is x number of years away and we'll discuss that when we come to it.

I remember the first major cut that I had to propose because it was obvious that we weren't going to get the money. As I recall, we went from the three squadrons on each coast, which was originally being talked about - I cut back the program proposed to thirty-six airplanes. Bill Martin was Admiral Burke's executive assistant then and Bill had been my boss at Patuxent River and was a great friend of mine. I used to go and see Bill frequently on this program because he kept calling me and telling me that Admiral Burke was really interested in this program. I kept him as informed as I possibly could. It wasn't a daily update but it was pretty frequent, and I frequently advised him that the program was in trouble. I didn't see how we were ever going to have the full quota that had been planned originally.

I did send two or three letters up the chain recommending program reductions and each proposal was approved. I finally made the proposal that we forget about a West Coast base at all, that with the dwindling aircraft that we apparently were going to buy we ought to consider only one coast for the remaining three squadrons, I think that was the number - thirty-six airplanes, and we finally got approval to have just the Harvey Point base, which is down in North Carolina, near Elizabeth City. It was chosen for a couple of reasons. There was almost unlimited space down there for the airplanes, water space, that is, and uninhabited areas around.

And about this time there got to be a considerable amount of interest generated in the possibilities of a nuclear-powered airplane, an atomic-powered airplane. The air force got interested in this idea, unlimited range, you know, the performance you wanted, and everything.

Q: The same principle that applied to a ship?

Adm. M.: Exactly, and, of course, as frequently happened, the air force had a totally different idea from the navy about what this airplane ought to be like. They wanted a supersonic-type airplane and the navy was more interested in a plane that could just stay on station indefinitely and could be used for anti-submarine warfare. The P6M was considered a possible vehicle to carry the heavy weight of the atomic-power plant that would be required. For that reason also Harvey Point was considered a logical base, so if the navy had gone to the atomic-powered plane the P6M and the atomic-powered plane would be at the same base. But it turned out that that never got any further and it was finally decided that the idea of an atomic-powered airplane was not a really feasible notion.

But in any event the program finally moved down to the thirty-six airplanes, with Patuxent River to be the first base that they would operate from until the squadrons were actually formed, and then Harvey Point would be the base from which they operated.

About this time Jimmy Flatley came to Op-55 and, while Dave MacDonald never ever told me that he was opposed to the program, I'd have to number Dave among those whom I thought were the least enthusiastic aviators about this program. Dave was a very capable, cagey individual, and he certainly kept his options open on this. He never discouraged me, never told me that the program was or wasn't going to go, but I just never did feel, once again, that he was very enthusiastic about it. The man who really kept the thing pretty much going at the flag level was Admiral Rees, and I'll mention him a little bit further.

Rees by this time had come in to be the Op-05 bravo. That's the Number 2 man to the Deputy CNO for air. And he really was one of the strongest supporters in the building. He did more to keep me going - well, in fairness, Dave MacDonald did, too, but Admiral Rees I think knew that he was going to be ComAirLant and he knew this program was going to come under him. So he had a keener interest in it maybe than might have been the case otherwise. In any event, he gave me more support and assisted me more in his position than had been the case before in the DCNO office.

Jimmy Flatley, as I mentioned, had come in to Op-55 and although he really questioned whether this airplane would ever function the way it was envisaged, he was very interested in it as a flying vehicle and wanted to see at least an experimental squadron of these airplanes established. He felt that even if it didn't ever operate as an open-ocean airplane or if it didn't operate as a minelaying aircraft the way it was designed, he was satisfied that it was enough of an advance in seaplane technology that he thought it was something that really was important. I'm sure that, had he lived and had he stayed around, he'd have had a big say-so in whether the airplane was discontinued, as it was under Bob Pirie and for good reasons.

In any event, the program just began to decrease in size and, of course, it was given a real blow by the loss of a second airplane. The first airplane was lost in a crash down near Patuxent and they never really determined fully what had happened, although they brought all the parts up from the river, the major parts, and reassembled them to try to post-mortem the crash and see what had happened.

Q: The crew was lost, I take it?

Adm. M.: The crew was lost. At that time, there were no ejection seats in the airplane. The plane apparently at low level, flying over the water, suddenly did a loop and crashed. The best evidence they had suggested a sudden malfunction in the hydraulic system which just tossed the airplane out of control. They did do a major hydraulic reconfiguration of the plane and the system. The second airplane was lost but the crew got out of this one so they were able to come back and give evidence. This second crash occurred over land.

Q: Was it a similar type accident?

Adm. M.: Similar type accident and this time they were able to identify pretty clearly what had happened because the crew got out safely. But the fact that we had now lost two aircraft, and we only had four total experimental aircraft actually built, showed the lack of wisdom in building such a small number of test aircraft. For fighter aircraft, you normally build quite a sizeable number, for test work, but this was a much more expensive airplane. Therefore, they felt they couldn't afford more than four X-type aircraft, the experimental type, before going into production for operating squadrons.

Admiral Jim Russell was the chief of the Bureau of Aeronautics at the time of the second crash, and there again is somebody that I have a world of admiration for. He was flying in from somewhere out of town when he heard about the crash and I got word to him in his aircraft that I'd meet him at I think it was Anacostia where he was coming in, and he said, "No, no, I'll come to your office." And he came to see me because we were faced with the necessity of getting a press release out right away, and what you're going to say and how you're going to say it, of course, is pretty important. The Martin people were all anxious to have the thing put in as good a light as possible but we had to be realistic in the sort of publicity the navy was going to get out of this. Admiral Russell came in and we sat down and worked out a proposed press release, which was approved up the line and we got it to the papers right away.

Q: And a situation like that is what Rickover has

avoided like the plague in terms of submarines, atomic submarines.

Adm. M.: Well, his record is a pretty good one except for a couple, I guess, the <u>Thresher</u> and a couple of others.

Thinking back to that program, I remember how supportive Admiral Russell was and how supportive Admiral Rees was, but I can't really say that there were many others in the senior aviation community who were really quite that attracted to it.

Q: At this stage in the game, what was your opinion about it, your private feeling about it?

Adm. M.: I really had some doubts about the feasibility of its operating the way we thought it was going to, but I think my doubts were colored by the fact that I felt this undercurrent of lack of support for the program in the navy. And it's interesting in this sense, too. There was quite a debate going on about who the pilots were going to be for this airplane. This started life as a seaplane and so, right away, you'd tend to think that patrol-plane pilots would be the logical choice. Well, when it looked as though it might be a real going concern, the jet jockeys wanted to get in on this thing, the carrier pilots.

They had the jet experience and they felt they should be the ones to fly the airplane and we really had quite a go-around with the Bureau of Naval Personnel deciding what the composition of the crew was going to be. How do you train the pilots for such a plane? Are you going to take P5M pilots who were flying around 150 knots and put them in a 600-knot airplane? But they've got the water experience. They're the guys who land seaplanes in the water, and the jet pilots aren't. Or, are you going to take somebody who knows jet aircraft like the carrier pilots do and make them the pilots?

The ramifications of this program were just sort of incredible, the way it spread across so many spectrums of the navy. And we had to have a training pipeline established so that at the time the plane would be in operation in the fleet you had your pilots and your crews ready to form operational squadrons. I had been told that I was to be the first wing commander, that was a verbal kind of a promise, I guess, and I was told that I would be allowed to choose top people for the program. BuPers finally settled on a mix between the VP and the carrier navy in identifying the first pilots that would go in to the airplane. By this time we'd begun to pull this thing together, but you asked me what my personal opinion was. I guess really I just had doubts about whether this airplane ever would be an operational unit.

What really gave me the doubts was looking at the <u>Albemarle</u>, which I commanded after leaving the Pentagon, and seeing how little really had been done to prepare that ship to take on the load of being the tender for this program. I just had the feeling all the way that the navy was simply going to shortchange this program in every way they could because it was an expensive program, and I guess my final conclusion was that it's never going to get the support at the level that it really requires, the enthusiastic support of the aviation community as a whole, and therefore it's apt to fall of its own weight.

As far as the airplane as an operating machine is concerned, I'm just sorry we never did really get the chance to proceed further with it. I'd like to have seen from a technical standpoint how it flew. I never flew in the airplane because it belonged to the factory at that time. We had one navy pilot I guess who actually flew in the airplane, other than the test pilots. I was at the factory frequently. I talked to test pilots frequently. Of course, I guess you'd expect them to be enthusiastic about their own firm's product but I got the feeling that they really did believe this airplane could do just about what it was supposed to do.

Q: Who at the Martin Company originated this idea, or

was it any one person?

Adm. M.: I don't know that you could single out a person.

Q: Was Glenn Martin still around?

Adm. M.: No. Jess Sweet, I think, was the president of the Martin Company at that time. Well, Martin is just like any other aircraft company. Their expertise pretty much had been in patrol planes and particularly in seaplanes, and I think this program might have been given a little additional impetus by the thought that it just might be that a jet seaplane would be a commercial venture worth considering. At that time there was concern about whether there was land enough for major airports in various places and there was a study done to show how many major cities could be serviced if you had jet seaplanes. New York City, for example -

Q: With water frontage?

Adm. M.: Yes, with water frontage. Many, many cities have this, and it was more than just a passing thought, I think, that a jet seaplane might be a commercial venture worthwhile. There are certainly many ports where you could use the airplane.

So it had a lot of impetus, but I think the long-range design people at Martin simply decided that the day of the prop-drive seaplane was just about gone and what do you replace it with? Well, you start looking at jets, and what do you do about a jet? Well, you have to have a hull that's strong enough to support an airplane of this type.

Q: Yes, and that's a major factor.

Adm. M.: Oh, indeed it was, and it had a new design of hull on it, a plane-tailed hull that was designed to get it up on the step faster and get off the water faster. It was designed to operate in very heavy seas. They never really operated in anything heavier than what happens out here in the Chesapeake Bay under controlled conditions. By that I mean they did not operate unless they knew what the sea state was, but they were gradually working themselves up to heavier sea states to operate the airplanes from.

It was an exciting idea and it could have gone. But I tell you they began to make the most fantastic claims, the Martin people, who became aware of the fact that the airplane production was going to get cut back. They kept coming over with all sorts of ideas, other ways the airplane could be used. They had even done a study that showed that the bomb bay, with a

Minter, Jr. #6 - 353

slight modification, could take a Polaris missile.

Q: Oh, my!

Adm. M.: And this was actually seriously proposed. The navigation system in the airplane was a very advanced one and was supposed to be able to give you your position with a very high degree of accuracy. This Polaris proposal didn't get too far but at least they had done a study to show that it might be worthwhile considering having this airplane as a launch vehicle.

I'm just telling you that you can't imagine the number of ideas that came out of the woodwork when it looked as though the airplane might be in some danger. They kept coming up with new ways the plane could be used and various procedures that might be proposed.

Q: Give me a ballpark figure on the supposed cost of a plane like this in contrast to a bomber or -

Adm. M.: I'd have to refresh my memory on this, Jack, but I believe we were talking in terms of production aircraft - let me see. The experimental aircraft were in the neighborhood of $50 million each and that's why they had such a limited number of them. But the production aircraft, once they got into production, and the original program was 108 aircraft, total, I think the cost was down somewhere in the neighborhood of maybe $10 million a copy.

Q: But it would soar if you went ahead with the Polaris idea?

Adm. M.: Oh, yes, sure. I never gave any serious thought to that. They simply pointed out that the bomb bay was just inches short for the Polaris missile and it could be tailored to get it into the bomb bay and, if you wanted to use if for that purpose, why, they were prepared to show you how it could be done.

Q: The Martin people sound like exceedingly good sales people!

Adm. M.: They certainly were.

I have never known how Admiral Burke was first hooked on this idea, and some day I guess even now I might go back and talk to Bill Martin about it sometime. But it was quite apparent that he really was sold on the airplane and the idea because it was such an innovative thing that it fired his imagination.

I didn't see Admiral Burke that frequently. I did have to brief him once or twice on the program, where we were going and what it looked like, but I didn't see him that much. My chain of command, obviously, was through the DCNO, Air, and he carried the ball. If he wanted me he sent for me, when he didn't, why, he didn't.

Q: In some quarters it's labeled with a name, I think the Seamaster.

Adm. M.: Seamaster.

Q: Where did that come from?

Adm. M.: The Martin people. That was their name for the airplane.

Q: I see.

Adm. M.: It was just sort of a descriptive term for what the airplane did. As I say, I was really sorry that we didn't operate about six of those airplanes out of Patuxent River, have enough people to put it through a navy testing program to see just what the capabilities were.

Q: There were still doubts about the effectiveness of the program?

Adm. M.: Oh, yes.

I went from the Pentagon to command of <u>Albemarle</u> and from <u>Albemarle</u> I went to AirLant, where Admiral Rees was the boss, and even when I was on the AirLant staff it was still a program that was sort of limping along. It was getting less and less attractive throughout the navy, and Bob Pirie finally took the step to kill the program completely.

Q: Slew the dragon!

Adm. M.: My recollection is that we had cranked roughly $400 million of navy money into that program and, the decision to kill it reverberated from one end of Washington to the other. I guess you have to say there was some real justification in the reaction. Here we had put $400 million in a program with only six airplanes to show for it. It was pointless, according to Bob, to crank additional aviation funds into a program that was never going to go any further, so he might as well bite the bullet, and that took a lot of courage on his part, I think, because, as I say, we took a real beating in the press, and in the navy itself. A lot of people said, "How in the world could we have spent that much money on an airplane and now we're not even going to use it?"

Q: Had the attitudes of the Congress, I mean the

appropriations committees, been explored? What was their idea?

Adm. M.: I wasn't privy to that, but I'm sure that Bob Pirie must have gone over and talked to people like Vinson and Stennis at that time. I feel sure this must have been explored with them before the decision was made because obviously you have to explain to Congress how you spent all that money and then have nothing to show for it.

I know I'm being a little unfair in this but every time I think about that program I get a little bit ill, because it just is almost like a Greek tragedy. You could almost sense from the start that something pretty bad was probably going to happen. I have spoken previously about the apparent lack of in depth senior aviation support for the program. I don't know. When I first went to the Pentagon I was told that it wasn't going to be a Polaris type program. In other words, we weren't going to really go all out for it. I had the uncomfortable feeling even then that we had stormy times ahead, and when I saw how little real, solid planning by an adequate staff, not by one guy, how little really had been done to pull the pieces of the program together in a comprehensive way, it became increasingly apparent that it was more a Martin dream than a solid Navy program. Martin had beautiful drawings and designs and everything, but they didn't have to operate in the Pentagon, in the atmosphere that I was associated with.

It was an interesting concept, there's no question about it. The support equipment for the airplane alone was just enormous. You should have seen the rubber docks that were prepared to have the airplane come in to - huge cylindrical, heavy rubber individual cylinders. They were coupled together to form a dock that the plane would taxi into and to get position for maintenance. The plan for maintenance at the buoy or in the rubber docks was novel for seaplanes. The enormous beaching gear that was required to get that airplane in and out of the water and the loading ramp for the tender were really advances but they were huge.

We took those rubber docks to sea in the Albemarle, for example, and it takes major heavy equipment to get the stuff over the side and get it back up again.

Q: What about their durability in salt water?

Adm. M.: Oh, there was no question about that. We had them for operational use down at Norfolk. The P5Ms were used a lot as test vehicles because we didn't have a P6M to test out these things. Of course, the beaching gear was totally different for the P5M and the P6M.

I tell you it was just too bad that the idea wasn't either killed at birth or properly staffed and the funding downstream identified so that you knew what it was going to cost and what you could realistically expect. Some day I intend to have a long chat with Admiral Burke about this program though he probably doesn't remember that I was the P6M project man. I've never had my time more occupied. Between the normal aviation ship branch work with the Ships' Characteristics Board - for example, we were working on Enterprise in those days, and that alone was sufficient to take most of your time. But that coupled with the P6M program made for some busy days.

Q: He said to you?

Adm. M.: I guess I would have to say that I had the strong feeling that this really represented a classic confrontation between the patrol-plane aviation navy and the carrier navy. It really did highlight - I shouldn't use the word conflict, I guess, because they're all members of the same team, but there's no getting around it, you're competing for aviation dollars and when this airplane was coming along it was in competition with carrier aircraft, and those who supported the carriers as opposed to the patrol planes for the navy obviously were not going to be very sympathetic to seeing large amounts of money spent for this.

I mentioned a moment ago even the conflict about who was going to fly the airplane, which was a very significant one and a very serious one, but it really did bring to the fore the difference and the feeling that the carrier navy was first and all other aviation comes behind, and this was behind.

Interview #7 with Vice Admiral Charles S. Minter, Jr.
U.S. Navy (Retired)
Place: His residence in Providence; Annapolis, Maryland
Date: Wednesday afternoon, 31 October 1979
Subject: Biography
By: John T. Mason, Jr.

Q: Well, Sir, last time you told me that very exciting story of the P6-M and I think you concluded with the details of that story. In August 1958 you went to take command of the Albemarle. Is that where you want to resume?

Adm. M.: All right.

I took command of the Albemarle in the Philadelphia Navy Yard in August of 1958. We were there just for a short time. The ship had been in for some minor repairs. I arrived to take command and we moved back to Norfolk, which was her home port. I was under the operational control of Fleet Air Wing 5.

Q: Tell me about the Albemarle herself.

Adm. M.: The Albemarle was the only ship at that time,

other than a diesel submarine, that was actually identified with the P6-M program. She had a ramp that was designed to actually bring the P6-M aboard her after deck though this never happened. We never had a P6-M actually operating with the Albemarle but that's what the design was for, and actually I think when I took command we were in the yard because there'd been a failure in this ramp fitting such that it had to be repaired. I was always suspicious of the darned thing. It was a very long metal ramp. It never looked very substantial to me. I checked with the engineers a number of times and they kept assuring me that it would do the job, but I had serious doubts that that ramp was ever going to work very well.

It was just an inclined ramp, really. There was a towing mechanism in the deck that was supposed to fit onto the bow of the P6-M and pull it up this ramp on beaching gear and put it on board so that you could have repairs done. But, in any event, as I mentioned, we never actually operated the P6-M because although Martin had some P6-Ms flying, they weren't at that time navy aircraft.

Q: So what did you operate with?

Adm. M.: We operated with P5-Ms and, on occasion, we operated with the Guavina, which was a little diesel submarine, that carried a modest amount of aviation gasoline and had refueling equipment aboard. Here, again, this was in preparation for ultimate operations with the P6-M.

Q: How much gasoline did it carry?

Adm. M.: Oh, very little. I've forgotten. Maybe 1,000 gallons, something like that. Nothing very sensational. It was purely an effort to see if the technique would work, because the P6-M ultimately was supposed to be able to be refueled from submarines that were designed for P6-M refueling purposes in various places around the world. This was purely an effort to see how you work out the technique of refueling a seaplane and, as I say, it was a very modest effort.

The Albemarle, other than the ramp for hoisting the P6-M aboard, had very little else in the way of specific modifications. It was one of the big seaplane tenders and a very logical contender to be sort of the flagship for operation of the P6-M. But other than that ramp there wasn't that much more that had been done in the Albemarle to make her capable of handling the P6-M. The P6-M was really somewhat down the way at the time I took command. We were still thinking in terms of maybe three years away before we'd have an actual operating fleet squadron.

Q: But you still had great expectations that something would happen?

Adm. M.: Indeed we did. Also, in operating the P5-M we used on occasion the rubber docks that had been designed for the P6-M. These were huge cylindrical, heavy, rubber - I'm trying to decide how you would describe them because you hooked them together individually to make a dock where a P6-M could actually be towed in or taxied in without damaging the hull. We could use those with P5-Ms, but they were terribly cumbersome equipment, heavy to handle. We had aircraft cranes on deck that could physically lift them in and out of the water, but they were certainly anything other than purely mobile.

Q: Sounds like a variant on the Mulberry?

Adm. M.: Well, yes.

Let me talk a little bit about some of the operations that we did do with the P5-Ms.

We had one period up the Rappahannock River when we conducted advanced-base operations, as we called them, with a P5-M squadron. That was only for about a ten-day period, but it was an effort to see how well the Albemarle could function in an advanced base and actually physically take care of an entire squadron of P5-Ms. We ran an operation under the sponsorship of Fleet Air Wing 5, and it worked reasonably well, but you must remember tenders were being used less and less. Seaplanes were operating from well established bases as opposed to really advanced bases the way they had before. This wasn't true as much in the Atlantic as it was in the Pacific, where we actually used the tenders to a greater extent. In the Atlantic the P5-Ms were operating from Norfolk, which is a big base. They operated from Bermuda, which is a big base. So tenders weren't really required the way they had been during the war when we operated out of Iceland, Argentia, and places like that. So we were sort of keeping the art alive in the Albemarle, once again just in anticipation of the time when we'd be operating the P6-M.

We went out to Bermuda and we operated with two of the seaplane squadrons out there, conducted operational-readiness inspections for them. We had them both aboard and spent I guess about three weeks out there.

It was not a really very active operational period when I had command of that ship.

Q: I suppose that was frustrating to you?

Adm. M.: It was frustrating because, you know, you just kept on wanting something to do. I'll give you an example of the most frustrating period I guess I ever spent.

The Albemarle became part of a task force that Lloyd Mustin had command of.

Q: This was in the South Atlantic?

Adm. M.: That's right, yes, but we were in the North Atlantic. This was a very hush-hush operation that took place.

Q: Argus or something, wasn't it?

Adm. M.: Yes, I think that was the code name of it. The Norton Sound was to fire some rockets 400 miles into space and they had nuclear explosives, and we, Albemarle, were put in the vicinity of the Azores. We had special equipment aboard designed for monitoring and research. The Research Institute had some vans aboard for electronic measurements, and I was told what we might look for physical activity in the sky when the firing was done. We went in to the Azores and refueled and then we were put in a 60-mile-diameter circle and we stayed for one month at sea doing 5 knots.

Q: That must have been pretty dull.

Adm. M.: It was just deadly dull. There was absolutely nothing to do. We didn't have any airplanes to operate. We were just at our wits' end, the exec and myself, trying to keep the crew halfway occupied. Here we were sitting out there, all those people with no planes to tend, our air department had nothing to do. We just ran out of ideas. We allowed the crew to have a beard growing contest to try to break the monotony. But I tell you it was a dull business. I guess they put us there that early because there was a serious question about just when these test shots could be fired from the South Atlantic, and they wanted us to be sure to be on station in plenty of time, and we were. Our total time at sea was just about a month and we finally got a message that the firings were going to take place, I guess it was the following night. We could actually physically see the aurora that developed from the highest-altitude shot.

The vans were manned by scientific personnel. As the captain, I could go in and out of the vans, but I had no idea really what measurements they were taking. But they used us for that entire month, and as I say, it was about the dullest period I ever had. We did a lot of sunbathing, but we certainly didn't do anything very productive.

I talked to Lloyd Mustin about this the other night, the first time I'd chatted with him since that particular operation -

Q: He put all of that on tape. They had a much more difficult time in the South Atlantic?

Adm. M.: Yes, they had bad weather.

Q: Very bad weather, which put the whole operation in doubt at times.

Adm. M.: Well, I didn't realize until the operation was all over just how little prospect for success a lot of people felt that operation had. Lloyd told me the other night that the analysts in the Pentagon had worked out a series of estimates and they came out with something like a 1 percent chance of success and tried to get Arleigh Burke to call off the whole thing. It was a success, though. It worked just as they wanted.

Q: They got the data.

Adm. M.: They got everything, so we participated, but I tell you it was anything but an interesting time for us.

I had one other experience in the <u>Albemarle</u> that was sort of a surprise. I got orders in the early spring to take <u>Albemarle</u> and be a task group commander for a small group of ships to go to Savannah for St. Patrick's Day. I never knew Savannah even knew what St. Patrick's Day was! I never realized just how much power Mr. Vinson had or maybe Senator Russell. In any event, it turned out that that was a yearly operation and the Atlantic Fleet always sent some ships in to Savannah, Georgia, for St. Patrick's Day, and, to my great surprise, it's a huge celebration there. They claim it's the biggest other than Boston in the United States, and the reason is that it goes back to the early days when Savannah was a major seaport and the dockworkers were Irish.

Q: Oh!

Adm. M.: They've got a very sizeable Irish population in the city of Savannah, and they kept St. Patrick's Day alive.

I was in there with a submarine and three little minesweepers, and we participated in their parade and all their celebrations and so on, which was an interesting little break in the routine. They had a senator from Utah down and we had a bunch of dignitaries aboard and had really quite a nice time but I must say I was astonished to find that Savannah figured in the Irish -

Q: Yes! I wonder if it still does.

Adm. M.: Yes, I think it does because I was talking to somebody the other day and they said, oh, yes, Savannah still has a big St. Patrick's Day celebration.

Actually, I wish I could tell you more about Albemarle that would be of interest but there just wasn't anything. I repeat we never once operated with the P6-Ms, which was a real disappointment to me. I was so in hopes that even as long as the airplane belonged to the Martin plant some time it might fly down and at least get accustomed to the ship that it was going to be operating with. But we never saw hide nor hair. My crew never even laid eye on a P6-M the whole time we were there.

About this time there were indications that the program was really beginning to have serious difficulties. I can't recall precisely when Bob Pirie pulled the plug on it, but it wasn't very much longer after I left Albemarle. I went to the AirLant staff, as I'll mention in a moment and I think it was while I was on that staff that they canceled the entire program.

Q: Was this your last fling with flying boats, the Albemarle?

Adm. M.: Yes, the last time I was associated with flying boats at all.

Q: Perhaps, then, it would be the occasion for you to comment on flying boats as such, their demise and their value to the fleet, to their discontinuance and that sort of thing?

Adm. M.: The PBMs and the PBYs played a pretty significant role in World War II in antisubmarine warfare, but they had really seen their day. It was obvious that these planes were not going to be really of major use in the future. There were too many more advanced airplanes coming along. The P2-Vs were beginning to supplant the flying boats. They had much greater capabilities for ASW purposes. There was no seaplane follow-on of any kind. They had several designs that were looked at for flying boats, but it just didn't generate the enthusiasm at the OpNav level that would be required to keep the flying boat going. There was less and less interest in that type operation.

It was a very difficult thing to do, too. It sounds attractive, to be mobile and to move around using tenders for support, but we had no tenders left.

Albemarle was about the last of the tenders, Albemarle and Currituck, and so all the support was leaving and there was no follow-on airplane, so it sort of died a natural death. It was obvious that the day of the flying boat had come and gone and wouldn't be coming again.

Q: You feel that it has gone definitely?

Adm. M.: Oh, I think there's no question about it. I don't believe we'll ever see a resurgence of that. As I mentioned to you before, I think, the P6-M was such an advance over all previous seaplanes that it was a quantum step ahead, but, of course, as we talked about before, it never made the grade and I felt that it just never had the support of the top level in aviation in the navy. Bob Pirie has told me since I talked to you last that he never thought the airplane as an airplane was any good. I would quarrel with him on that. I don't think the airplane had been proven or disproven at the time the program was discontinued.

Q: Martins thought it had value or they wouldn't have put so much effort into it?

Adm. M.: Oh, yes. And as I mentioned also, Admiral

Burke was just totally enamored of the idea. He really thought this was a program that had great promise and whether his senior aviation admirals just never did completely try to convince him that this program wasn't going anywhere or not, I was in no position to say, but I've always felt that their hearts weren't in the program. They weren't prepared to support it and, of course, Bob Pirie just stopped it cold after $400 million of money had been spent on the program.

Q: A lot of tax money!

Adm. M.: Oh, it was just an incredible thing. I think I can look back on that and say honestly that was the worst time of my career because I could just sort of feel that that was the way it was going and yet I felt helpless to do anything about it. I was ordered as a captain to run this thing, not to run it but to keep track of it for the CNO and I did the best I could, but I just never could get the feeling that there was any enthusiastic acceptance of it in senior aviation circles. It was just one of those things that you could just see heading for a bad end and yet so much effort went into it. We had so many people who were associated with the program. Even the personnel efforts, as I mentioned to you before, to get the training for the pilots who were going in this program. I had a tremendous interest in it, naturally, because I was told I'd be the first wing commander. I'd have the first command and I was really excited about it, but it just became so obvious that it wasn't going to be supported by the senior aviators that I guess when the time came I wasn't nearly as surprised as a lot of epople were when Bob decided to call a halt to it.

I don't really think of anything more about the Albemarle trip -

Q: It was less than a year?

Adm. M.: Oh, less than a year. I was relieved, interestingly enough, by Vince De Poix who had just been selected as the prospective first commanding officer of Enterprise and approved by Rickover. He came aboard the ship with a stack of books under his arm because this was to be sort of his makee-learn cruise as a shiphandler, but they knew he wasn't going to be doing very much operating and there'd be plenty of time for study and there obviously was. So he relieved me, I've forgotten precisely when but in the summer of '59.

Q: In April.

Adm. M.: Yes, that's right. I had less than a year aboard.

Q: But you got a more interesting job coming up?

Adm. M.: Yes. Actually, I enjoyed my <u>Albemarle</u> tour other than the fact that we just weren't kept busy enough. I kept going to the wing commander's office to ask if there wasn't something they could use us for. We did as much in the way of operations with the P5s as we could, but they were sort of limited in total operating funds. There wasn't any real point in sending us to sea and using us for programs that weren't going to be very productive and so it just was not a very active period of operation.

We did have one experience, as I recall. We were alongside the pier in Norfolk when a hurricane was heading up the coast. I guess for a very junior commanding officer I was a little bit surprised to find that it was totally up to the commanding officer whether he went to sea or whether he went up to what they called the hurricane anchorage up in the bay. <u>Albemarle</u> could only make 18 knots and I debated about taking her to sea because if the storm had done what the predictions were I'd be able to go behind it and come right back in the next day. As it turned out I would have been able to do just exactly that, but if the storm hadn't done what was predicted for it, at 18 knots you could be in some real serious trouble, so I decided to go up the bay and anchored in the hurricane anchorage. We had a tremendous blow that night. We dragged anchor for a time and we kept steam up the entire night, but came back the very next day. There was no great problem.

Q: That certainly was the safest thing to do, wasn't it, because those predictions on the course of a hurricane are always inaccurate?

Adm. M.: Oh, yes, exactly. You just can't be sure of them. But I was a little bit surprised to find that each commanding officer had that choice. The fleet commander didn't attempt to tell you where to go. It was up to you. You had these choices to make and, as I say, I just went up the bay and anchored.

Jack, I think that's just about it on Albemarle.

Q: All right, then we go to assistant chief of staff for readiness?

Adm. M.: That's right.

Q: On ComNavAir Atlantic.

Adm. M.: Yes. That was an interesting tour. In the first place, ComNavAirLant was Admiral Rees who was a most unusual man. I had certainly known him since I first started being involved in the P6-M program when he was Op-05 Bravo, number 2 man to the deputy chief of naval operations for air, and the one who really kept closer to the program than any other aviation admiral. Of course, at the time he was in the Pentagon I'm sure he must have known he was in line to become ComNavAirLant and, had the P6-M program gone, it would have been part of his aviation organization. So he naturally had a very keen interest in the program.

When I was assigned to it first, I was ordered in to him and I kept him closely advised. When he left the Pentagon while I was still there and went to ComNavAirLant he told me specifically to drop by as frequently as I could and keep him briefed on how the P6-M program was going as long as I was in the Pentagon. I did that and, of course, when I took command of Albemarle I still made it a point to go up to see Admiral Rees occasionally to let him know what I was hearing about the P6-M program.

So I knew the man fairly well. I've never known anybody quite like him. He was a man it took a lot of time to get to know and he never got very close to very many people. On the AirLant staff I guess we had 150 or 160 officers and I don't think Admiral Rees personally knew more than maybe eight or ten, just the very senior ones, the department heads. He dealt directly with them. Occasionally an action officer from a lower level would get up in the front office to see Admiral Rees, but he wasn't one of these hail-fellow-well-met types. He was a very aloof individual and it took a long time to get to know him.

I remember the man that I relieved told me when I first got aboard not to be surprised if Admiral Rees didn't send for me for anything, advice or information or anything else, for just an indefinite period. And that turned out to be almost the case! I guess I was there more than a month - I would see Admiral Rees at staff meetings, but I wasn't sent for and asked for any advice. However, some of my more senior subordinates were and it turned out that one or two of these were people who'd gotten very close to the admiral, so he had a lot of confidence in them. I had no objections to that way of doing business. It began to chafe me just a little bit that I wasn't being called in as frequently as I thought perhaps I should be, but after a sort of break-in period I did get to be one of those who I think was about as close to the admiral as most of his senior officers were.

He had two chiefs of staff during the time I was there and he was very fond of both of them. They were both top-notch officers. Tommy Booth was his first chief of staff and he left the staff to take command of the Saratoga, which was a real plum for anybody to get. She was a brand-new ship and she was finishing building in Newport News. He was relieved by Smoke Strean, who also was a top-notch individual. I'd known Smoke slightly out in Honolulu when I was on the Fleet Air Wing 2 staff but I never had close association with him until we were together on the AirNavLant staff.

That staff operation was a sort of an eye-opener for me. I'd been in aviation, of course, for a long time but I'd never previously served on a staff, an aviation staff, other than a patrol wing staff and a staff which is primarily carrier oriented was a little different setup for me.

Admiral Rees, I think, operated differently from many others in that position, too, because he wasn't just interested in airplanes. When he would go out to an aircraft carrier for an inspection, almost the first thing he did was to go to the engine room, the engine spaces, and talk to the chief engineer. He'd spend some time down there and see how the engineering plant was working, and he knew an awful lot about it. He also stayed very, very close to the operations of the Portsmouth shipyard where our aircraft carriers would go in for overhaul. Admiral Rees just kept right on top of those overhauls. I tell you they didn't get away with a thing in the Norfolk yard, and if they ever missed their estimates on when a carrier was coming out smoke would come out of the third deck of our building, I can tell you.

He had a very good materiel officer, Emerson Fawkes, who was an outstanding man in his field. Emerson got to be a great favorite of the admiral, too, because Emerson was not only a terrifically hard worker but a very, very competent, knowledgeable fellow, and he stayed pretty close on the carrier maintenance program and the overhauls.

I've seen a lot of people in those air type commander assignments but normally an aviator in that job is more interested in the airplanes, the airplane end of it, than he is in the ships themselves. That's maybe too broad a statement, but all I'm saying is that Rees had a little different view, I think. He really knew that no matter how many airplanes you had they weren't going to do you much good if your carrier didn't operate properly.

Q: Well, he was of that school that learned to be a shiphandler and everything else first before he became a flyer, wasn't he?

Adm. M.: Absolutely, but he was brilliant and he was

very, very knowledgeable. He would spend weekends at sea. Frequently he'd just decide on Friday afternoon that he wanted to fly out to one of the carriers operating out of Mayport or somewhere and he'd go aboard and just spend the weekend, take one or two staff people along with him.

Q: He had no family obligations.

Adm. M.: He had no family, just his mother who stayed with him. She'd act as his hostess in his quarters. But he was certainly free to come and go as he liked and did. He frequently got aboard.

Q: As you talk about him, he seems to be a man with certain characteristics that wouldn't naturally appeal to a selection board?

Adm. M.: I never heard anything about Admiral Rees from senior officers I've talked to that wasn't complimentary in the sense that they all recognized his brilliance. I think there were those who thought he was somewhat eccentric. He was not cut from the common bolt. I mean he was a different kind of a man. He simply functioned differently.

Q: But his brilliance was overriding so -

Adm. M.: It was. He didn't seem to have a lot of close friends even in his own age group. He used to play a lot of tennis with Admiral Sabin, I remember, and he had two or three intimates who were really close to him, but I don't recall him being that frequently in the company of people of his age group in the aviation community. I didn't see him in that light as much as I perhaps thought I would have, but I think he was highly regarded. I know he was highly regarded by Admiral Wright, who at that time was SACLant and CinCLant.

I remember very well Admiral Wright went to the West Coast and on his way back through Omaha he was given a briefing by the air force and he was tremendously impressed with the briefing, the technique that was used in the briefing. There were four colonels who did the briefing and as far as I know none of them knew very much what he was talking about because the generals answered all the questions, but they did it in a Hollywood style that really appealed to Admiral Wright. The only reason for telling this story is that as soon as he got back he announced to his staff that he wanted a briefing team set up like that because he knew that in two or three months' time the secretary of defense and the Joint Chiefs of Staff were all to have a meeting in Norfolk and he wanted a briefing just as good as the air force.

Well, the reason I know about this is because I was called in and told that I was to do the AirLant part of the briefing. Without going into great detail, I'll simply tell you I don't think I ever spent more time on any single project than I did on that one because Admiral Wright was just absolutely insistent that everything be absolutely letter-perfect, and I can't tell you how many hours we spent in that CinCLant compound running over this thing.

The surface sailors had to have a part of the briefing, the submariners had part of the briefing, I did the air part of the briefing, we had an intelligence part of the briefing, we had a nuclear-weapons part of the briefing, and it was to be exactly one hour, exactly, and it was honed right down to the minute. I think I had twelve minutes, my part of it, and I could have done it in my sleep. I never got so sick and tired of anything in my life, but when it was over - it must have gone fairly well because Admiral Rees called me in and he wasn't a man given to lavish compliments, he just said that he had had a call from Admiral Wright and Admiral Wright said he thought we did pretty well. He said, "That was a very high compliment."

But, to get back to Admiral Rees, I admired the way the man did his business. He was so knowledgeable about every aspect of the AirLant operation and he simply wouldn't let his commanding officers get away with a nickel, or his flag officers, for that matter.

A commanding officer of an aircraft carrier can always make his ship look an awful lot better if he operates with a smaller number of airplanes than the ship is really designed to handle because you have room enough to move them around. If you have a dud on the flight deck you can get it below, but if you have a ship that is right chock-a-block with airplanes, it takes a lot more doing on the part of your aircraft-handling people and your maintenance people to make the thing go, and there was almost a constant battle between the AirLant staff and the deploying ships' commanders about how many planes they were going to take to the Medterranean when they were going to deploy. Admiral Rees was an absolute bearcat on that subject. You didn't cross him. He knew how many airplanes he wanted aboard, and the operations people and I and others would sometimes go in and talk to him about taking one or two off. His whole point was if we ever got to the point where we started operating aircraft carriers with far less planes than they were really designed to handle, they would become subject to the very obvious question as to how valuable they are. I mean if you have a carrier that only operates sixty planes, why, somebody can say that's not a very efficient operation. So Rees really held their feet to the fire. When the ships would deploy to the Mediterranean, they had just about every airplane aboard they could possibly cram, and he insisted on that.

Q: He avoided the cosmetic!

Adm. M.: Right.

He also was awfully good - he had a very good staff system. Of course, each department of the staff had to keep track of the carriers as they were getting ready to deploy the ship, how well was it manned, how well trained was the air group, the ship's company, were the officers up to snuff, et cetera. We would have a very major predeployment conference where the staff would go down and get together with the ship's company and we'd have a slugfest right there in the wardroom because that was the ship's last chance to tell the staff what the staff had not done. If they were short of spare parts or if they had any deficiencies of any kind that were because the staff hadn't done its job, the Admiral would hear about that at that time. He also was briefed on deficiencies that were the result of failures on the part of the ship or air group. So it was a healthy thing all around because everyone had a chance to sound off. Of course the staff had been keeping the admiral informed all the way through about how the ship was doing, how close she was to being up to snuff, what her percentage of readiness was, and so on.

I don't mean to say these were knock-down drag-out fights. That's an extreme kind of a statement and it isn't quite the way it was, but it was the last opportunity for the commanding officer to have his say to the admiral. And Admiral Rees would get on us just as quickly as he would on the ship's company if we hadn't done our jobs.

Once again, I think his planning efforts and routine paid big dividends because I can't recall ever seeing a carrier leave Norfolk or Mayport that really you could say was not ready for operations in the Sixth Fleet. And, of course, as soon as she chopped in to the Sixth Fleet and as soon as she'd operate for a few days, we'd get a feedback from the fleet commander to AirLant as to how X carrier was doing, and seldom did we have any flarebacks that came from the fleet commander saying that "we've got a ship that wasn't ready to go."

In fairness, I believe the carriers went better prepared than the other ships that were going to the Sixth Fleet. There were problems that others would have and perhaps we didn't have. With the destroyers, manning was the problem in those days, in some instances. The destroyers were getting pretty old and tired and we were beginning to get new carriers in. Even so, we were still operating with a number of World War II carriers. The one that I eventually got, Intrepid, was an old one. Shangri-La was another one. We were just starting to get the Forrestal class in operation, but we still had a lot of old carriers and a lot of tired carriers, so it took some doing to keep them up.

Another thing that Admiral Rees kept his eye on. DCNO (Air) about this time came out with a new and somewhat complicated system for determining the actual operating costs of the aviation branch of the navy. Without going into tremendous detail on that, they had worked out the number of pilots you had in aviation squadrons and the number and type aircraft and from this mix figured the total flying hours you were supposed to have available per month. For example, fighter pilots were supposed to get twenty hours a month, you were supposed to have so many carrier landings, and so on - and based on all those figures, they decided how much aviation fuel should be expended in a month's time. They did this for all the squadrons in the navy, the patrol squadrons as well as carrier squadrons.

Q: This was a reflection of the economy drive in the Eisenhower administration?

Adm. M.: That's correct, and actually the system basically was pretty good. It led to some sort of odd conclusions occasionally, but we were simply given a certain amount of fuel per quarter that AirLant had control of for all of these ships and all these planes and we, in turn, would then allocate to individual squadrons. The squadron commander knew he had so much aviation fuel available for a month, and we kept definite charts to see how they were going, because at the end of the time period we wanted that amount at least used. If it wasn't used, maybe we could take it from a patrol squadron and make it available to a carrier squadron. But we were constantly having the carriers that were operating with the Sixth Fleet, where we had no control, you see. They were operating for somebody else and if any kind of an emergency arose, the Sixth Fleet commander would fly these fellows right around the clock, so all of a sudden they were running out of fuel and they were coming back to us and saying, "What do we do, we're twenty-one days into the month and we've just about used all our fuel."

Rees used to keep very, very close tabs on that. I'm sure Washington was watching us pretty closely, too, but he did a masterful job in that. Every week we would brief him on the OpTar funds, the expenditures, and where we stood at this time in the quarter. He was just a bear on keeping tabs on those things and did a terrific job of it.

I keep talking about Rees so much but he really was the man that I think everybody on that staff really had a world of admiration for. As I've mentioned, many of the people came and went from that staff and never laid eyes on him. They saw him coming into the building but never really had occasion to see him. He was tough in many ways. I remember I made a trip with him when I was the senior officer aboard the plane. We went to Guantánamo. We were going to inspect one of our carriers down there and see how the training group was making out. He had a great interest in the fleet training group, by the way, at Guantánamo, and he wouldn't just sit in his office and hear about it, he'd fly down and go aboard and see how the fleet training group was conducting its business down there.

This was in the wintertime and after we arrived I checked with the admiral to see what time he wanted to take off for our return. We were going to be there two days before we were to take off and go back to Norfolk. I notified the pilot to plan for 0930 Monday morning. We all knew to be aboard by 9:15. We all boarded except one man. Our CEC officer had somehow gotten tied up with one of his friends down there and the time came for the plane to go.

Admiral Rees came to the plane, and the CEC officer wasn't there. We were all down there, by the way, in tropical khaki, that's all we wore down. Of course, it was pretty hot down there but cold back in Norfolk. We got in the airplane and the admiral was very impatient. When he set a time he meant wheels up and away at 9:30. He didn't mean 9:32 either.

I'd just started to tell him that Commander whatever his name was was not aboard and I saw a jeep coming a mile a minute around the corner of the hangar and heading for us, but by that time we were starting to roll out on the taxiway. I said to Admiral Rees, "There's Commander So and So." He said, "Too bad," and we took off!

Q: He can walk!

Adm. M.: That poor fellow came back. He'd bummed a ride back to Norfolk. He landed at Washington in tropical khakis in the middle of a snowstorm and had to finally work his way back down to Norfolk! I tell you, nobody ever missed a flight after that. Not one.

I also remember on that particular flight, there had been a real scandal and a major court-martial that was taking place in Jacksonville as a result of a ferry pilot coming in from Guantánamo with a plane just loaded with whiskey. The customs people got wind of it. Somebody tipped them off, and they got the pilot and found - oh, I've forgotten how many cases of whiskey were aboard that airplane, but there were indications that a lot of people were going to be recipients of it. Well, this thing was getting to be a major investigation that Admiral Rees had ordered conducted. This was going on at the time we made this trip to Guantánamo. I remember one of the staff people came up to me and said:

"Are you going to ask the admiral if we can bring any whiskey back with us?"

I said: "Are you out of your mind? Don't you know about this investigation that's going on?"

The truth of the matter was we were legally authorized to carry in the airplane the legal amount - I've forgotten whether it was a gallon or what it was. But we came back to Norfolk on that particular ship and the customs man came aboard - of course, even the admiral couldn't get off until the customs man completed his check. We all had our declaration slips and the customs man went through them, and he went through them again, and finally a third time, and he said to me:

"You mean no one on this airplane has any whiskey?" And I said, "I don't think you're going to find a drop on this airplane!"

Admiral Rees had a very keen interest, of course, in the people who were the commanding officers of his aircraft carriers and I know he had a major input into those who got the commands. I remember one instance, however, where if he knew about this particular officer he certainly gave no indication to me. This was an officer who had had a very significant wartime background as a dive-bomber pilot. He was well known in the navy, in aviation circles particularly. A somewhat unorthodox individual, and a real character who had been an ex-aviation cadet and was a sort of hero in that community. He got assigned to command one of our ASW carriers and to the best of my knowledge he had never had any background in ASW whatsoever. He'd always been an attack carrier pilot and had attack carrier background.

I was acting chief of staff. I guess it was before Smoke Strean got aboard and after Tommy Booth had been detached. So it was my job, of course, to bring any visitors in to see the admiral if he was free, and this particular officer reported aboard. He was an old friend of mine. I'd known him from Patuxent River days, so he came in to see me first. He was on his way to the Mediterranean to take command of this ASW carrier and asked if I thought we could get in to see the admiral. I said yes, I thought so, so I stuck my head in the door and told the admiral that I had this prospective commanding officer outside. I felt sure he would know the man because he was so well known in aviation. I think perhaps he did, but he acted as though he didn't. I took this officer in and said, "Admiral Rees, this is Captain So and So. He's got orders to command <u>Lake Champlain</u>."

The admiral looked up and said: "What do you know about antisubmarine warfare?"

This officer said: "Admiral, I hardly know how to spell it. I've never had any antisubmarine warfare experience."

I don't think Admiral Rees thought that was funny at all. He just said:

"Well, I hope you have a nice cruise," and that was it. We didn't sit down and have a cup of coffee or anything else.

The main point of interest about this story is this fellow had command for only about three months and the continuation board humped him, and it created a great stir in aviation circles. Here was a man who on the one hand had been given command of an aircraft carrier, which was a real feather in your aviation cap, and they turned right around and had him humped out of the navy. I tell you, it created quite a furor in aviation circles, particularly in the ex-aviation cadet community. They just saw one of their heroes being summarily relieved and couldn't understand it.

Q: Was the fine hand of the admiral suspected?

Adm. M.: No, I don't think Admiral Rees had anything to do with it. As a matter of fact, I'm quite certain he didn't. The board that sat on this thing, I've heard varying stories about it. I know there was a senior aviator on the board who simply didn't care for this individual. He said he knew he wasn't flag material and he didn't think he was even captain material and they had him relieved. But I was always astonished that Admiral Rees appeared not to know this man despite the fact that he had quite a reputation in aviation circles. If Admiral Rees had been opposed to him getting command I'm certain he would have said so, and I'm certain also that he normally had a lot of sayso in who got command of the carriers, certainly of the Atlantic carriers.

He stayed very knowledgeable about his captains. He watched them very closely and, of course, he had a large part to play in who made flag rank because your performance under him as an aircraft carrier commanding officer was a big part of your aviation career, and Rees was in a position to do you an awful lot of harm or an awful lot of good.

Q: After you left Admiral Rees, you got a big command?

Adm. M.: Yes, I got orders to be commanding officer of Intrepid.

Q: Did he help you in this?

Adm. M.: I think he did. I'm satisfied he did. I think I may have mentioned before that it used to be that senior aviators controlled the aviation community as far as detailing was concerned. Op-05 essentially made all the assignments of commanding officers for the carriers and I know he did it in conjunction with AirLant and AirPac commanders and so in this particular case -

Q: You mean in cooperation with BurPers?

Adm. M.: Oh, yes, but BuPers simply rubber-stamped what he wanted done. Op-54 used to control all aviation personnel.

I assume that Admiral Rees suggested that I would be capable of having command of a carrier. In any event, I got ordered and I was quite happy to get command of a carrier. In those days, if you didn't have command of a carrier you could just kiss flag rank goodbye.

Q: And this was almost a certitude that you were

going on to flag rank?

Adm. M.: Well, not completely, but it was a long step forward, if you didn't have a problem with your carrier.

Q: Yes.

Adm. M.: But I got command. Intrepid was a World War II carrier. She had quite an interesting World War II history.

Q: What was her tonnage?

Adm. M.: She was 40,000 full load displacement. I took command in Fuimincino, the port for Rome, in Italy. This was at the time the Olympic Games were being played and the only time in my life I got to see some Olympic Games.

This was far and away the most interesting sea command I had up until that time certainly. I had a top-notch crew. I had an exceptionally good air officer, which made life very pleasant for me. He became later a flag officer himself. As a matter of fact, he was so good that when the fleet was asked for nominations for the first air officer to go to Enterprise, I called John - this fellow's name was

John Dick - and I said:

"You probably think I'm going to sabotage you but you're so good and they need an absolutely first-rate man for the Enterprise and I'm going to nominate you for it," and I did. He was the first air officer of the Enterprise and he eventually succeeded and got command of a ship of his own. But he was simply representative of a department head who was just top-flight in every way. I was very fortunate I had him. I had a wonderful chief engineer, an ex-enlisted man who really knew that engineering plant backwards and forwards. I had an arresting-gear and catapult officer who was just superior and I'll talk about him in a few minutes.

All in all, I thought I had just a first-rate organization.

Q: What complement did you have on board?

Adm. M.: We had about 2,300, I think it was, and, of course, we had the air group. We had a veteran air group aboard and, once again, really wonderful people. One of the pilots in the air group, one who came just about the time I was leaving, is now ComAirPac, Bob Coogan. He was the commandant of midshipmen here and subsequently and currently is ComAirPac.

So I started off with a fine ship's company, and I relieved an old friend, Eddie Outlaw. We had been shipmates in Op-55 at the same time and I'd known him since Naval Academy days. He was two years ahead of me here at the Naval Academy, and Eddie really ran a good ship. He had them shaken down so that it was a pleasure for me to operate.

George Anderson was the Sixth Fleet commander and I remember at the time I took command, Eddie Outlaw said to me:

"The ship operates well but I have to warn you about two things. George Anderson is an absolute bug on proper uniform and conduct ashore for your crew. He really insists upon your people really looking shipshape at all times, even operating at sea you want to keep your people looking sharp.

I mention this because I'd hardly taken command when we went to sea for about a three-week period. We were operating with the Sixth fleet and I had not had an opportunity to call on Admiral Anderson, although it was customary for him to helo aboard a new carrier command or when a new commanding officer was there. So I was sort of anticipating a call from him at most any time. Meanwhile, we got involved in a NATO exercise. I didn't normally have a flag aboard for which I was just grateful beyond all measure because

I could run my operation. But during this particular operation a cruiser admiral who was coming through the Med on his way back to the East Coast was assigned Intrepid as his flagship for three days of this operation. He came aboard just before the operation started. We highlined him from the cruiser to the carrier. I had his flag quarters all set for him. I had known him slightly before and I went down in the flag quarters to talk to him, just tell him what the ship was prepared to do and the way we saw the operation. I was in tropical whites, which was the customary uniform, and he said:

"Charlie, this operation is going to be a difficult thing. We're going to be operating day and night for the next three days. I just think it's ridiculous for us to be in tropical whites. Let's make the uniform tropical khaki." And I said:

"Well, Admiral, whatever you say, but I understood that Admiral Anderson wanted the deck watch and the commanding officer to be in tropical whites."

"Well," he said, "no, George really does want your uniform to look sharp in port but he recognizes that for operations at sea you don't look this way, so I think we can do this. I had dinner with him and we talked this over."

So I said, "Well, Admiral, it's what you think." I told my exec and he said:

"Captain, I've never heard of anybody being in tropical khaki as we've been told Sixth Fleet regulations require tropical whites."

Anyhow, we shifted to tropical khaki, and the last morning of the exercise I got a message at 6:30 that White Charger, which was George Anderson's call, wished to come aboard to observe flight operations and to please advise the earliest time suitable. Well, we had a launch that was scheduled to go around eight o'clock, so I rushed down to the admiral's cabin and told him the Sixth Fleet commander was coming aboard and was he sure we wanted to meet him in tropical khaki.

"Oh, yes, sure," he said, "we'll do just what we've been doing."

So I sent word back to White Charger that we could take him at 7:30 and let him observe an eight o'clock launch. He came aboard in his helicopter and I've never seen a more gleaming suit of whites in my life than Admiral Anderson was wearing, and his accompanying staff members stepped out in whites and here we were in tropical khaki. He didn't say a word. He greeted me, I'd known him before, and he congratulated me on having assumed command. We went up to the flag bridge, we had a cup of coffee, we watched flight operations. Everything went fine, landings and takeoffs went well. He went back down and got aboard his helicopter. The operation ended about this time and about the time he was leaving in his helicopter we were highlining the cruiser Admiral back to his flagship and Admiral Anderson had hardly gotten aboard the Sixth Fleet flagship when I got a flashing-light message which called my attention to Sixth Fleet uniform regulations.

Well, of course, I was just caught. I couldn't very well go back and tell him that Admiral Taylor had told me to do this -

Q: Was this Whitey Taylor?

Adm. M.: No, this was J. McNay Taylor.

In any event, Anderson had made Taylor an information addressee in this same message, so I knew I didn't have to do anything except sit tight. After that I got a personal message from Admiral Taylor telling me that he would explain to Admiral Anderson that it was at his direction that we were in tropical khakis.

But George was absolutely a bearcat on these things, on these uniforms, and also on conduct ashore. Shore-patrol reports were something that he watched very, very carefully, and I can tell you you'd hear if your crew misbehaved ashore.

Q: He must have suffered terribly in Zumwalt's days!

Adm. M.: Oh, yes! He really did.

We had some very interesting operations during this time. We did several NATO exercises. This was at a time - I guess I feel sorry for the people who operate in the Mediterranean today because in those days there were so many wonderful ports that the Sixth Fleet could visit.

Q: In North Africa?

Adm. M.: You could work right around the Mediterranean. We went in to Istanbul, we went in to Athens, and we went down to Beirut. We didn't go in to any North African ports. I didn't, anyway, but Barcelona, Spain, Naples, occasionally Cannes. That whole Mediterranean area was sort of open to the Sixth Fleet in those days.

Q: Haifa was tabu, though, wasn't it?

Adm. M.: Yes. We didn't go to Haifa and we didn't go to Alexandria, but we did have all those other very interesting ports and, to me, it was just a wonderful operation. I enjoyed every bit of it. I do remember many things about it though.

I've never been any place where weather made up as quickly as it seemed to in the Mediterranean, with as little warning. At the time I was there we had three carriers operating there, the Saratoga, the Independence and the Intrepid, and, as I mentioned, I was the fortunate one in not having a flag aboard so I ran my own show. I didn't have anybody to tell me what to do. As long as I did my job I didn't have to worry. The people who had flags aboard constantly had the staff looking over their shoulder at what they were doing and I was happy that I was able to operate on my own.

I remember specifically one night that that we had flight operations scheduled, and we had light winds. I called the weather guesser down to ask for the best information on the weather and he said there was nothing, no frontal activity in the area, nothing unusual. But I just had an uneasy feeling about the weather. Well, just before the last afternoon flight came in I had them scout about 150 miles ahead of the ship and they reported there were a few little clouds but nothing of any significance, we we went ahead with our night launch, but I felt uneasy about it and I can't tell you why. I just had a feeling that things were not good. Then I began to hear Saratoga. We were getting some relays from Saratoga that they were running into some weather and they were fifty miles north of us. She was starting to recall her aircraft, so I started calling our planes back in.

Meanwhile, the wind had dropped and we had to crank up flank speed to get our planes back aboard. Well, by the time we got the air group recalled and had gotten our ADs aboard, the weather began to really deteriorate and we began bringing them in on GCA. Finally, we were into rain, heavy rain, by this time and the wind was shifting back and forth - and trying to maintain a course and a pattern for the pilot to hit the deck properly took some real doing because the wind was shifting so frequently. We were finally left with one A-4, one little light attack airplane, the only one. Pitch-dark now, clouds right down on the deck practically, rain coming down, the wind shifting, and no bingo field. We had no place to send this fellow. He had made three passes and he had to get aboard or he was going to have to ditch. And on his fourth pass, in a blinding rain and an A-4 is not a very good cockpit to see from to begin with, this kid caught the third wire and we had him down.

I might just mention we didn't lose a pilot the entire cruise, but I've never been so happy to see anybody as I was that young fellow.

I called the weather guesser down and said:

"How could you have been so far wrong?" When we talked to him at six o'clock he was still saying no signs of weather.

"I can't tell you. It just makes up very quickly in the Med," and it certainly does.

It taught me a lesson. We had it happen once after that. I was ashore in Naples. The ship was at anchor. We had the ship's company ashore, on liberty. The executive officer called me about eight o'clock. I was at a friend's house for dinner, and he called me and said if you're coming back you'd better come quick because the weather is really beginning to make up.

I just was barely able to get back in my gig and by this time the seas had picked up to such an extent that we couldn't get our liberty party back from the beach in our motor launches. They could make it out just to the breakwater and that was as far as they could go. We had to leave about eighty members of our crew ashore because we were sailing the next morning and they had to be brought out in a cruiser which was inside the breakwater. We highlined them to the ship the next day.

Q: That's phenomenal!

Adm. M.: The next morning I got the ship under way and I got as close to the breakwater as I possibly could to make a lee for the motor launches coming out. We got one motor launch hooked on. We got one liberty party aboard but we simply couldn't get the others. The wind was getting worse and the waves were getting worse.

Q: What is the scientific explanation for the weather coming up so rapidly?

Adm. M.: Jack, I just cannot tell you. They have a weather phenomenon that hits along the coast of France, the mistral, and a mistral hit along the Cannes area while we were there. It will blow for three days, and you just can't seem to predict it. I've never been any place where it was quite like that. I talked to other people and they'd had similar experiences. I don't know how to describe it to you. You can just sort of sense it when it's going to happen. If you've been there for a while, you get the feeling that this weather is going to -

Q: Is there some indication in the barometer? Does it drop?

Adm. M.: It would happen very quickly. You wouldn't

get enough advance indication that it was going to happen.

I made a point from there on every afternoon, the last flights scouted as far as they could away from the ship not only the way we were going, what our point option was going to be, but actually all around the ship because you might have to change, might have to run back for various things. I don't recall another recovery where conditions got quite as bad as that one where we could have lost a pilot.

Q: Well, if he'd ditched his plane he'd have been lost, too, wouldn't he?

Adm. M.: He might well have been. Of course our CIC would have kept a real close plot on him and I would hope that we would have gotten him back, but I was happy that we didn't have to try.

Normally, when you're operating there you have a bingo field that you can get into if weather starts to close in or something happens to an aircraft. There were fields around the area but once in a while you get so far away that you have no choice other than to get them back aboard as best you could.

I mentioned the catapult and arresting-gear officer and the air officer as exceptional people. We had something happen but I'll bet you it never happened before or since and it gave me a very uncomfortable twenty-four hours.

We were in the middle of a launch and our port catapult failed. The cable broke and while that meant a rereeving job - well, you've got two catapults on the old carriers like we had, so we could keep operating. Then the starboard catapult failed. So I had both my catapults down, both with cables that we thought might have been cut. We were just -

Q: Sabotage, you mean?

Adm. M.: Well, it was one of these crazy things. There was no reason why two catapult cables would fail simultaneously. You know, these cables are inspected daily to see to it that you don't have any breaks in them or anything and it's very unusual to have even one fail.

Our catapult crew worked round the clock for fortyeight hours and during the time they were doing the work we found the causes. In the case of the port catapult, one of the fairleads had broken in such a way that the cable running through it kept chafing at that particular point which was not available to normal inspection, and it failed. As for starboard catapult, somebody had dropped a screwdriver and it had fallen in such a way that it wedged below a cable with the sharp edge up and the cable ran back and forth over it until the cable failed. It was just a one-in-a-million kind of an accident.

Q: What's the thickness of a cable like that?

Adm. M.: Oh, they're about three quarters of an inch thick. They know from experience how many shots you can expect from a cable before normal replacement and, as I say, they inspect the part that they can see frequently and if they don't see any broken strands or anything they presume everything is okay. That catapult crew of mine worked around the clock for forty-eight hours getting both cats back in commission. But I tell you they did a remarkable job. Most people wouldn't understand just what a job that is.

I sent a message saying that both catapults were out and, at first, I was very reclutant to send anything else because we didn't know the cause, but I tell you the air officer and I sweated it out for a little while because you never know. You could have somebody disgruntled aboard or something and he could sabotage you, but as it turned out that wasn't the case. I breathed much more easily when I found out that we could rule out sabotage.

Q: It's remarkable that you had that kind of a spare part or in duplicate?

Adm. M.: Oh, we had spare cables. We were able to replace the cables, but I tell you the job of rereaving a catapult is a pretty significant operation. There's nothing very simple about it.

I mentioned to you we didn't have a flag aboard. I was a part of a carrier division, but the admiral was either in <u>Independence</u> or <u>Saratoga</u>. He did fly down on one occasion and spent a night and watched our air operations and then flew back. And for one other period I had an admiral aboard. He was aboard for about ten days, but he was not an aviator.

I think of one other episode that occurred during this particular time. I was exposed for the first time to the drug problem on a ship. I'm sure we didn't have any significant difficulties before we visited Istanbul.

Q: In the eastern Mediterranean?

Adm. M.: That's right. We were at sea operating and the flight surgeon came up to the bridge and told me that he had taken a young sailor off the flight deck and down to sick bay because he had seen what he thought were evidences of drug use on the part of this young fellow.

Q: Cocaine?

Adm. M.: No, it wasn't. It was marijuana, but he observed his pupils and there were other indications that the young fellow was high on something. So he took him down to sick bay and, sure enough, he found that he'd been smoking pot.

Well, here was a man on the flight deck. He was a seaman, a young fellow, and I couldn't believe that he was into this by himself, so immediately, of course, we had to have an investigation to see how widespread this problem was. We got the naval investigative service aboard also to assist us, and after about a week of investigation we found that we had I think it was a total of seventeen people aboard who were involved, and as apparently usually happens in these cases, there were ringleaders, fellows who had been doing this for a long time and got others into it. They apparently had bought the marijuana in Istanbul.

Then we had the problem of trying to categorize usage. It was pretty evident that some of these fellows were fairly old hands at it, others were fairly new at it -

Q: It had been going on?

Adm. M.: Yes, it had been to a minor extent, because it wasn't something that happened on a routine basis in those days the way it seems to be now. In any event, we ended up with my recommendation to the Navy Department. Of course, I reported it right away to the Sixth Fleet commander that we had drugs aboard and what we were doing and that went back to BuPers and we discharged - I think it was eight. Those who I decided were using it just for the first time and just for a thrill we gave them lesser punishment.

Q: But the veterans -

Adm. M.: The veterans, the guys who were really involved in it, had been, and knew what they were doing, we discharged them.

As I say, I really had not previously had any experience ever aboard ship with anyone who had used drugs.

Q: The navy at that point had no provisions for rehabilitation?

Adm. M.: No, because it wasn't a problem in those days, and frankly I guess either we didn't recognize or we just weren't advanced enough to do anything about alcoholics, either. A lot of people drank an awful lot and I'm sure we must have had the same degree of alcoholics aboard, or that I understand they claim are alcoholics in the service in these days, but we had no rehabilitation centers for people like that either. If a man was a chronic drunk, he was discharged, but as far as the drug use was concerned, this was an eye-opener to me. I watched it very carefully after that and I saw no further evidence of it the whole time we were in the Med. As a matter of fact, I think that the fact that we'd gotten seventeen of them got to be such widespread knowledge around the ship that this alone had a pretty -

Q: Surprising that the marijuana came from Istanbul?

Adm. M.: Yes. Of course, there were hard drugs available there, too.

Q: Yes, and that's what I would have thought of.

Adm. M.: Yes, and these were not actually hard drugs.
  By the way, you mentioned earlier - this is something that might be of interest to you. I had Allan Nevins aboard for about three days.

Q: Oh, did you really? Did you get a chance to talk with him?

Adm. M.: Oh, yes. I had him stay in my cabin because usually when I was at sea I stayed in the sea cabin instead of my cabin down below.

He had been doing a history of the Sixth Fleet in the Mediterranean over a period of time and he would come back periodically and spend a few days aboard a ship and get with the Sixth Fleet staff in various places just to sort of bring himself up to date.

Q: I'm not familiar with that history.

Adm. M.: He told me that he had done - I don't think that's the name of it, but I think he actually had done a historical background paper of some kind on the Sixth Fleet and my recollection is that he was back for a refresher course to bring himself up to date on its operations.

Q: He was on the SecNav's history advisory board.

Adm. M.: I don't know the background of it but I know that he was aboard for about three days.

Q: A very interesting chap he was.

Adm. M.: Yes, indeed he was.

I really don't think of much more about <u>Intrepid</u>'s operations in the Mediterranean. I had her for the entire deployment and when we came back to the navy yard -

Q: Six months were you there?

Adm. M.: Yes, just about six months.

Q: Did you have any contact with the Royal Navy? Was it much in evidence at that time?

Adm. M.: No, I didn't have much contact with them. In some of the NATO exercises some of their ships would operate with us. Occasionally ashore - for example, I went to a luncheon that was given in honor of George Anderson in Beirut and some of the Royal Navy captains were present.

Q: Did you have access to Wheelus?

Adm. M.: No, I did not. We never had an airplane go in there and I never had any occasion personally to go.

I'm trying to think of other areas we went in to.

Q: Malta?

Adm. M.: We did not go in to Malta on that cruise. We had planes that landed there occasionally. Once in a while we had flights in a out of there just to pick up things and bring them back to the ship.

No, we didn't really have that much in the way of operations with the Royal Navy.

We eventually did get in to Barcelona. We were scheduled to go in to Barcelona on the 1st of January. I remember that well because on New Year's Eve we were refueling underway anticipating being in Barcelona the next morning, and during this refueling operation, by the way, we had a man who fell overboard while I was hooked up to the tanker. It was at night and we had a life-guard destroyer directly astern, 1,000 yards. It wasn't really bad weather but a pretty fair sea was running and the minute this boy went over the lifeguard watch aft dropped a life buoy to him but, of course, there were some anxious moments because I couldn't break away from the tanker and there was nothing much I could do. I waited desperately, hoping to hear something from the destroyer astern, and the minute this fellow went over CIC notified their CIC, so they were on the lookout for him. He told me later when we got him back on board the next morning that he thought that destroyer was going to run him down. He saw her bow moving up out of the darkness and he was shouting his head off. He was picked up and we brought him back aboard the next morning.

That night, right after we finished refueling, some sort of emergency arose in the eastern Mediterranean and I was given dispatch orders to proceed at flank speed to the vicinity of Sicily and stand by for further orders. Well, that was perfectly all right except for the fact that quite a number of wives who were following the ship around the Medterranean to various places were waiting for the ship in Barcelona. We knew when we were scheduled to be in certain places so we could tell them. We were authorized to tell them that we'd be in port at a certain time.

This was just before pay day and all these girls that were coming over to Barcelona expecting their husbands to meet them there the next morning and expecting also to have some money, and all of a sudden we were several hundred miles away.

A classmate of mine, Dick Colbert, who later was CinCSouth, had command of <u>Altair</u>, a supply ship. He and his wife took these wives of ours in tow and really did a wonderful job of taking care of them and keeping them posted. I got a message in to him that I didn't know when we'd be back in. It was a tremendous help -

Q: Was your family there?

Adm. M.: No, my family wasn't there. My family wasn't in the Med.

Incidentally, speaking about Dick Colbert reminds me of one other thing that happened during this cruise.

Dick and I may be the first to work very hard at development helicopter replenishment techniques. Of course, we did go alongside for replenishment, but you could helo supplies over and we worked this thing out pretty well. It was a very feasible operation. You could bring over ammo, you could bring aboard fresh provisions, you could bring an awful lot of things with a helicopter that would save you much time alongside.

Q: What did you have at that time in the way of helicopters?

Adm. M.; We had two aboard. I had a couple. These were not designed for that sort of thing but they were used, UHs, I guess they were. But we did develop what they call vertical replenishment there and did quite a bit of that during this time in the Med.

Jack, I don't think of anything else in particular about our time in the Mediterranean. I'm just trying to think about other instances where I worked more directly with the Sixth Fleet commander but really, as I say, I was sort of an independent operator and

Minter, Jr. #7 - 419

thankful to be. I had my own destroyers and was able to operate just about as I thought fit, except when I was specifically tied to an operation like a NATO excercise or something like that.

Q: This was somewhat after the Suez crisis. Were repercussions still in evidence?

Adm. M.: No, not evident to me, at least. The political repercussions would have been something that, say, George Anderson would handle.

Q: Yes, the cauldron was still boiling, certainly.

Adm. M.: Yes.

I remember one other incident. We were in Genoa over Christmas that year and two of our sailors got involved in an episode ashore that had some overtones that made for a pretty sticky affair for a little bit. They had been ashore and were starting back to the ship when suddenly they found themselves being chased by a group of Italian men, a little mob of some kind. These two sailors realized that they were going to be overpowered by the group that was chasing them, so they ran down an alley and finally went into an apartment building and raced up to the top. These people were right behind them, according to their story, and they worked their way out on a ledge and found their way into another apartment, raced through this apartment, and it was the apartment of a worker and his wife. The man woke up, and his wife screamed, when these two sailors ran through their place.

The crazy part about their story is that the next day at work this man dropped dead of a heart attack, and the communists in town maintained that he was frightened so badly by these two sailors that it brought on his heart attack. Well, of course, the embassy got involved in this and I got ashore right away, the next day after we'd done our own investigation. Incidentally, the two fellows were picked up by the police of Genoa and were released when they told their story and they were returned to the ship. I went ashore and talked to the consul there about what we should do, and meanwhile had fired off a message to Admiral Anderson because, as I mentioned earlier, he was absolutely death on misconduct ashore and I wanted to be sure that our side of the story got to him first, because it looked as though there might be political overtones in this. It did get in the press, the communist press. I also asked for advice from the consul there about whether the ship should do something. The ship's company really felt pretty sorry for this Italian. They wanted to chip in and send a donation but we were told that this would probably be the wrong thing to do because they might think we felt we were guilty.

Q: Yes, that would be vertification!

Adm. M.: Yes, so we simply got some flowers, I guess.

Q: A very tricky situation.

Adm. M.: That's the only incident that I can recall having any sort of political overtones.

Q: Were there any repercussions from Anderson?

Adm. M.: No. I got the whole message to Anderson and I followed up on it and we got a message back saying that they accepted the whole story and appreciated my telling him in time.

Meanwhile, I had the consular people ashore get a message off to the State Department so we were both in gee as to how this story developed. As I say, it did get into the newspapers and the communists tried to make something out of it but nothing further really.

Q: That's where you had to be ever on the alert for that kind of reaction?

Adm. M.: You did, yes.

Q: They were looking for things to twist and turn.

Adm. M.: I'll tell you just one final thing.

Intrepid was relieved by Shangri-La, and we were scheduled to go back to the States via Rota. We were in Gibraltar first for an overnight stay and then through Rota, where we picked up some dud aircraft, some planes that had been banged up and needed transportation back to the States. While I was in Rota, I had the ship's navigator go ashore and get onward routing from the Fleet Weather Central in Norfolk. This was a new service that was being offered and they would give you the best transoceanic routing, based on long range weather forecasts. Now, remember, this was in February and the navigator came back and told me that they had routed us north of the Azores and I said, "I can't believe – "

Q: The North Atlantic.

Adm. M.: That's right. "Well," he said, "they say that's their best prediction for the next five days."

So we started and the first day we had beautiful weather, absolutely magnificent. Then we hit four days of the worst weather. We went through four severe fronts in succession. We had such heavy snow that I couldn't really see the end of the flight deck from the bridge on occasion. Of course, we had to slow down. We took heavy water over the bow, and the wind was so strong on occasion that I couldn't keep my search radar going without danger of burning it out. We had to increase our lookouts. After the second front I got a message off to Fleet Weather Central asking if they could recommend a track either north or south to improve our conditions and we got the discouraging reply back that for 600 miles on either side of us the weather was just the same!

We lost some catwalks. We didn't lose any aircraft but we certainly could hardly get anybody on the flight deck for a day or two because of the wind and the inclement weather. It was the worst crossing I've ever made, I must say, but we finally got in to Norfolk in late February and we were scheduled to the navy yard, anyway, but she was one more banged-up ship when we pulled alongside.

Q: Was your faith in the so-called weather guessers restored in the future?

Adm. M.: I can assure you that one of the first calls I made after I got ashore was to Fleet Weather Central to find out how they could possibly have predicted that going north of the Azores in February was the proper thing to do. I told the fellow there:

"You know, I almost disregarded your suggestion completely because I just couldn't believe that that was correct." And he showed me the weather maps from six days back and, sure enough, it looked like the recommended track was best but it was a total disaster as far as I was concerned.

Index to Volume I

Interviews with

Vice Admiral Charles S. Minter, Jr.
USN (Ret.)

USS ALBEMARLE: seaplane tender - assigned to the P-6M program, p. 337; p. 342; p. 350; Minter takes command (Aug. 1958) - ship identified with P-6M program, p. 361 ff; she operated with P-5Ms and with the submarine Guavina, p. 362-3; becomes part of a task force for the ARGUS operation in the South Atlantic, p. 366 ff; in Savannah for the St. Patrick's day celebration, p. 369; p. 375;

ANDERSON, Adm. George W., Jr.: 6th fleet commander - his insistence on proper uniform and conduct ashore, p. 398-9; p. 420;

ARGENTIA: VP-73 based on Argentia when Atlantic Charter was signed by FDR and Churchill, p. 60-61;

ARGUS OPERATION: a special operation in the South Atlantic to test weapons, p. 366 ff;

ATSUGI, Japan: see entries under: PATROL SQUADRON 28; also p. 258.

USS AUGUSTA: flagship of Admiral King - had FDR aboard for the Atlantic Charter signing, p. 60;

BAER, RADM Donald G. (Pinky) - Minter's roommate for four years at the Academy, p. 10;

BAKER, RADM Felix L.: skipper of the new RANDOLPH, p. 122, p. 127; his impatience in getting the ship to the Pacific and into combat - resultant state of un-readiness, p. 127-9; p. 155; p. 169-70;

USS BELKNAP: converted 4-piper - seaplane tender with VP-73 in Argentia, p. 60-61; p. 72; p. 78;

BELLINO, Joe, Commander, USNR: the navy bends a bit to let him play on weekends with the Boston Patriots, p. 316-7;

BLUIE WEST I: an army base in Greenland - used for ferrying planes to U.K. - p. 84-7;

BOONE, Adm. Walter F.: (Freddie) - p. 295-6; p. 301; as Superintendent of the N.A. he refuses to approve civilian sports jackets for members of the football squad after their success in the Sugar Bowl game, p. 302;

BOOTH, VADM Chas. Thomas II (Tommy): Chief of Staff to Adm. Rees, p. 379;

BURKE, Admiral Arleigh: head of Op.23 - p. 220; special test data from the tactical test division of Patuxent furnished Op. 23 - p. 220-1;

    his enthusiasm for the P-6M program, p. 335 ff; p. 354; p. 372-3;

CHIANG Kai-shek: p. 287;

USS CHICAGO: p. 47;

CHURCHILL, The Rt. Hon. Winston S.: piped on the AUGUSTA for Atlantic Treaty signing, p. 61; his stop in Trinidad, p. 101;

CLARK, Admiral J. J. (Jocko): his reaction (7th fleet) to the loss of the intelligence plane off the Chinese coast, p. 281-2;

COLBERT, Admiral Richard G. (Dick): skipper of the ALTAIR in the Mediterranean, p. 417-8; works at idea of helicopter replenishment, p. 418;

COMNAVAIR Atlantic: Minter becomes Assistant Chief of Staff for readiness (1959), p. 376 ff; conservation of aviation fuel, p. 387-8;

USS CORAL SEA: Trapnell gets command - invites Minter to be his Exec., p. 229;

CROMMELIN, Comdr. Charles L.: air group commander who got assigned to RANDOLPH and replaced the group with whom the ship had trained, p. 130-1;

DAHLGREN PROVING GROUNDS: p. 238;

DAVIDSON, RADM John F.: p. 290;

DAVIS, VADM Wm. V.: Deputy CNO for Air, p. 334-5;

EDDY, RADM Ian C.: Director of Athletics at the Naval Academy, p. 290-1; succeeded by Elliott Loughlin, p. 293;

ERDELATZ, Ed.: head football coach when Minter came to Academy as Exec to the Director of Athletics, p. 291; p. 301-2; p. 305;

FITNESS REPORTS: comments on the system, p. 26 ff;

FLATLEY, VADM James H., Jr.: As Op-55 he wanted to see an experimental squadron of the P-6M established, p. 344-45;

FLEET AIR WING 2: p. 273-4; p. 276; the mission of the Air Wing, p. 277; responsibility for training the Chinese Navy in Kaoshung, p. 277-8;

see also: entry under: WILLIAMSON, RADM T.B.

FLYING BOATS: (PBMs and PBYs) Minter comments on their value to the fleet, p. 371-3;

GALLERY, RADM Daniel V.: In command of Icelandic base (1942), p. 79;

USS GUAVINA: used for practice fueling of seaplanes - also intended for use with P-6M, p. 337; p. 342; p. 362-3;

HALSEY, Fleet Admiral Wm.: p. 162; p. 166-7;

HAMILTON, RADM Thomas: an inspiration for Minter at the Academy where Hamilton was head football coach, p. 10; p. 315-6;

HANNA, Dr. John: very helpful in convincing the Congress the Naval Academy needed a field house, p. 303-4; p. 306;

HEADQUARTERS SQUADRON 9-1: Minter becomes Commanding Officer of this newly formed maintenance outfit, p. 105-6;

HEBERT, Congressman Edward: his attempt to get tickets for the Sugar Bowl game, p. 297-8;

HEWITT, Admiral H. K.: head of math department in Minter's day at the Academy, p. 22-23;

HIROSHIMA: bomb drop, p. 161-2;

USS HOUSTON: Minter's first tour of duty (1937), p. 26 ff; the skipper and fitness reports, p. 26-28; p. 33; FDR' cruise (1938) on board, p. 33 ff; Minter comments on the value of his two years aboard, p. 39-40; the wardroom experience, p. 44-5; sports in the fleet, p. 46;

HYLAND, Admiral John J. (Johnnie): his eventual flight over Patuxent in a F-9-F, p. 224-5;

ICELAND: U. S. units in Iceland (1941), p. 69 ff; in 1970s the Cod war with the British and Icelandic threats against the U.S., p. 76; lack of reliable navigation charts - for flight of three PBY-5As from Argentia to Greenland to Iceland, p. 84-6;

USS INTREPID: Minter gets command, p. 396-424; operations in the Mediterranean, p. 396 ff; a drug problem aboard, p. 410;

ITALIAN POWs: p. 180 ff;

ITAMI (Osaka), Japan: assigned as base for Patrol Squadron 28, p. 250-4; the squadron's initial flight from Guam to Itami, p. 254-5;

KAOSHUNG: headquarters for the Taiwanese Navy, p. 278;

KIVETTE, VADM Frederick N.: his reaction to the proposed cost of the P-6M program, p. 341;

KOREAN WAR - night interdiction flying - see entries under: PATROL SQUADRON 28.

LeTOURNEAU CRANE (Tilly): the incident on the deck of the RANDOLPH that involved conflicting orders, p. 200-1;

LOUGHLIN, RADM Charles Elliott: succeeds Ian Eddy as Director of Athletics - his rapport with Erdelatz, p. 293-4; p. 298; p. 302;

MacARTHUR, General Douglas: The Japanese reaction to Truman's dismissal of the General, p. 270-1;

MAGIC CARPET: The RANDOLPH's first encounter, p. 171-3 ff; her real preparation for this duty - in Norfolk Navy Yard, p. 178; returns Italian POW's - resultant loading task in Naples, p. 185 ff; the return trip to Staten Island, p. 185 ff;

U. S. MARINES: assistance given them in Korea by Patrol Squadron 28, p. 261 ff; changed relationship with members of Patrol Squadron 28, p. 268;

MARTIN AIRCRAFT CO.: see entries under: P-6M.

MARTIN, VADM Wm. I.: Director of the Tactical Test Center, Patuxent (1948), p. 213-4; Executive Assistant to Adm. Burke as CNO, p. 342; p. 354;

McDONALD, Adm. David Lamar: keeps his options open on the
                P-6M program, p. 344;

MINTER, VADM Charles S., Jr.: family data, p. 1-7; marriage,
                p. 44; Pensacola days for newly weds, p. 56-7;

MITSCHER, Admiral Marc: forced to come aboard the RANDOLPH
                because two previous flagships at Okinawa were hit
                by kamikaze, p. 151-2; p. 157;

MUSTIN, VADM Lloyd: p. 366; p. 368;

NATIONAL WAR COLLEGE: p. 318 ff; subject of Minter's thesis:
                "The Future of Red China as a World Power," p. 324 ff;
                the South American trip, p. 329;

U.S. NAVAL ACADEMY: appointment to, p. 7-8; experiences during
                the four years, p. 9 ff; sports at the Academy,
                p. 10-11; summer cruises, p. 12 ff; aviation summer,
                p. 17; comments on the curriculum, p. 20-1; p. 208-9;
                Minter ordered to the Academy as Exec to the
                Director of Athletics (June 1953), p. 289 ff; Minter
                credited with extensive knowledge of intramural
                sports, p. 290; the Sugar Bowl triumph, p. 294 ff;
                Superintendent Boone makes a rash promise about seats,
                p. 295-6; Minter discusses the problems that arise
                when the head coach is not an academy graduate and
                does not quite understand the ground rules of the
                academy, p. 299-300; efforts to get a field house
                for the academy, p. 303-6; importance of Army-Navy
                games for the athletic programs at the Academy,
                p. 308-9; comments on the influence of the media
                on game time, etc., p. 309 ff;

NAVAL AVIATORS: Minter comments on two "distinct breeds"
                of naval aviators, p. 242-3;

NEUTRALITY PATROL: as it pertained to VP-73 operating out
                of Quonset Point and Argentia, p. 65 ff; Iceland,
                p. 70 ff; the Joint Intelligence Squadron in Iceland,
                p. 79-80; Minter's one-half of VP-73 returns to
                Quonset Point in Jan. 1942, p. 82;

NEVINS, Professor Allan: his visit to the 6th fleet, p. 413-4;

OP. 55 - AVIATION SHIP'S BRANCH: Minter, in addition to P-6M
                program, given job as Head of Aviation Ships Branch -
                responsible for input into Ship's Characteristics
                Board for all ships relating to aviation, p. 336;

P2-V: fleet patrol plane - test project at Patuxent for Minter, p. 216; Minter takes one to the Lockheed factory - Trapnell goes along, p. 229-30; Minter tests a model with skis - in Minnesota, p. 230 ff; testing in weather, p. 233;

P-5Ms: operated with the ALBEMARLE in anticipation of the P-6M program, p. 362 ff;

P-6M PROGRAM: Minter notified at National War College that he would be called early to coordinate the program, p. 330-1; p. 334 ff; Adm. Davis, deputy CNO for Air - not too enthusiastic about the program, p. 334-5; Minter's account of the concepts, costs, p. 335-60; Minter has responsibility of a program manager - also responsibility for planning for ships to be used in the program, p. 338-9; dilemma over the proposed crews for the plane, p. 349; Martin Company proposes plane to carry a POLARIS missile, p. 353; p. 361-3; p. 373 ff; p. 377-8;

PATROL SQUADRON 28: Minter takes command at Barber's Point, Hawaii (1950) with purpose of taking squadron to Korea, p. 244 ff; problem of 15 new ensigns assigned when the squadron was half through the training cycle, p. 246 ff; squadron deploys in March, 1951 for Japan, p. 250; orders changed from Atsugi to Itami (Osaka), p. 250-1; p. 254-5; initial missions out of Itami, p. 256-7; weather reports to the 7th fleet, p. 258-9; reconnaissance, p. 259-60; night interdiction work with marines in Korea, p. 261-6; operates out of K-9 (Pusan), p. 266-67; p. 270-1; p. 276;

PATUXENT NAVAL AIR STATION: Minter's great desire to go to Patuxent - and reasons for so doing, p. 202-3; first assigned to the Naval Air Station (1946) under Capt. Abe Vosseller, p. 202-3; the complexities of command at Patuxent, p. 204; the role as management coordinator, p. 205 ff; Minter becomes attached to the tactical test division in June 1948, p. 213; assigned to test project on the P2-V, p. 216; various planes being tested around 1948, p. 217-8; the fly-by provided by Patuxent for the Presidential dedication of Idelwild, p. 221-3; a school for test pilots, p. 235 f testing a B-29, p. 238-9; use of A/F climatic hanger at Eglin Field, p. 239-40;

PATUXENT - TEST PILOT'S SCHOOL: p. 235 ff; Captain Sydney Sherby sets up the school, p. 236;

PENSACOLA: Minter to Pensacola after two years on the USS
             HOUSTON, p. 38-9; Minter reports for training
             (1940), p. 47-59; specialization is introduced -
             Minter chooses patrol planes, p. 48-9; the "thousand
             aviators" and special tests, p. 50-1;

PIRIE, VADM Robert Burns: as DCNO for Air finally kills the
             P-6M program, p. 356-7; p. 372-3;

USS PRINCE OF WALES: brings Churchill for the signing of
             the Atlantic Charter, p. 60;

QUONSET POINT: commissioned as air station in July 1941, p. 59;
             the facilities, p. 62; Minter returns to be exec of
             headquarters squadron 9-1, p. 105 ff; AVS School,
             p. 108-9; remarks on the calibre of the men involved
             in the program, p. 109-110; few disciplinary problems,
             p. 111 ff; value of this command for Minter, p. 114-6;

RADFORD, Admiral Arthur: impatient with the newly arrived
             RANDOLPH in the Pacific because at first she did
             not keep pace with the more seasoned carriers, p. 128-9
             his trip to Korea and his help to the marines in
             their efforts at night interdiction of Korean land
             convoys, p. 262-3; p. 270-1; Minter goes back to Pearl
             in an effort to report (on behalf of his boss) on
             loss of plane off China coast, p. 282-3;

USS RANDOLPH: Minter reports as Assistant air officer on the
             newly commissioned carrier, p. 122 ff; pre-commission-
             ing details, p. 123-6; captain's impatience to get
             into combat, p. 127 ff; Crommelin's air group, p. 130
             success in melding air group and ship's company,
             p. 132-3; Tokyo raids, p. 135 ff; hit by a kamikaze in
             Ulithi harbor, p. 136-7; ship again operational
             by April, p. 139; participation at Iwo Jima, p. 144 ff
             Okinawa, p. 147 ff; RANDOLPH has three flags on board
             at same time, p. 151; morale is maintained in spite
             of frenzied pace of operations off Okinawa, p. 154-5;
             the medical crew and their efficiency, p. 155; tragic
             crash of an army P-38 on her deck in Leyte Harbor,
             p. 158; p. 163-4; typhoon in summer of 1945, p. 164-5;
             concern about topside weight - armor plating, radars,
             etc., p. 175; reception in Baltimore, p. 176-8; prep-
             arations for the real MAGIC CARPET work, p. 178 ff;
             back to Boston and repairs and preparation for duty
             as a carrier, p. 194-5; her initial duty as a carrier
             qualifications ship, p. 195; a midshipman cruise,
             p. 196-8;

READ, RADM A.C.: p. 56; p. 58;

REES, VADM Wm. Lehigh: had an active interest in the P-6M
          program, p. 344-5; p. 348; as ComNavAirLant,
          p. 377; p. 395;

RICKOVER, ADM Hyman: p. 9; p. 12;

ROWCLIFF, RADM Gilbert J.: ComCruScoFor (1938) - his attitude
          towards naval aviation, p. 37 ff; an estimate of
          the Admiral as given by his communications officer,
          p. 41-2; p. 47;

RUBINO, Tony: Professor in the Physical Ed Department of
          the Naval Academy, p. 306-7; p. 316;

RUSSELL, Admiral James: Chief of Bu Air, p. 347; supportive
          of the P-6M program, p. 348;

SEAMASTER: The Martin Company name for the P-6M, p. 355;
          see entries under: P-6M.

SOUCEK, VADM Apollo: heads the three-admiral contingent that
          provided a high speed fly-by for the dedication of
          Idlewild Airport, p. 221-3; p. 228;

SPRUANCE, Admiral Raymond: comes aboard the RANDOLPH in
          Ulithi harbor and inspects her damage, p. 137; p. 167;

STAUBACH, Lt. Roger T. (USNR): p. 316;

STREAN, VADM Bernard M.: (Smoke): Chief of Staff to ADM
          Rees, p. 379;

TAIWAN: p. 286-7;

TATE, Captain Jack: new skipper of the RANDOLPH (1945) -
          his characteristics, p. 168-9; p. 199-201;

TOKYO: raids on from USS RANDOLPH and others, p. 135-6;

TRAPNELL, VADM Frederick M.: one time head of Patuxent Test
          Center - story of how he saved Johnnie Hyland is a
          near disastrous flight over Patuxent, p. 224 ff;
          his penchant for correct English, p. 227-8; p. 229;
          his backing for a test pilot school at Patuxent,
          p. 235-6; p. 274;

TRINIDAD: see entries under: VP-53.

TURNER, RADM Frank (Freddie): p. 218-9;

TYPHOON: the big blow in the summer of 1945, p. 164-5;

ULITHI: a kamikaze hit the RANDOLPH at anchor in the harbor, p. 137-8; p. 140;

VP-53: Minter and several others detached from VP-73 (Iceland) and sent to Norfolk to commission VP-53, p. 88; new squadron operated in South Atlantic, p. 89; Minter serves as Operations Officer, p. 90; winter of 1942-43 based on Trinidad, p. 91 ff; a discussion of night patrols and what they could accomplish, p. 101-2; wolf packs, p. 104-5;

VP-73: PBY-5 squadron - Minter reports in 1941 - first to Norfolk, then Quonset Point and then Argentia, p. 59; on to Iceland in Sept. 1941 until Jan. 1942 - p. 62;

VOSSELLER, VADM A. B. (Abe): C.O. of Naval Air Station, Patuxent, p. 203; p. 211;

WIDHELM, Captain Wm. J. (Gus): succeeds Martin as Director of the Tactical Test Center, p. 214-5; p. 227; p. 229;

WILLIAMSON, RADM Thomas B.: p. 247; invites Minter to be operations officer on his staff (Fleet Air Wing 2), p. 273-4; p. 277; a downed intelligence plane off the Chinese coast - incident costs Williamson a promising career, p. 279 ff;

WRIGHT, Admiral Jerauld: p. 382-3;